Daniel Libeskind

radix–matrix

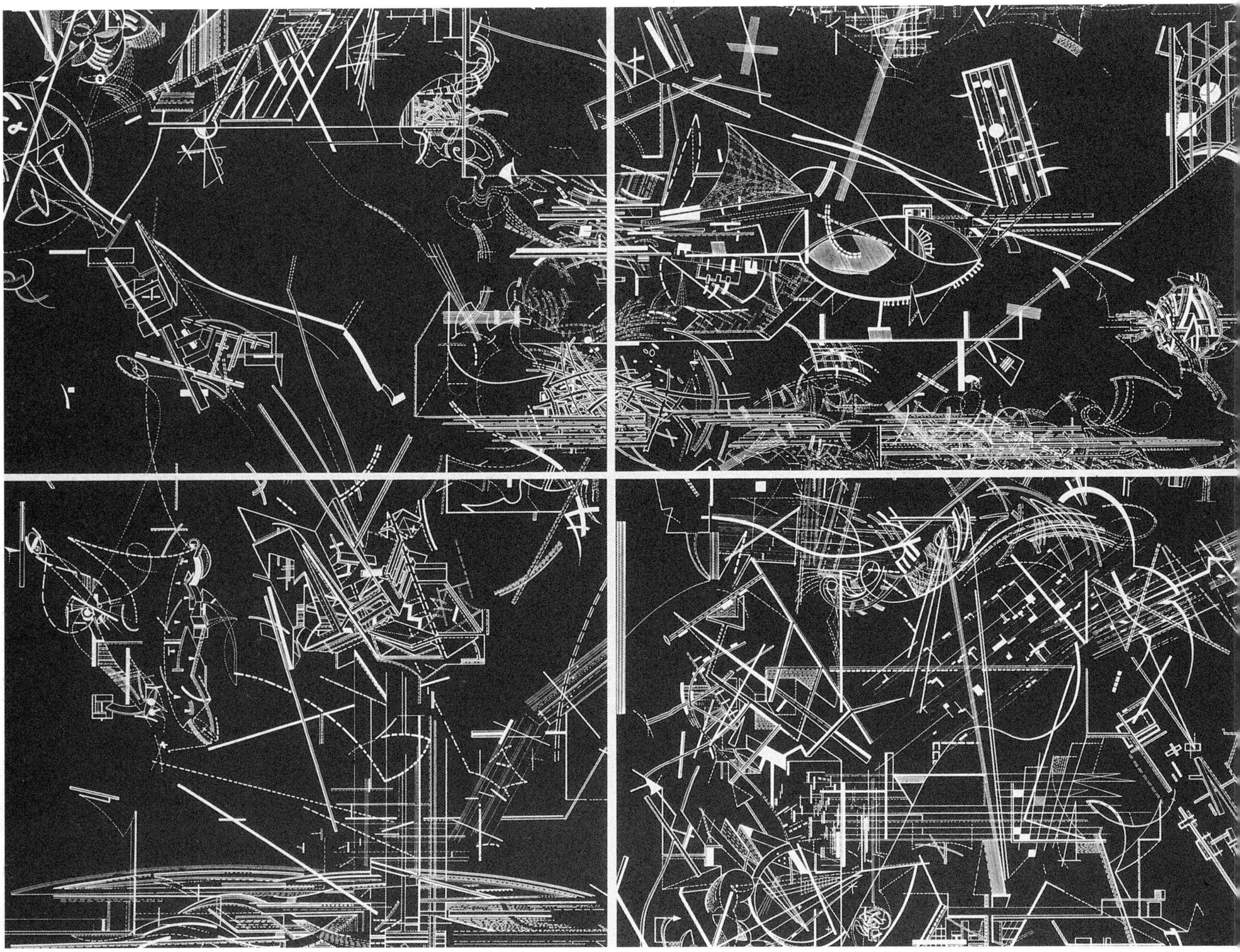

Daniel Libeskind

radix–matrix

Architecture And Writings

Prestel Munich · New York

Many thanks to Alois Martin Müller, Matthias Reese, Barbara Holzer and Elizabeth Govan for the following material republished from the German edition and to Teresa Go for her extraordinary perseverance and care in the production of this new revised edition.

Daniel Libeskind

Front cover: Berlin Museum with the Jewish Museum by night
Courtesy of Bitter Bredt Fotografie, Berlin
Frontispiece: Four Ages of Space, 1982

Library of Congress Cataloging-in-Publication Data is available.

Die Deutsche Bibliothek - CIP-Einheitsaufnahme
Daniel Libeskind : radix – matrix ; architecture and writings /
[transl. from the German by Peter Green]. - Munich ; New York : Prestel, 1997
Dt. Ausg. u.g.T.: Daniel Libeskind
ISBN 3-7913-1727-X

Prestel-Verlag
Mandlstrasse 26, 80802 Munich, Germany
Tel. (+049 89) 38 17 09 0; Fax (+49 89) 38 17 09 35
and 16 West 22nd Street, New York, NY 10010, USA
Tel. (212) 627 8199; Fax (212) 627 9866

Prestel books are available worldwide.
Please contact your nearest bookseller or write to either of the above addresses for infomation concerning your local distributor.

Translated from the German by Peter Green
Manuscript edited by Andrea P. A. Belloli

Designed by WIGEL, Munich
Lithography by Fischer Repro GmbH, Frankfurt

ISBN 3-7913-1727-X

TABLE OF CONTENTS

'Mildew Green is the House of Forgetting'[1]

Intrinsic to Daniel Libeskind's architecture, as indeed to all architecture, is a unity of materiality and virtuality. In contrast to the self-sufficing act of building, architecture reveals the contours of an idea which goes beyond concrete forms. What this idea represents is usually obscured from immediate view. Nevertheless, the essential nature of the building cannot be understood without taking the idea into account.

In this case, the idea is not about something vague or arbitrary. It has to do with concepts which are neither concrete nor abstract, which, by their very nature, are concepts, not pure ideas. In other words, they sound the distance which exists between themselves and what stands physically before us. Concepts of this kind are always borne by emotions. Instead of being a purely logical construct, the idea manifests itself in combination with an irreducible affect. It may seem odd that architecture of all things — in every respect a technical entity — should be the object of concepts which elude objective and logical definition; but even in the past, different names were given to this discrepancy between concept and physical manifestation. For example, an excess of ideas in comparison with the actual built construction revealed itself in what was described as the 'character' of a building. Those features which gave a building its characteristic appearance, which lent color to each of its parts and added up to a concept of the whole — these distinctive features constituted its individuality.

Libeskind's designs always show signs of exceeding their objective parameters. In the collages and lithographs he created in the '70s, he activated random typological characters and familiar techniques against themselves. In his early models, he veiled sculptural forms beneath a layer of written (paper) scraps, or he inserted indecipherable signs in the gaps. In this respect, his models were still reproductions of concepts, since their lack of apparency denoted an excess of meaning or signification. The discrepancy between a wealth of signs and what the signs conceal settles like a layer of snow over his objects. A blanket of icy stillness spreads over everything, even where — and the title heralds it — a line of fire has drawn a shaft of light. Perhaps the Jewish Museum in Berlin is so irresistible because it is also Libeskind's inaugural work and at the same time an almost unsurpassable masterpiece. In this work, outward unwieldiness and inward restraint meet and condense the presence of this remarkable building into a cipher of its secret.

People with a sensibility for these kinds of characteristics in a building — characteristics which have their origins in the realm of inventive conception and which affect the latent imagination of visitors — have repeatedly observed that the Jewish Museum is an angry work: angry at the inexorable way in which the destruction of the Jews in Europe confronts us in it; inexorable in its angry insistence on the recollection of this destruction. As an analogue to the *sefer hashoah*, this building has to perform the impossible task of making the boundary of that which can be portrayed function as a healing boundary; and it must do so without allowing an event to be concealed that we must always remember and that we are obliged to expound, both to ourselves and to those who grow up unknowingly in its shadow.[2]

There are hardly any buildings, with the exception of the *Carceri d'Invenzione* by Piranesi, which bear this double burden of representing both actual buildings and mental structures, and which therefore have to submit to being measured by both standards: the durability of their ideas and the imaginative faculty of their designer. Libeskind's first building work begins with a final act: not so much an approach which a work has to follow as a work which for a long time will expose the reason for its erection in the unanswerable question: How was the inconceivable possible?

Notes

1. Paul Celan, Gedichte in zwei Bänden (Frankfurt am Main, 1975), vol. I, p. 22; from the 1952 cycle of poems Mohn und Gedächtnis.

2. Geoffrey H. Hartman, The Book of Distinction, quoted with a commentary by Dominick LaCapra in Representing the Holocaust: History, Theory, Trauma (Ithaca, 1994); see esp. the chapter entitled 'Historicizing the Holocaust', pp. 69ff.

WORKS

Alexanderplatz, Berlin

Urban Planning Design

I am working today in Berlin with a project I have termed Traces of the Unborn — a term to describe the need to resist the erasure of history, the need to respond to history, the need to open the future — that is, to delineate the invisible on the basis of the visible. The scheme developed certain planning and architectural concepts which reflect my interest and commitment to the memory of the city, to the time in which it dwells and to the freedom it represents.

Even though the competition for Alexanderplatz took place in a particular area of Berlin, there were certain fundamental points which were addressed, which relate to issues of other urban centers, whether devastation has taken place because of war, political catastrophes or economic disasters. I followed Paul Valéry's axiom that 'humanity is permanently threatened by two dangers: order and disorder.' I have tried to make a scheme which navigates between the Scylla and Charybdis of nostalgic historicism and the *tabula rasa* of totalitarianism.

Alexanderplatz constitutes the largest urban area for development in post-war Germany. Alexanderplatz is the place where well-worn as well as completely new sections of the city meet, where a new centerpoint of a united Berlin must happen — the dynamic vortex which has remained untamable and undeniable from the time of the entrance of Czar Alexander to the exiting of the Russian troops in 1989.

The distance separating my scheme from the first-prize scheme was only one vote; however, there was an unbridgeable spiritual gap in the attitude towards urban space.

I proposed a scheme which opens the area and emphatically rejects the idea that public space needs to be closed in an urban room. My design for Alexanderplatz does not enclose the center, but relies on the history of Alexanderplatz to resist willfully imposed planning concepts. It calls for immediate interaction with what already exists by supplementing and subverting, stabilizing and destabilizing, the network of traffic, street patterns and building.

A radical feature of the scheme in view of Berlin politics today was to advocate the acceptance of the existence of the DDR, which represents almost fifty years of building. Even the prefabricated ill-conceived buildings of the DDR, which have little architectural merit, should not be singled out for demolition, but should be incorporated in an ecologically responsive manner. The contradictions inherent in bringing together mass housing of the former DDR with high-density commercial development is mediated by a major urban park, which would act as a field thematizing the ruin of time.

Having rejected the option of erasing the history of the city, the proposal put forward a gradual the improvement of public spaces traffic and organization of Alexanderplatz without relying on some hypothetical 'time-in-the-future' when Alexanderplatz would be perfect. The given is not treated as an obstacle or seen as a form of pathology, but understood as an opportunity pregnant with new relations and new urban experiences.

This scheme rejects contextualism and utopianism, advocating instead the transformation and metamorphosis of what exists. There is an important need in every society to identify the icons which constitute a particular area, the structures which form the texture of living memory. Thus, in refuting the past and the future alike, the eternal present of transformation is used as a strategy for the creation of unpredictable, flexible and hybrid architecture disseminated both horizontally and vertically. This structure introduces a connection or a knot between buildings and their sites. From this structure emerge forms whose individual expression and representation are indistinguishable from the political space they occupy.

The city is the greatest spiritual creation of humanity; a collective work which develops the expression of culture, society and the individual in time and space. Its structure is intrinsically mysterious. It develops more like a dream than a piece of equipment. In this competition, I have challenged the whole notion of the 'master plan' with its implied totalism and finality, its misguided ambition of eternal recurrence of the same-through-replication. Instead, I have suggested the open and ever-changeable matrix which reinforces the processes of transformation and sees the dynamic of change in a diverse and pluralistic architecture. Such an approach is an alternative to the traditional idea of planning, which implies continuity based on projection rather than an approach which treats the city as an evolving, poetic and unpredictable event.

Model, aerial view

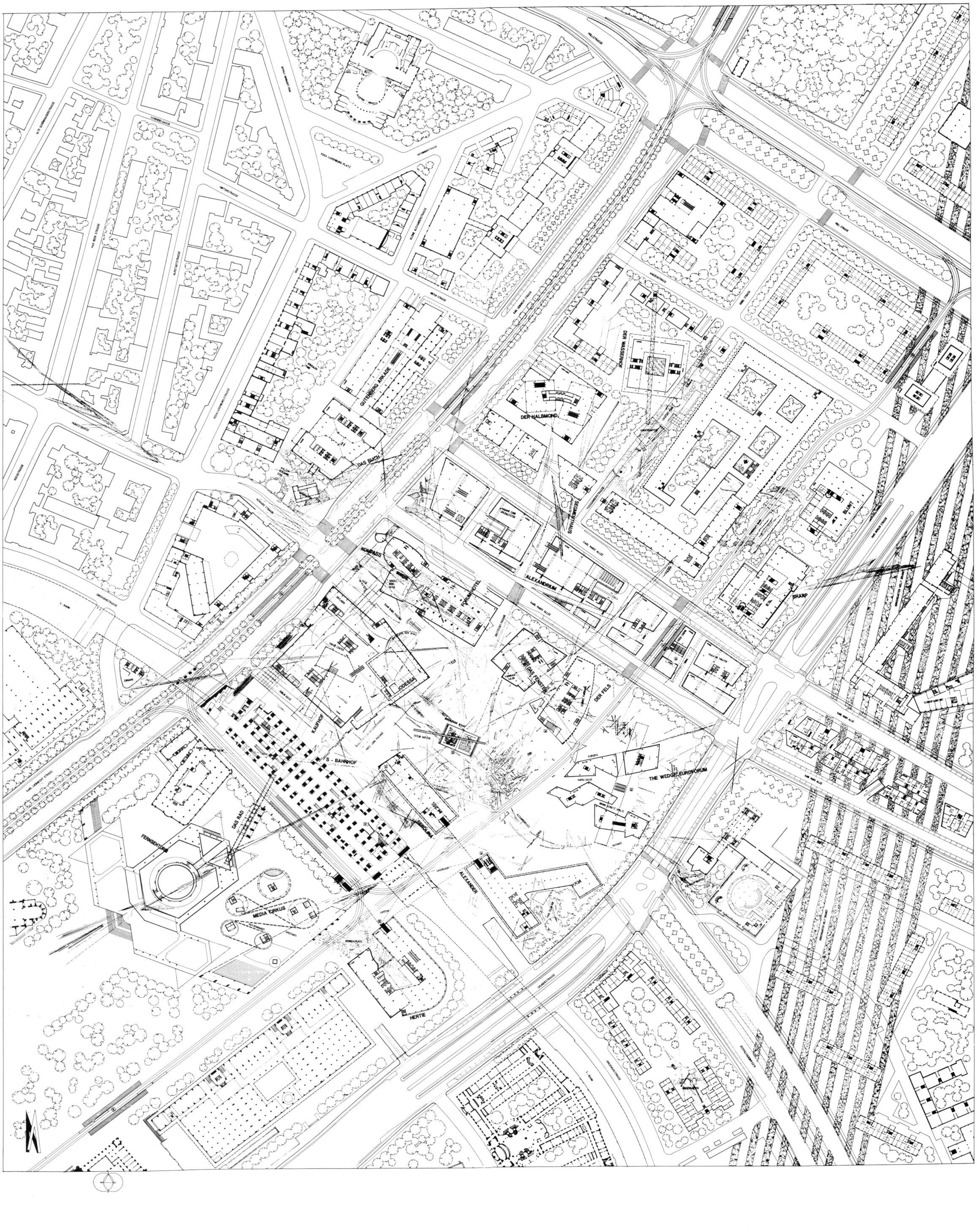
DAS BUCH
GUTENBERG ARKADE
DER HALBMOND
DER WASSERHOF
KOMPASS
ALEXANDRUM
ODESSA
KAUFHOF
S - BAHNHOF
DAS RAD
FERNSEHTURM
MEDIA CIRKUS
HERTIE
ALEXANDER
DER FELS
THE WEDGE
EUROFORUM
SHARP

Site plan

Model, view towards West

Section/Elevation

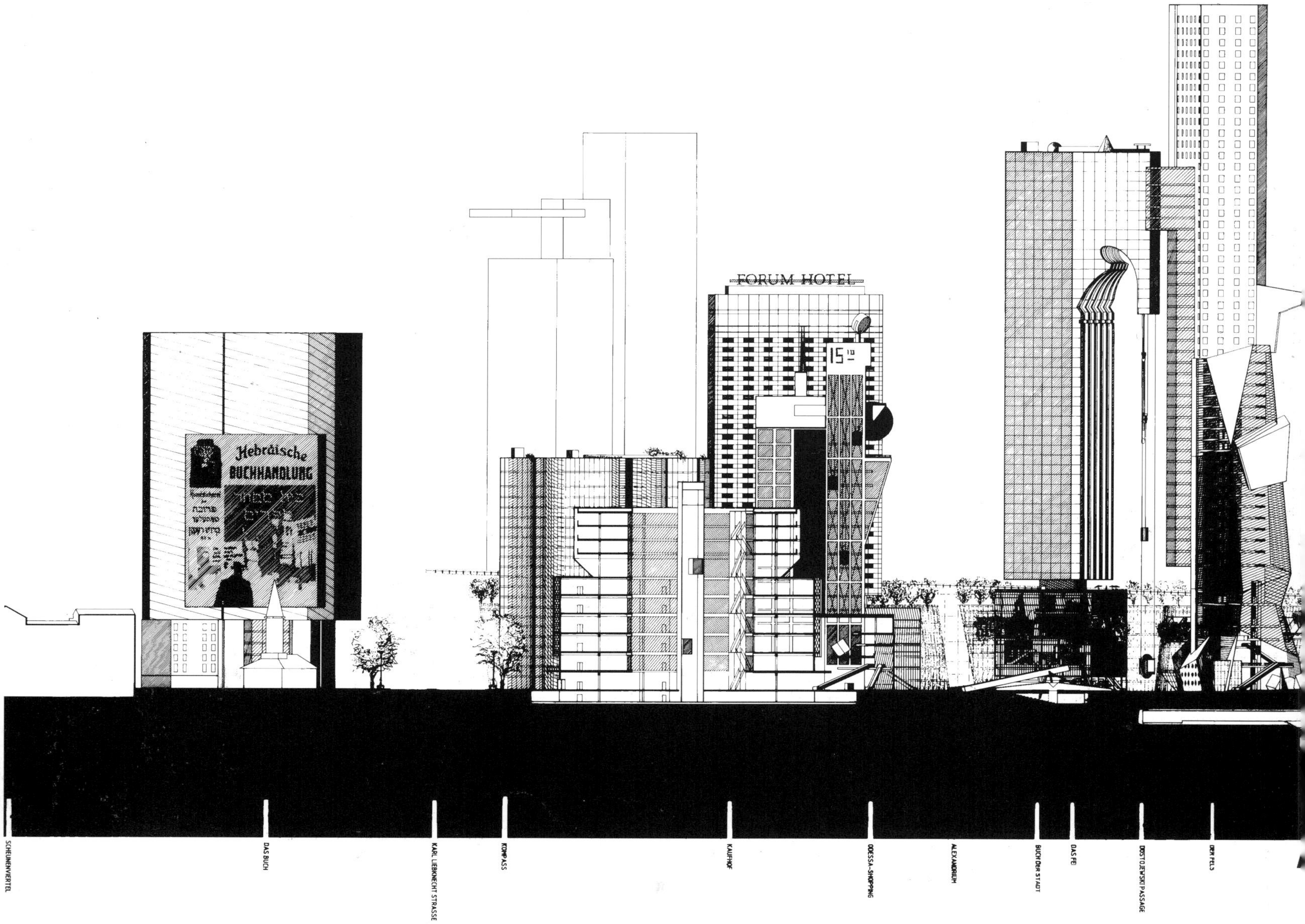

View of Alexanderplatz, in background EuroForum

View of Alexandrium and EuroForum

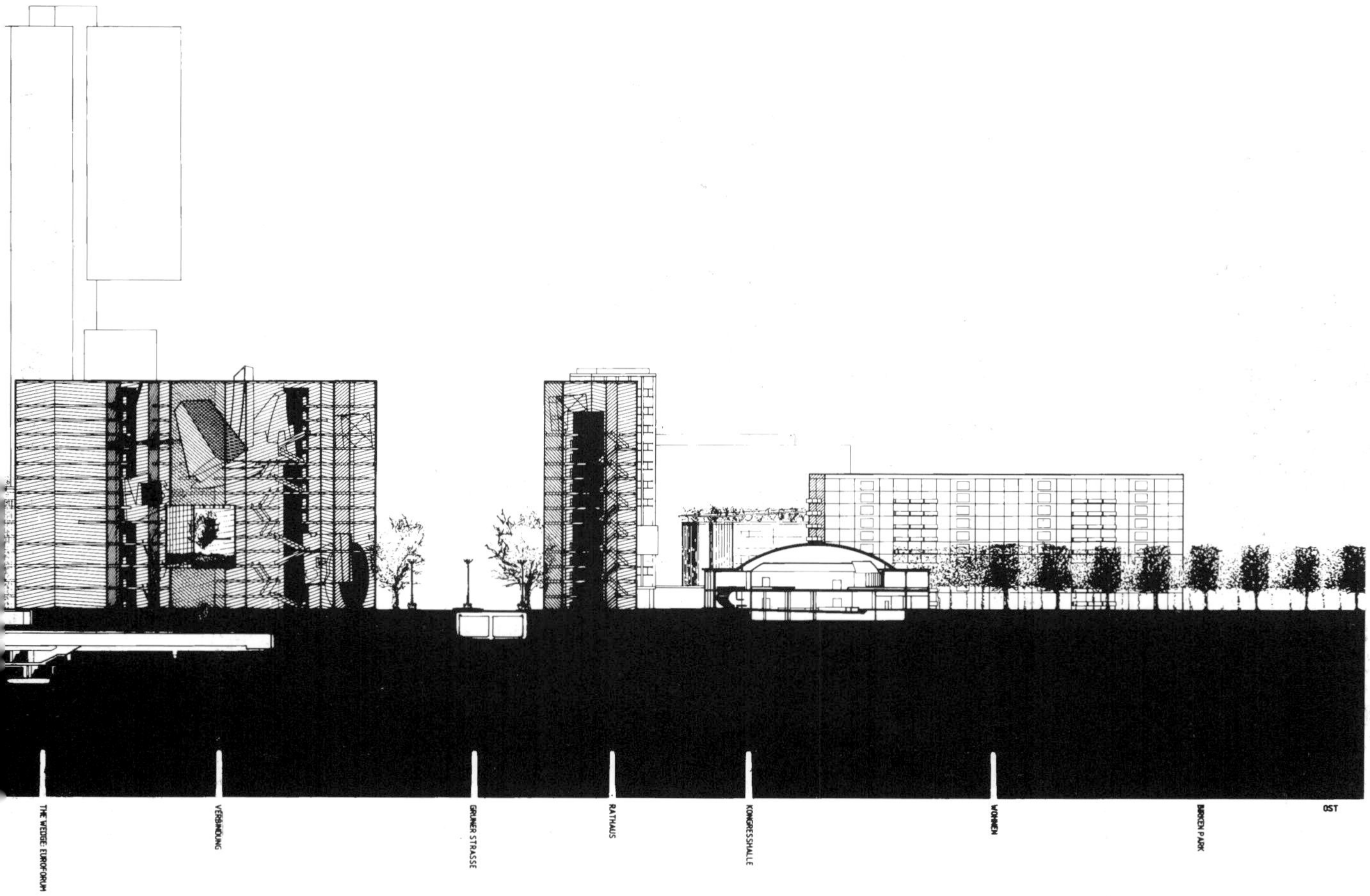

GUTEN MORGEN
GUTENBERG ARKADE
DER WASSERHOF
DER HALBMOND
MOSES
AARON
DAS BUCH
BLUNT
SEGMENTHAUS
KOMPASS
ALEXANDRIUM
SHARP
FORUM HOTEL
EINGANG
ODESSA
DAS FENSTER
DER FELS
ALEXANDRIUM
KAUFHOF
THE WEDGE : EUROFORUM
WOHNEN
DAS RAD
BEROLINA
ALEXANDER
S - BAHNHOF
DAS TOR
HERTIE
FERNSEHTURM

Typical groundfloor plan in proposed buildings

View of Alexanderplatz

City Edge, Berlin

Ancient vistas of cities and buildings, like memorable places and names, can be found on maps — the books of the world. Each appears in a different color on a different background, though any color can be exchanged for another by a traveller whose destination is not found on the map.

A voyage into the substance of a city and its architecture entails a realignment of arbitrary points, disconnected lines and names out of place along the axis of Universal Hope. Very thin paper — like that of architectural drawings, Bibles, maps, telephone books, money — can easily be cut, crumpled or folded around this indestructible kernel. Then the entire unwieldy construction can be floated on water like the tattered paper making its Odyssey on the Liffey. Finally, the water itself can be adhered to the mind, provided that one does not rely on the glue. In this way, Reality as the substance of things hoped for becomes a proof of invisible joys — Berlin of open skies.

In exploring the shape of this sky which continually refuses to come into identity or equivalence, one discovers that what has been marked, fixed and measured nevertheless lapses in the dimensions of both the indeterminate and the spherical. This space of non-equilibrium — from which freedom eternally departs and towards which it moves without coming home — constitutes a place in which architecture comes upon itself as beginning at the end.

1. Erased line: Historical axis. A public space.
Edge, limit, delusion. Speer's ordered disorder. Underneath the ground, the city traces its own schizoid memory and protects it by insulating and covering the site. What is unforgotten cannot be eradicated, concealed. Opening unbuildable realms which stretch directly into the foundation, the block discloses a public space. By cutting off the presence of fragments, both the street and the area of building are reconsecrated.

Reconstructing that which cannot be filled up, the site abruptly turns its own emptiness into an Archimedian point.

2. The fulcrum: No. 24 Am Karlsbad. A monument in the park.
A turning point. Crisis towards which possibilities return in order to revolve an invisible lever. Proposal for the Fulcrum of Universal Ideals. Chiasm of direction whereby an X grounds itself in the sky. Mies van der Rohe hanging pieces of glass outside his window in order to study their reflections.

3. Solid line: Dwelling in its totality. Housing, offices, public administration.
Building as crossing the site, blocking the historical (always ready to leap again ...), cutting the remaining fragments, unhinging the horizon. Re-establishment of a City without Illusion, an architecture without limits. To realign the sky against diagonal intersections: the ground-prop instead of a sky-hook. By opening the space between the fulcrum and its virtual arc, the solid line grounds itself in the sky. Now the unsupportable supports the support: new techniques at ground level. Intermingling of life and work by retrieving Utopia from the pit.

4. The field: Intersecting nature. A garden in the city.
The spared preserves what is to come. Four quarters of the ancient sky reflected upon the Earth establish common points: necessity in contingency, chance in axioms. The framing of variety cinematically suspended in an acrobat's leap.

5. The throw: Child's play. Children's day facility.
Reorienting the site towards its own play of place. A child's hope as a way of knowing and ordering the site across lines which cut themselves off from the web. Paths across and out of the block. Buildings whose vectors emerge, criss-cross and roll on the ground.

6. Compressing curves into straight lines. Commerce, Industry.
The space production. Imploding a curve into an angle — horizontally.

7. A final point: The beginning of a new diagonal.
Moving out of dark crevices and corners. Walter Benjamin's unexpected encounter with the locomotive in the clouds.

Collage: Site plan showing seven points

"Cloud Prop" model. Project in urban context. Wood and paper

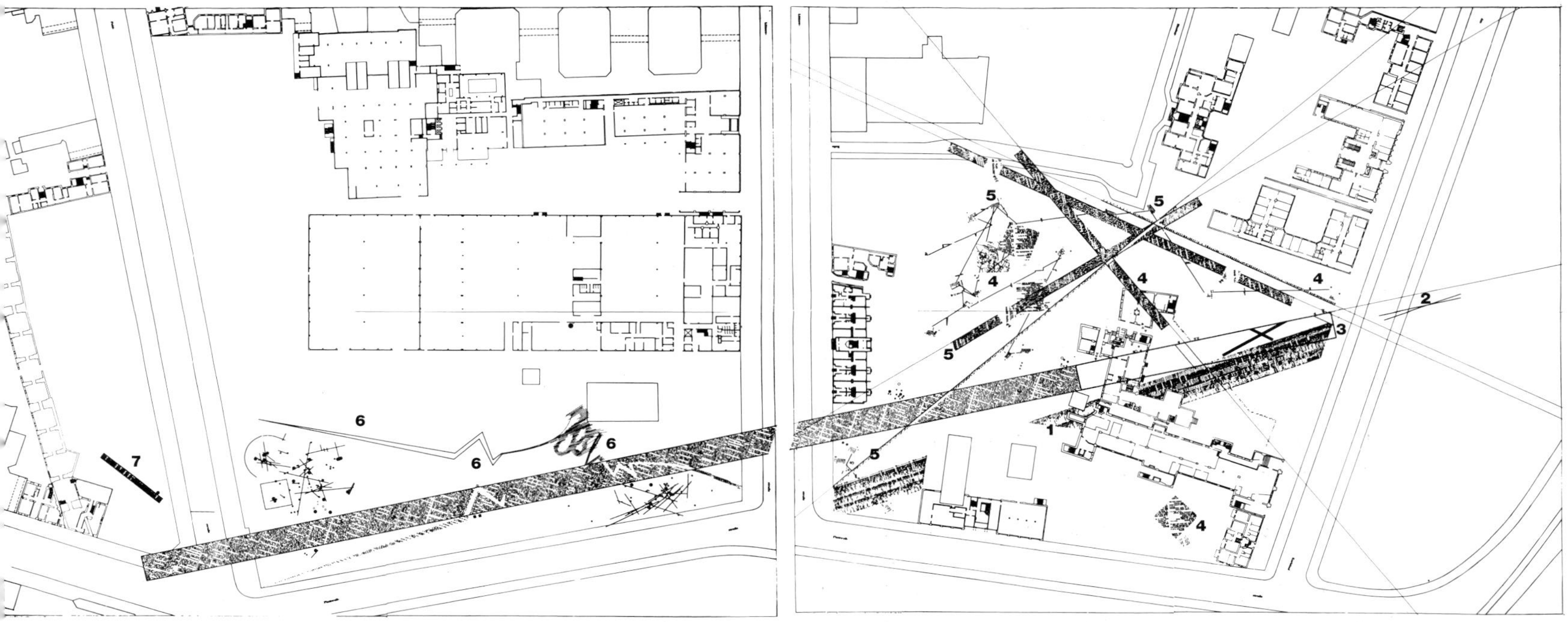

7
6
6
6
5
5
4
4
4
2
3
5
1
5
4

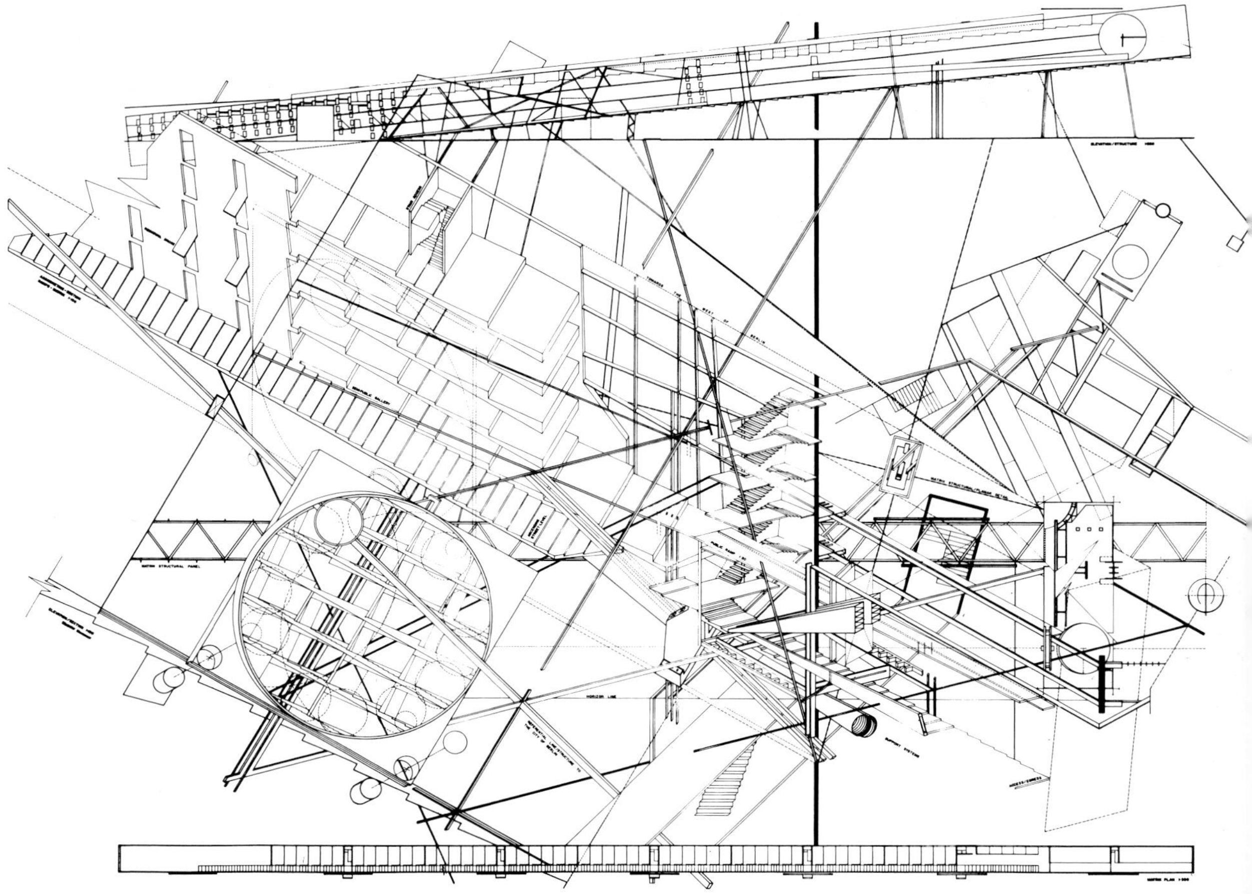

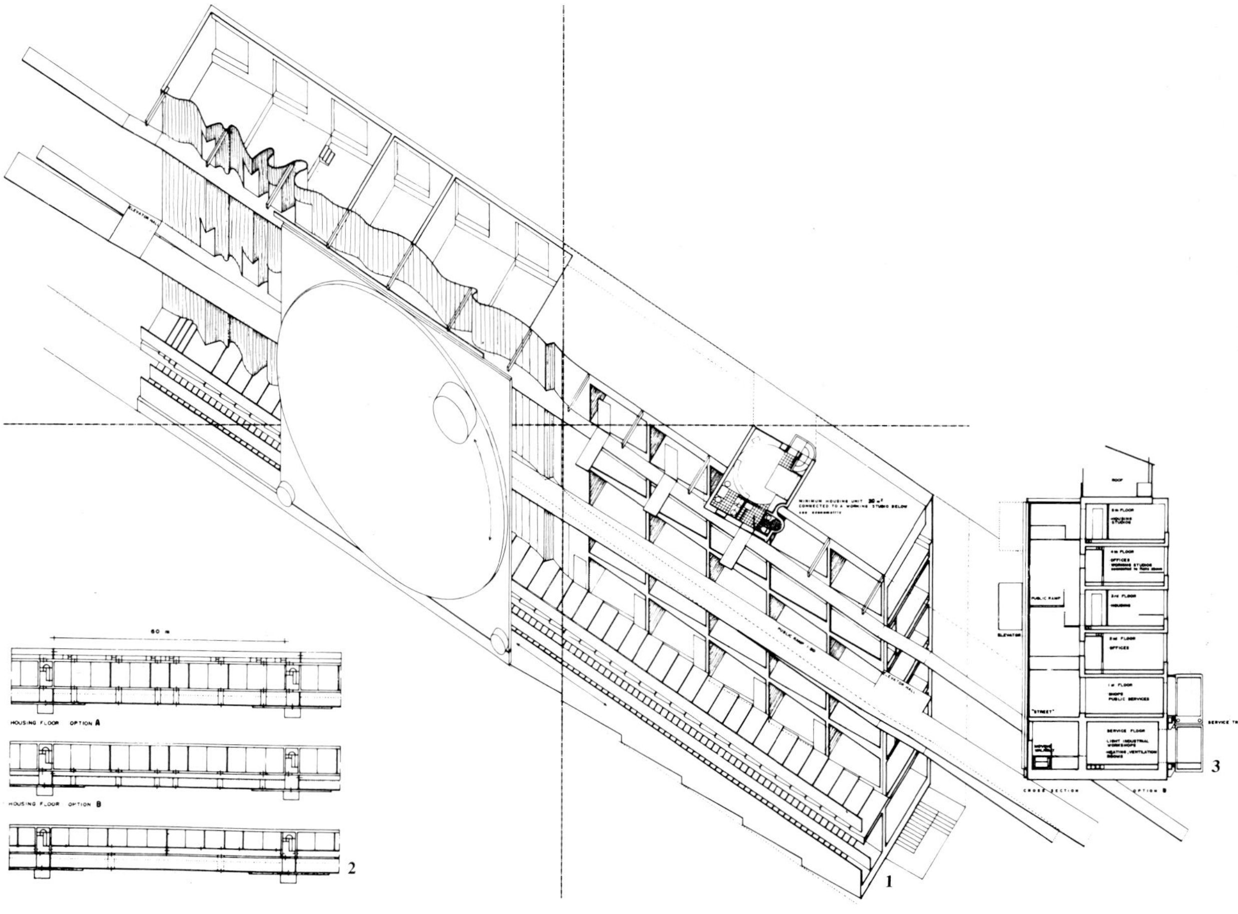
MINIMUM HOUSING UNIT 30 m²
CONNECTED TO A WORKING STUDIO BELOW
60 m
HOUSING FLOOR OPTION A
HOUSING FLOOR OPTION B
ROOF
5th FLOOR
HOUSING STUDIOS
4th FLOOR
OFFICES
WORKING STUDIOS
3rd FLOOR
HOUSING
2nd FLOOR
OFFICES
1st FLOOR
SHOPS
PUBLIC SERVICES
PUBLIC RAMP
ELEVATOR
"STREET"
SERVICE FLOOR
LIGHT INDUSTRIAL WORKSHOPS
SERVICE TRAINS
CROSS SECTION
OPTION B

1 2 3

Elevation/Axonometric plan: close-up with schematic circulation, entrances, staircases and elevator

Axonometric plan of office and living spaces with bridges in the open Hall and elevator

Detail model "Cloud Prop." West elevation, Terrace system with staircase and 'open space'

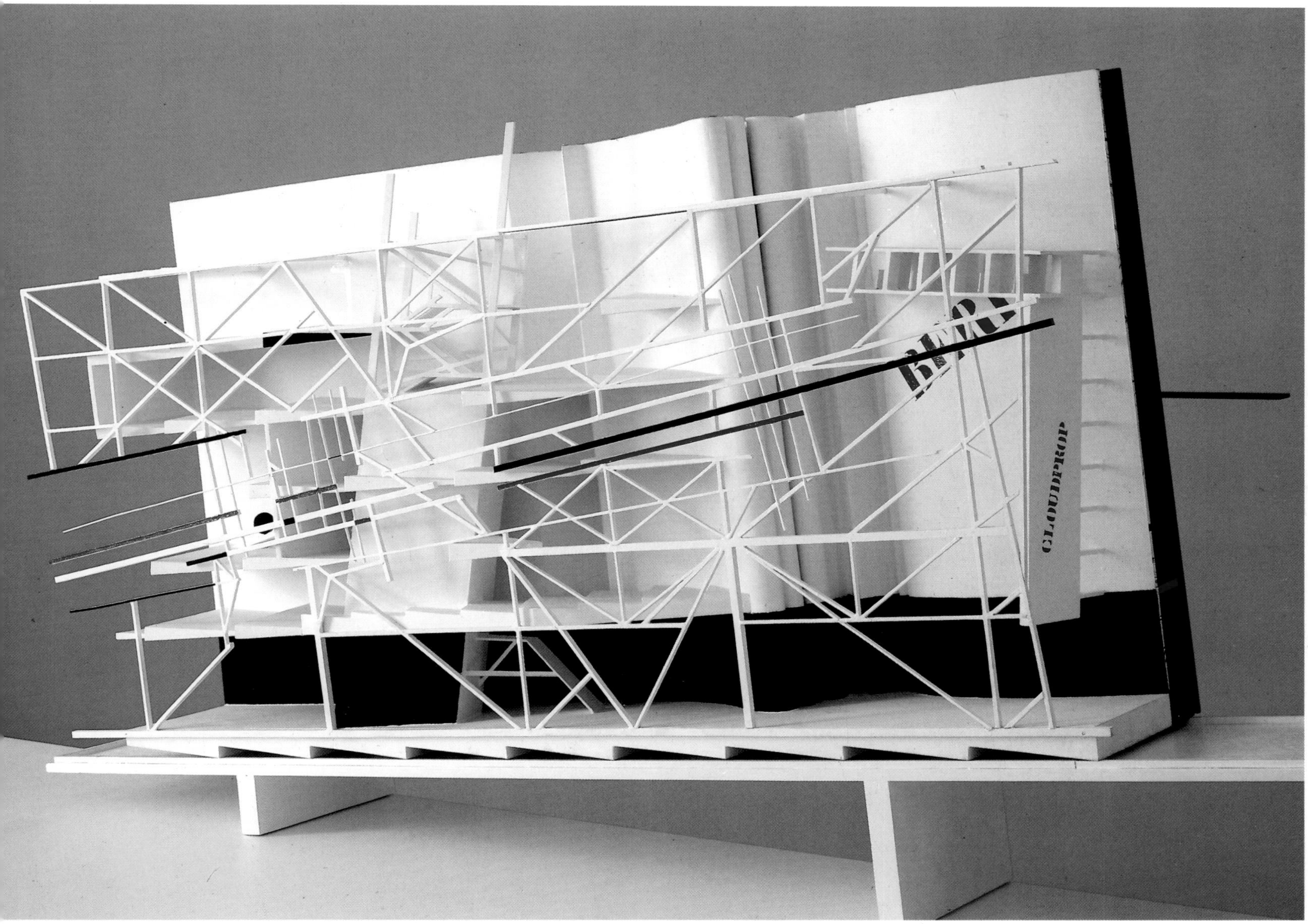

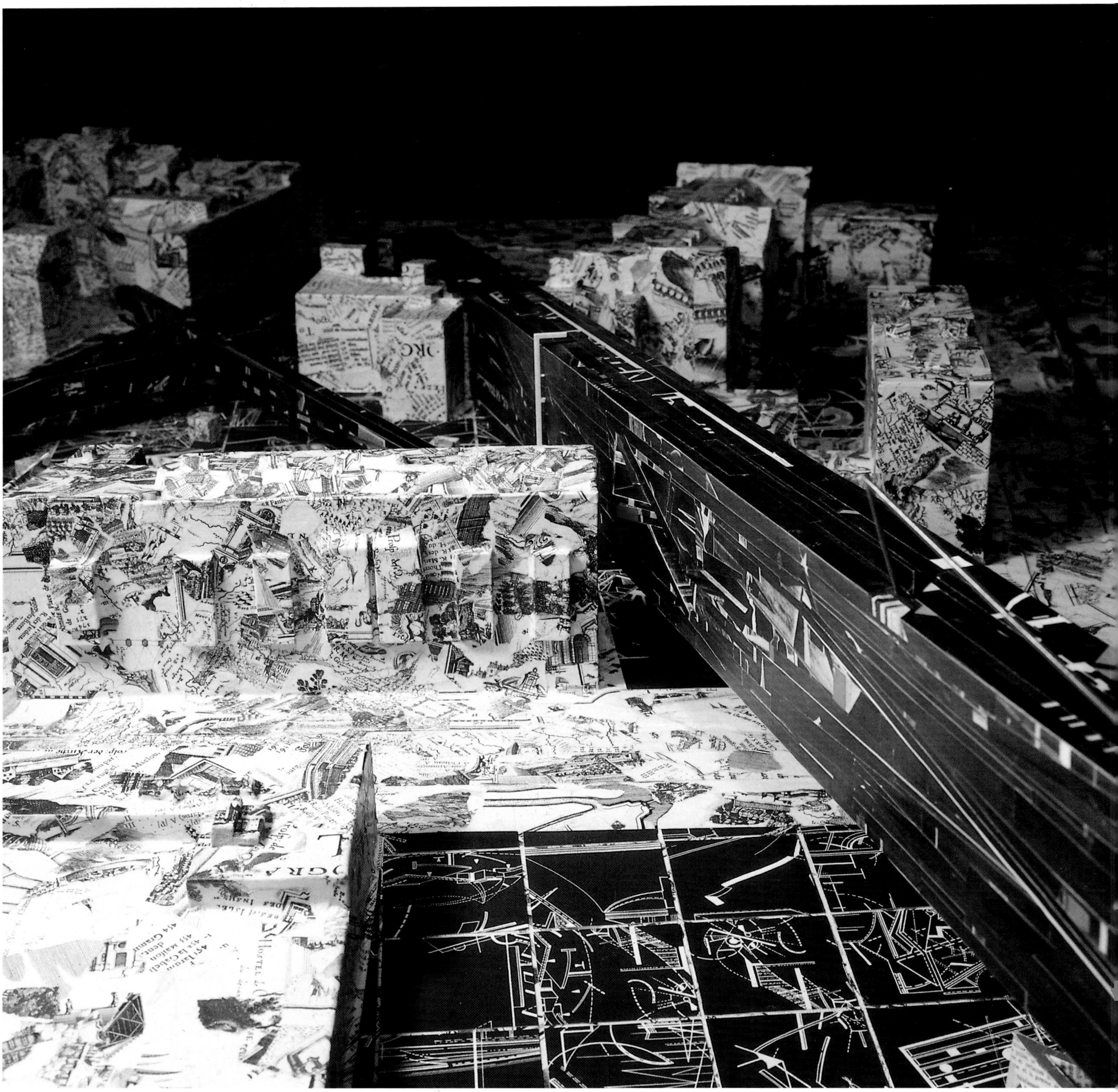

Cloud Prop Model

Axonometric

Primary structural frame with elevator

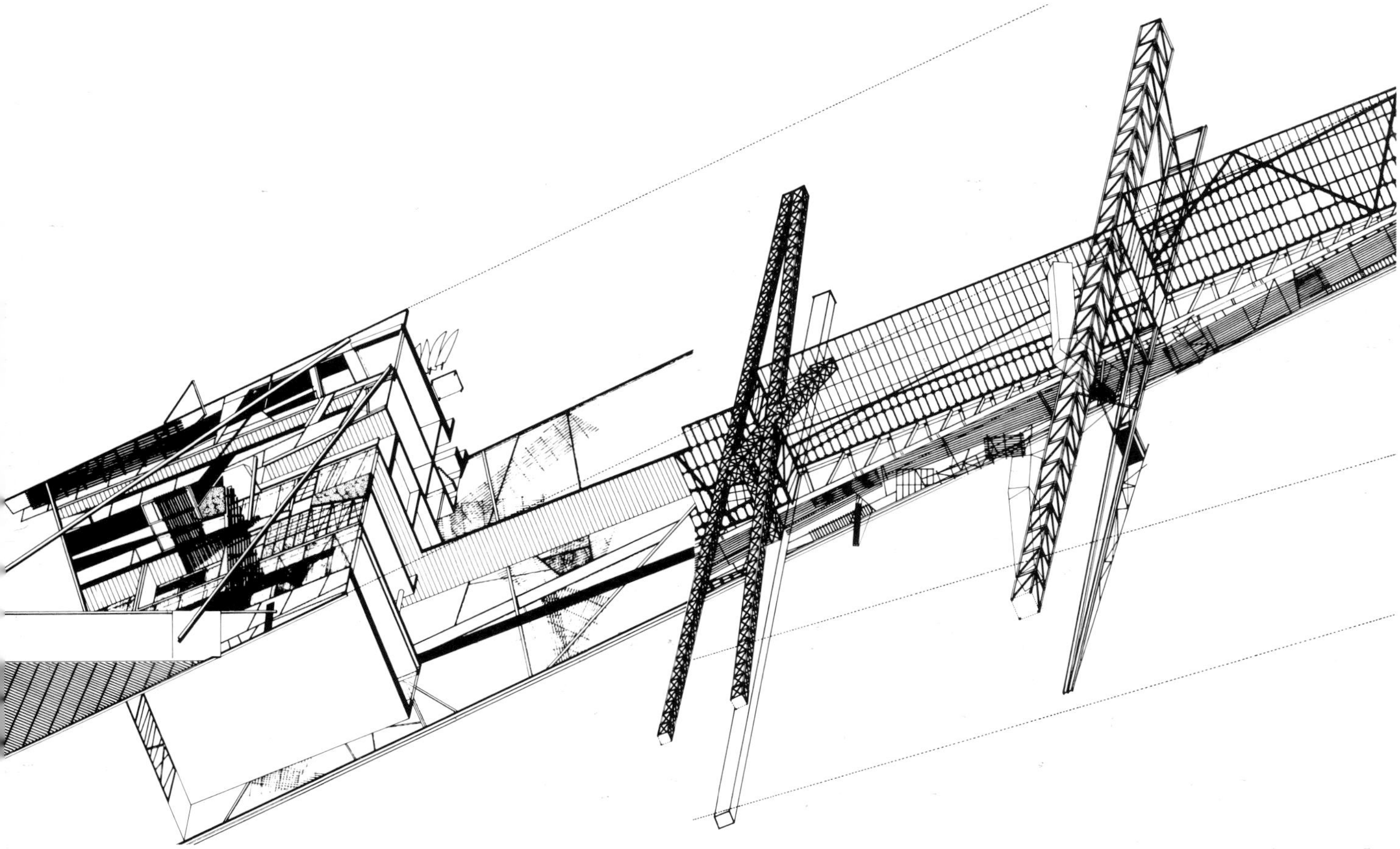

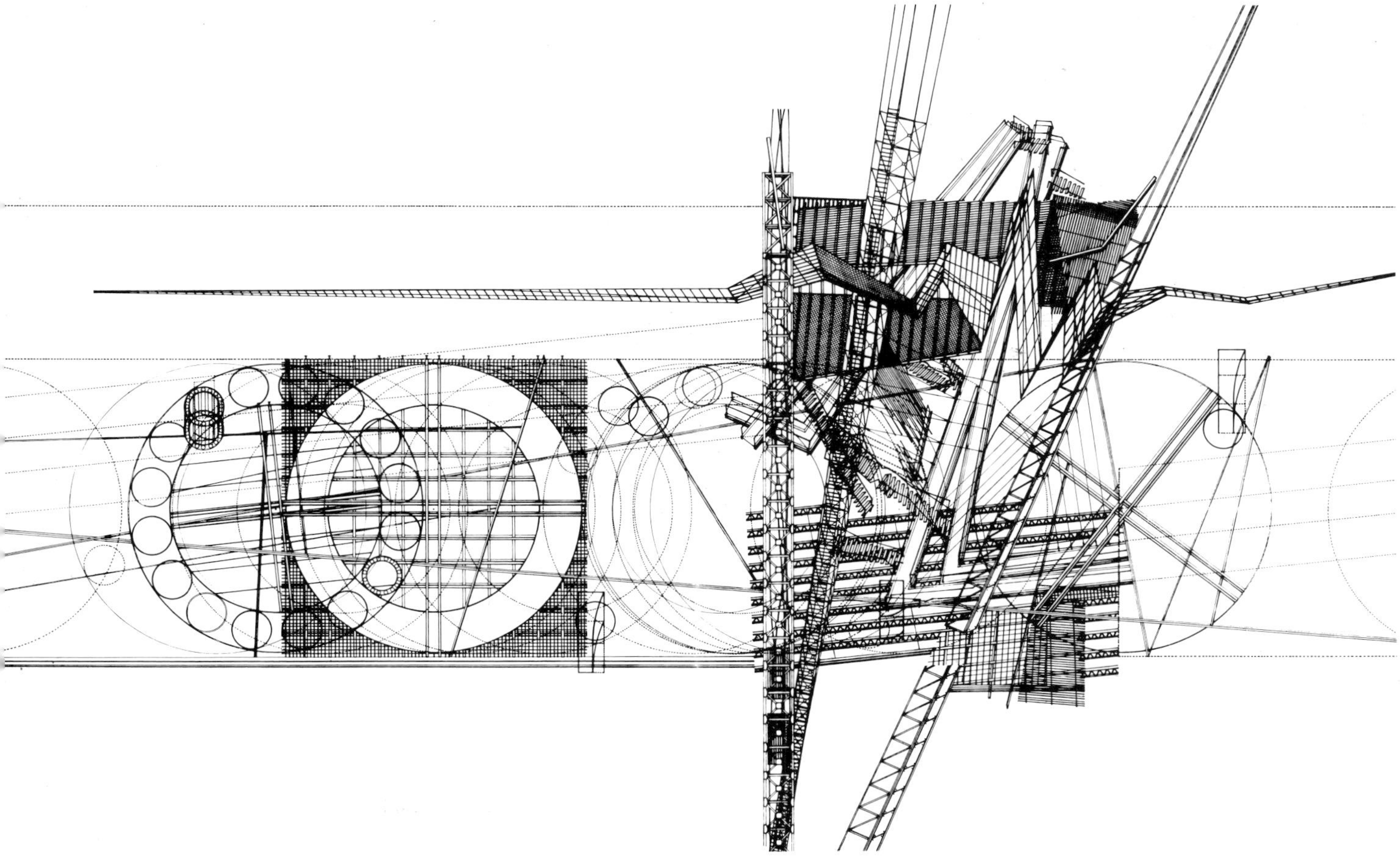

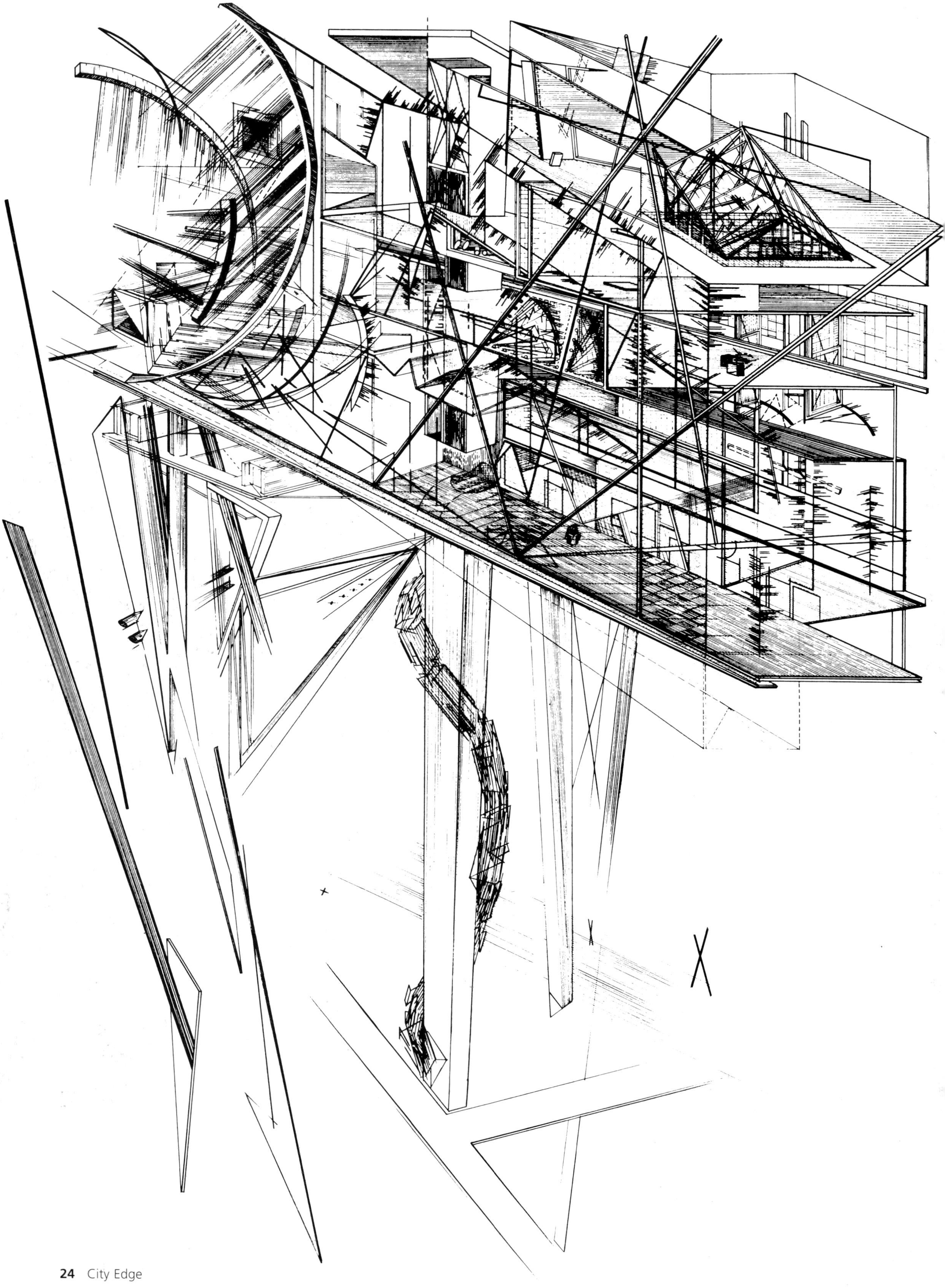

"Lightness" pencil drawing

Joyce model
"Never is the Center" 1988
("Mies van der Rohe memorial")

Out of Line, Berlin

Site plan with "Aleph Wing"

ANGEL TRAPPING HISTORY
Berlin could be seen as an exemplary spiritual capital of the 21st century, as it once was the apocalyptic symbol of the 20th century's demise. The identity of Berlin cannot be re-founded on the ruins of history or on the illusory 'reconstructions' of an arbitrarily selected past.

The design echoes the contortions of the non-existent angel; but the contortions are as real as those of all the other deported archangels: Franz Kafka, Walter Benjamin, Primo Levi, Osip Mandelstam, Paul Celan .... The ten thunderbolts of absolute absence are deployed to alter the physical image of Berlin and to open joyous channels of communication, re-membering the future.

RELEASING THE VIEW
The concept of the site-as-puzzle has been derived from the symbolic fragments of memory of Potsdamer Platz as they have been recorded in nine projective/hysterical viewpoints. These accelerated time perspectives develop a momentum which finally cancels the very notion of perspective.

Like Humpty Dumpty's shattering act, this spot cannot be 'put together again' even by 'all the King's horses and all the King's men.' The site-puzzle is in fact the entry into a tenth 'gate': the post-contemporary city, where the view is cleared beyond the constriction of domination, power and the gridlocked mind.

PLACE MOSAIC TIME
The transformation of the shape of the (future) city must be accompanied by corresponding changes in the mentality associated with pre-war lot lines, anachronistic visions, dreams which money can buy. What is necessary is an optimistic view of the 21st century: a radical rethinking of zoning, function, property and program. These categories are no longer appropriate to the changed relationship between capitol, capital, public responsibility and the end of ideology. Thus 'totality', 'uniformity' and 'master planning' are over twice—once in the East and once in the West. The pieces of the mosaic come from around Europe: Paris, Venice, Vienna, Berlin ... and Elsewhere.

The profound undertaking of refounding Potsdamer Platz must be taken at its face value, through the presence of witnesses, dates, anniversaries—*Places out of Time.*

ILLUMINATED MUSE MATRIX
What is needed is a connection of Berlin to and across its own history. This connection, this movement goes through the relation of the old and the new, capitol and capital, full and empty, the 'no longer' and the 'not yet.'

The (9 + 1) x (Muse) lines embody a diverse set of programs related to their use and function. These structures are buildings going over, on and below the streets containing housing, production, cultural and leisure functions. Apartments, factories, markets, hospitals, kindergartens, cemeteries, speakers' corners, cafés, libraries, communication and information centers connect to office buildings, housing and transportation systems throughout the city.

The Muses constitute a diurnal and nocturnal journey through the geography of Potsdamer Platz, as well as through the topology of Berlin's culture. Historical places and old streets have been left as they are, removed from the realm of the monumental and left to the eye of past history.

MAPPING THE IN: VISIBLE CITY
The lost center cannot be reconnected like an artificial limb to an old body, but must generate an overall transformation of the city.

Potsdamer Platz can be the place where the East-West, center-periphery division can overcome the conflicts which were born and witnessed and which died in this very place.

These conflicts cannot be resolved by reconstructing a hollow past, but by laying new foundations and new images which are open to concrete dynamics.

Thus no style or system should be given priority over others. A heterogeneous, pluralistic reality is the goal.

The only priority manifested in this scheme is that a small child should be able to discover a dream and an imaginative future.

RESONATING PLATE
The New Potsdamer Platz contains a myriad of diverse world-spaces and is symbolized by the 'prytaneion-field-building' supporting a tranquil and flexible space which is based on the simple principle that people from around the world form the 'shareholder's association,' thus owning a share of Potsdamer Platz. Soil from the World on the roof, wilderness of Berlin on the ground.

This elevated structure hovers like a plow over the land. Everyone now has the right to a space in the wilderness, the possibility of cultivation, streams of seeds powered by wind and sail, the eye-I-cure, thunderstorms, sky-books, artificial sun-rain, spark-writing, plantation in the clouds, the waterfall, inspiration ... all necessities in the Berlin of tomorrow.

THE CITY IS NO LONGER **MAN** WRITTEN LARGE BUT MAN IS CITY WRITTEN VERY SMALL—AND ALMOST ILLEGIBLY: CITY.
THE NEW VISION FOR BERLIN IS NOT UTOPIAN IN NATURE; RATHER IT ENVISIONS CONCRETELY A PLACE WHICH HAS LEARNED FROM ITS PAST AND WHICH LOOKS TO THE FUTURE. THE CHANCE TO RESTRUCTURE, REPLAN, RETHINK, REDO SHOULD NOT BE LOST IN THE SIMPLISTIC SOLUTION OF SELECTIVE RECONSTRUCTION, SINCE EVEN ORPHEUS DID NOT SUCCEED IN WALKING BACKWARDS INTO THE FUTURE.
LEARNED FROM ITS PAST AND LOOKS TO THE FUTURE. THE CHANCE TO RESTRUCTURE, REPLAN, RETHINK, REDO SHOULD NOT BE LOST IN THE SIMPLISTIC SOLUTION OF SELECTIVE RECONSTRUCTION, SINCE EVEN ORPHEUS DID NOT SUCCEED IN WALKING BACKWARDS INTO THE FUTURE.
THE FEELING FOR AN ATMOSPHERE OF SANCTITY AND DETACHMENT WILL NOT MAKE AN APPEARANCE AGAIN WITH THE PARAPHERNALIA BELONGING TO AN APOTHEOSIS OF AN ETERNAL STYLE DETACHMENT WILL NOT AGAIN MAKE AN APPEARANCE WITH THE PARAPHERNALIA BELONGING TO AN APOTHEOSIS OF AN ETERNAL STYLE. I DON'T CARE FOR DISORDER AND I DREAD POLICE PROTECTION AS WELL.

O U T O F L I N E
1 9 9 1

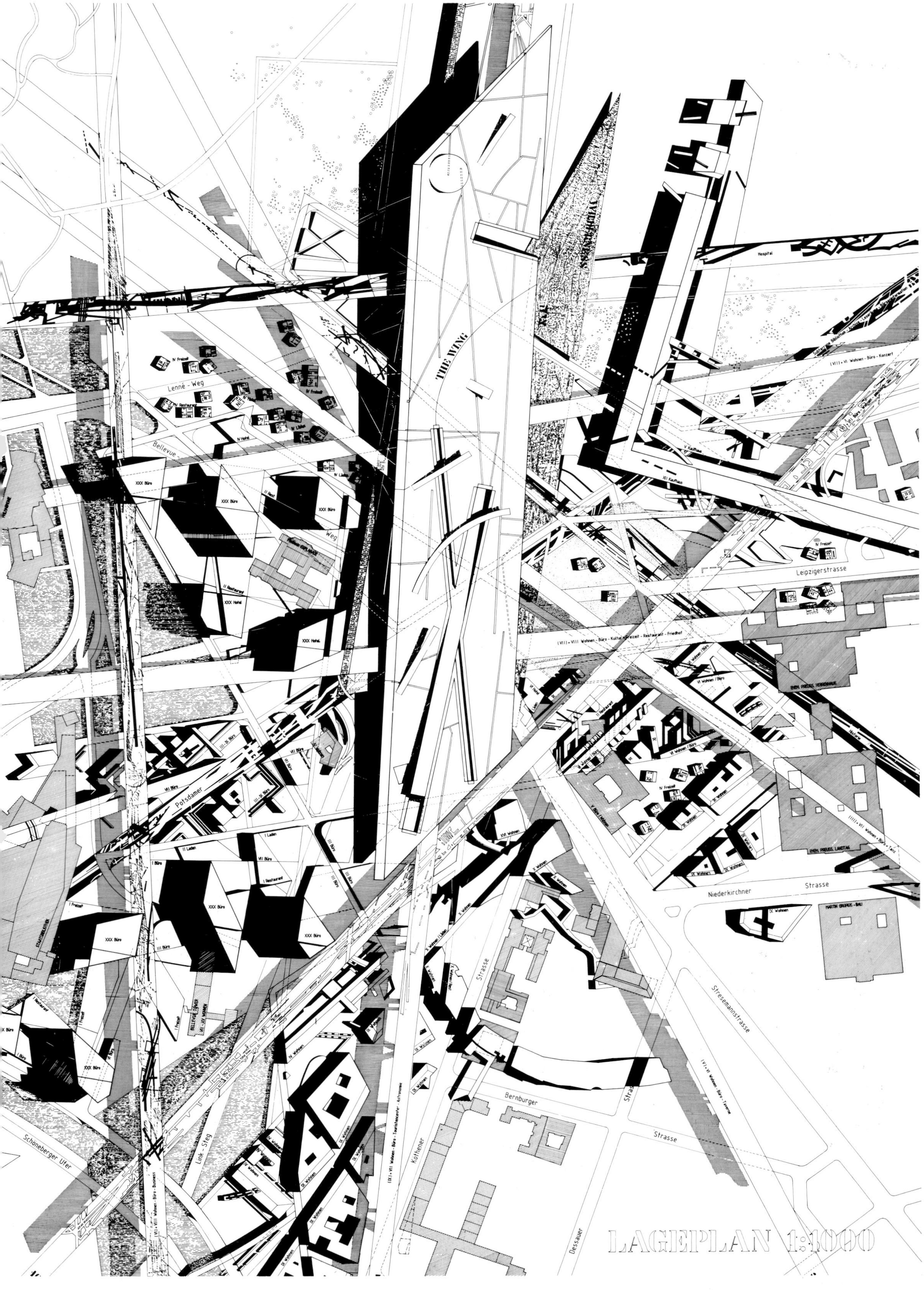

THE WING
Hospital
Lenné - Weg
Bellevue
Weg
Leipzigerstrasse
(VIII) • VIII Wohnen - Büro - Kultur - Freizeit - Restaurant - Friedhof
EHEM. PREUSS. HERRENHAUS
Potsdamer
EHEM. PREUSS. LANDTAG
Niederkirchner Strasse
MARTIN GROPIUS - BAU
Strasse
Stresemannstrasse
Bernburger
Strasse
Köthener
Link - Steg
Schöneberger Ufer
Dessauer
LAGEPLAN 1:1000

Puzzle pieces model

"Illuminated Muse Matrix"

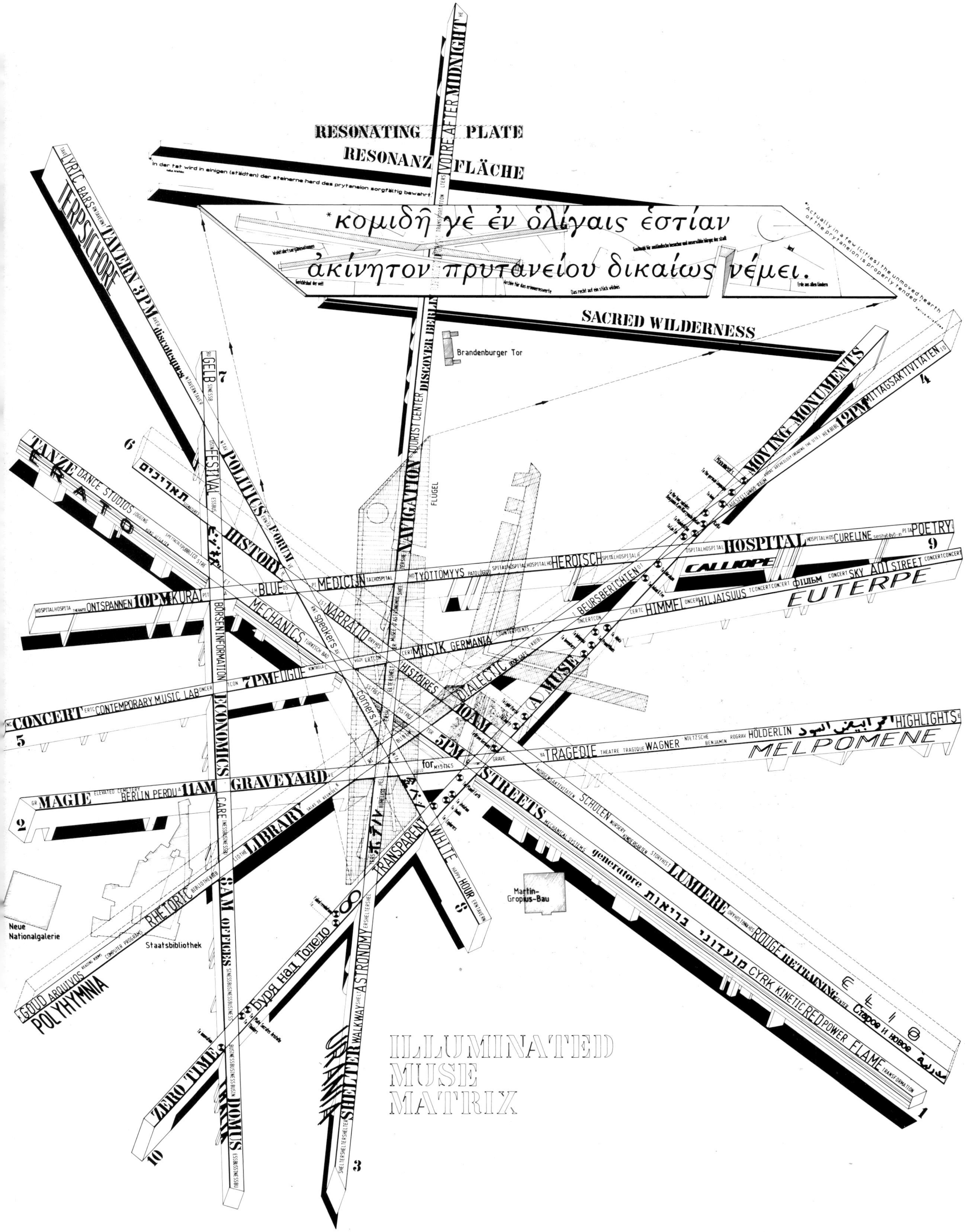
RESONATING PLATE
RESONANZ FLÄCHE
VOIRE AFTER MIDNIGHT
*κομιδῆ γὲ ἐν ὀλίγαις ἑστίαν
ἀκίνητον πρυτανείου δικαίως νέμει.
*Actually in a few (cities) the unmoved hearth of the prytaneion is properly tended
SACRED WILDERNESS
Brandenburger Tor
LYRIC BARS
TERPSICHORE
TAVERN 3PM
DISCOVER BERLIN
TOURIST CENTER
NAVIGATION
FLÜGEL
MOVING MONUMENTS
12PM
MITTAGSAKTIVITÄTEN
TANZE
DANCE STUDIOS
ERATO
GELB
FESTIVAL
POLITICS
FORUM
HISTORY
POETRY
HOSPITAL
CURELINE
CALLIOPE
HEROISCH
BEURSBERICHTEN
EUTERPE
SKY ART STREET
HIMMEL
HILJAISUUS
ONTSPANNEN
10PM
KURA
BLUE
MEDICIN
TYÖTTOMYYS
MECHANICS
NARRATIO
MUSIK GERMANIA
BÖRSENINFORMATION
CONCERT
CONTEMPORARY MUSIC LAB
7PM FUGUE
HISTOIRES
DIALECTIC
MUSE
10AM
ECONOMICS
5PM
TRAGEDIE
WAGNER
HÖLDERLIN
HIGHLIGHTS
MELPOMENE
MAGIE
BERLIN PERDU
11AM
GRAVEYARD
STREETS
SCHULEN
LIBRARY
TRANSPARENT
WHITE
HAPPY HOUR
generatore
LUMIERE
Martin-Gropius-Bau
RHETORIC
9AM OFFICES
ROUGE
RETRAINING
CYRK KINETIC RED POWER FLAME
CLIO
Старое и новое
Neue Nationalgalerie
Staatsbibliothek
COMPUTER PROGRAMS
GOUD ARQUIVOS
POLYHYMNIA
Буря над Толедо
ASTRONOMY
SHELTER WALKWAY
URANIA
ZERO TIME
DOMUS
ILLUMINATED MUSE MATRIX
1
2
3
4
5
6
7
8
9
10

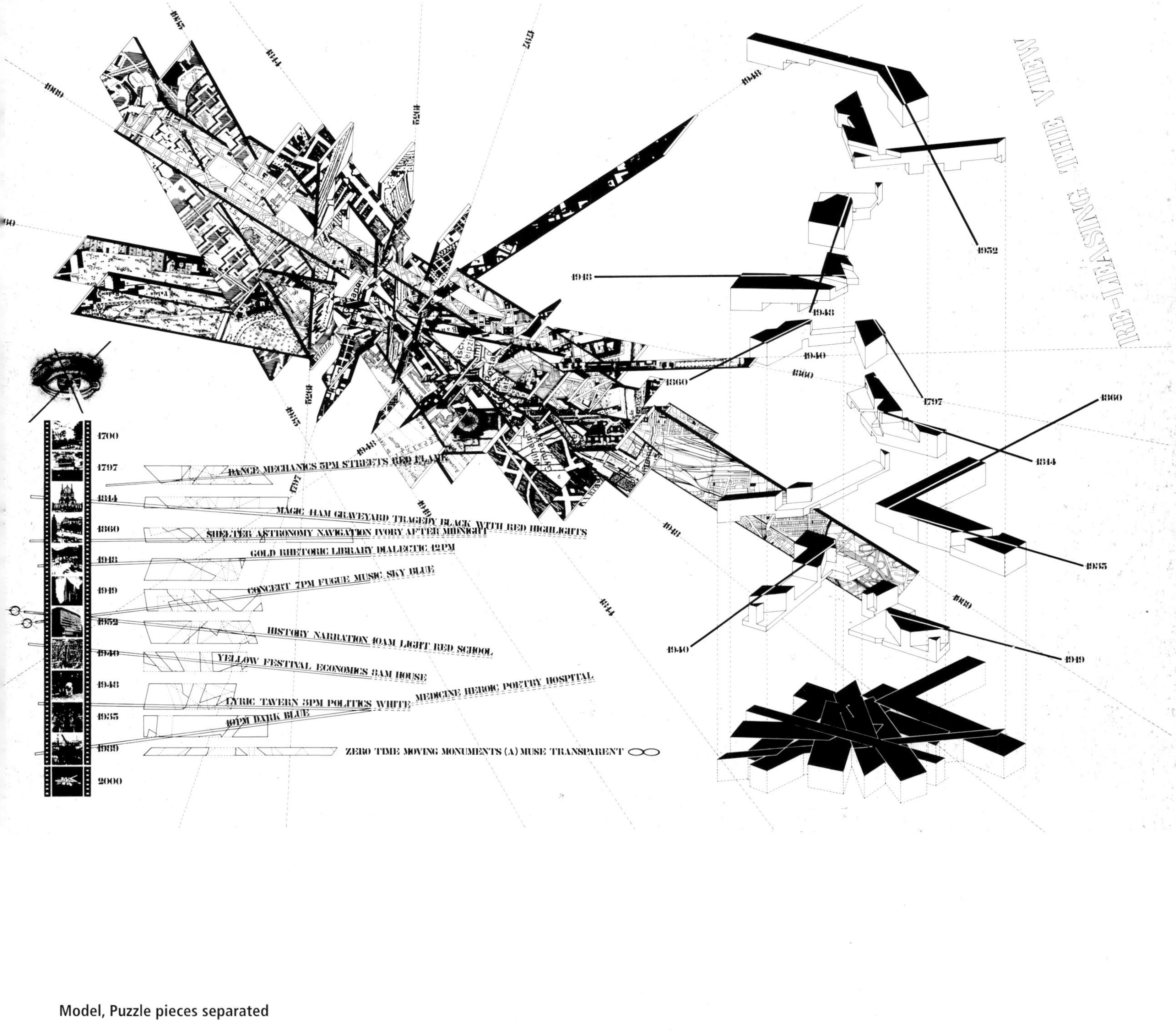

Model, Puzzle pieces separated

"Re-leasing the View," construction site as puzzle

Habitable Bridge, London

Out of Water: X-web with a point

In this competition for a habitable bridge over the Thames, I have sought to rethink the idea of a bridge for the 21st century. The traditional notion of the bridge has been to overcome water — conceived as a barrier — by constructing an element linking the two banks of the river; a binary logic AB, creating by its sheer exsistence the separation of the banks it sought to overcome. This scheme proposes to celebrate the Thames through a multivalent and non-linear connection to the many places of London. The proposal no longer points to the separation of the north and south bank, nor to outdated economies, but rather makes this strategic site central to London as a whole.

The proposal includes two interrelated components: the first is a vertical inhabitable bridge in the form of an undulating tower coming directly out of the water and reaching a height equivalent of the width of the river. The second is a web of pedestrian walkways, which on both the first and second levels create a delicate public filigree connecting many different points of the riverbank.

The vertical bridge is conceived as a slender column which in its form and position connects London as a city of vertical spires with its horizon, the Thames. The tower represents a twenty-four hour beacon of life, activity, and economy making itself visible as an orienting point from all over London. It is deliberately decentered, shifting the virtual center line of the river towards the south bank. The vertical bridge takes its bird-like sail form in order to reflect light, deflect views and modulate the winds, while presenting a dynamic and ever-changing silhouette.

The pedestrian web in an intricate, delicate urban structure dematerializing the horizontal weight of the connections. There are diverse and unexpected pathways, forming a membrane of public activities. The structure is a combination of pylons and tensile member creating a mutually supportive heterogeneous tensegrity structure over the river.

The web contains pavilions, cafes, recreational places for winter and summer (covered and open), distributing a field of diverse spaces and events suspended over the water. There is a functional pathway to service the tower hidden amidst the pedestrian routes. The web and the bridge generate a sense of adventure and excitement, celebrating the water without obliterating or obscuring the drama of the Thames and the city around it. The proposal lifts the bridge from the horizontal to the vertical position emphatically opening the Thames to the people of London.

View from the South Bank

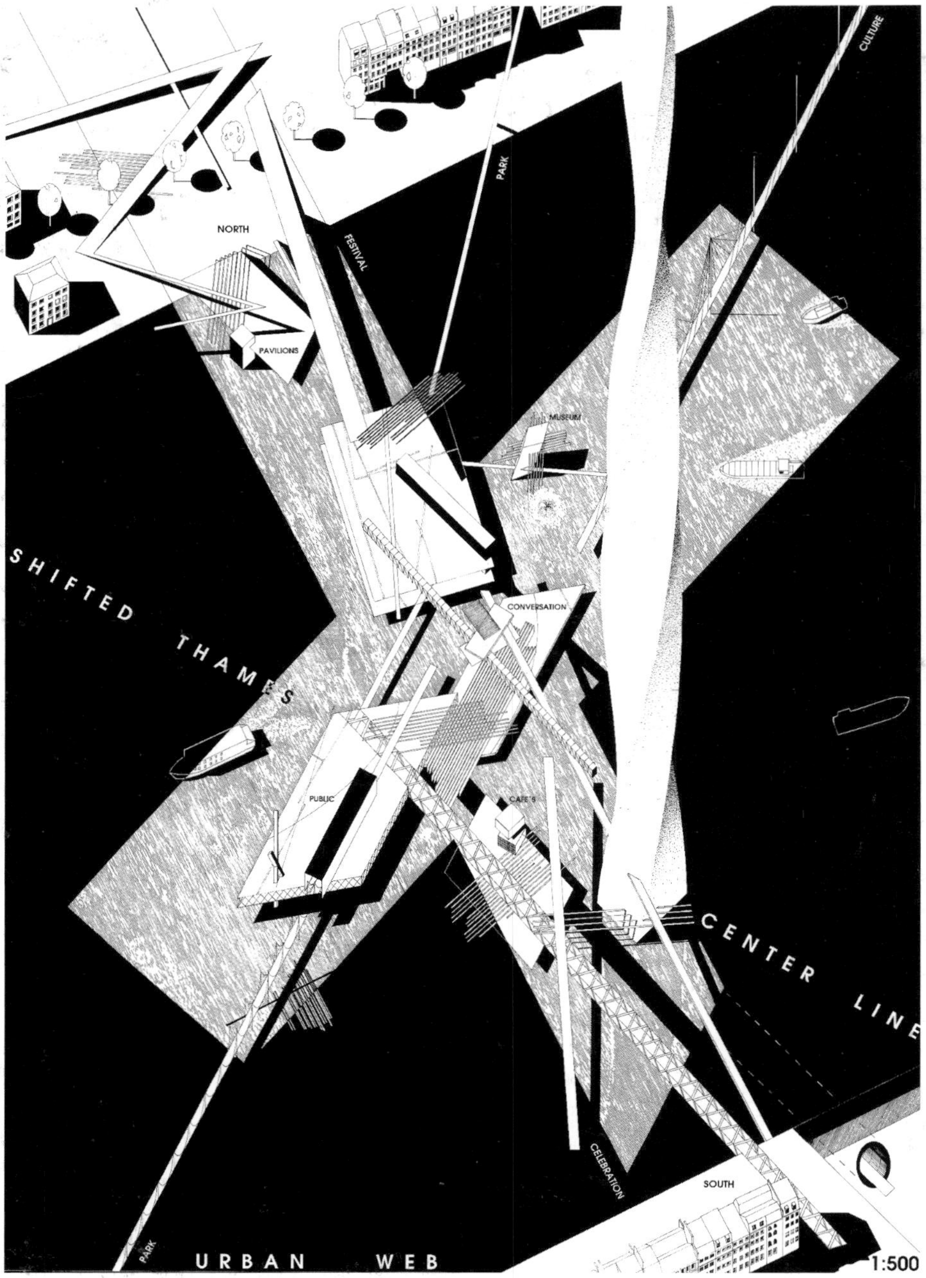

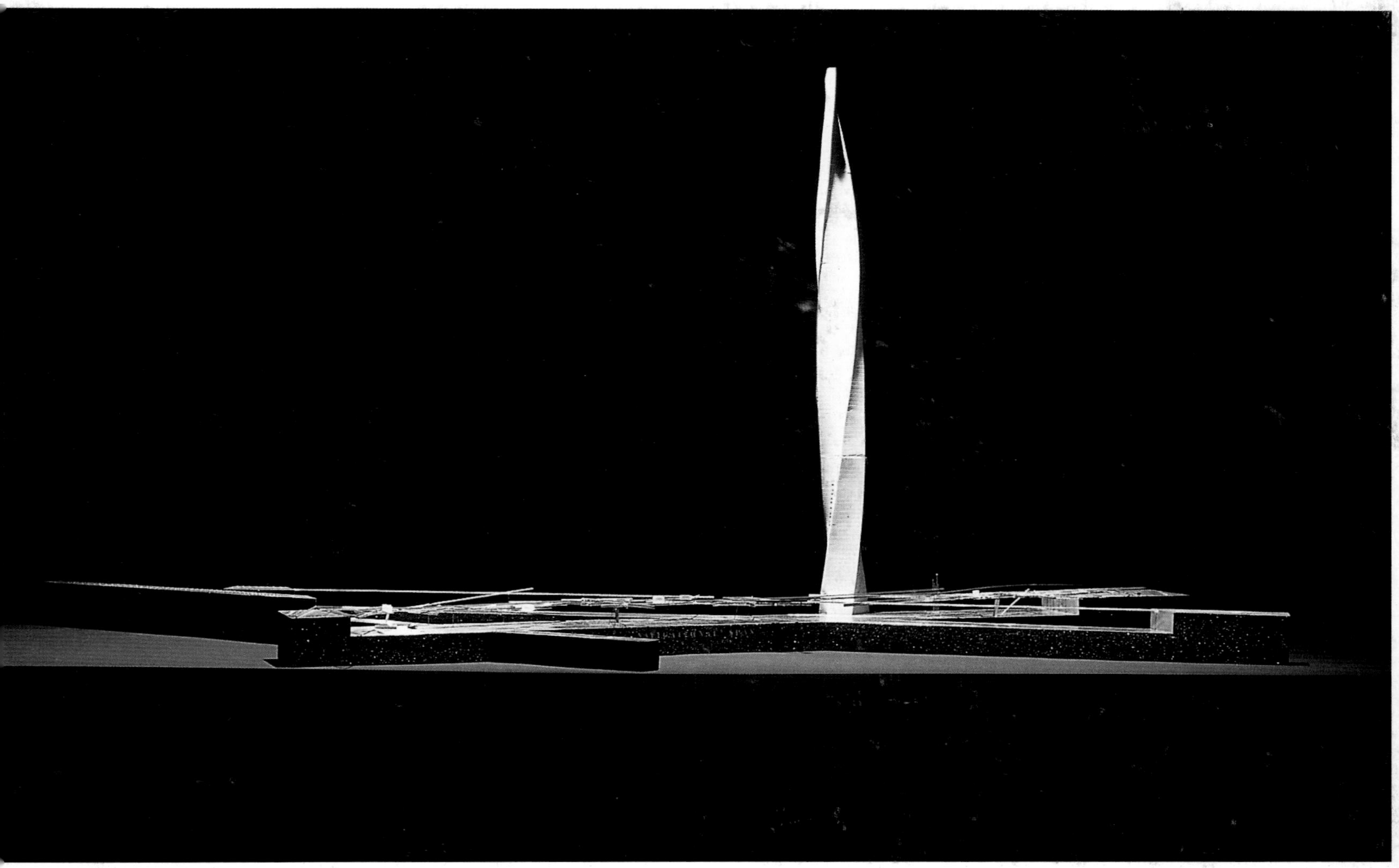

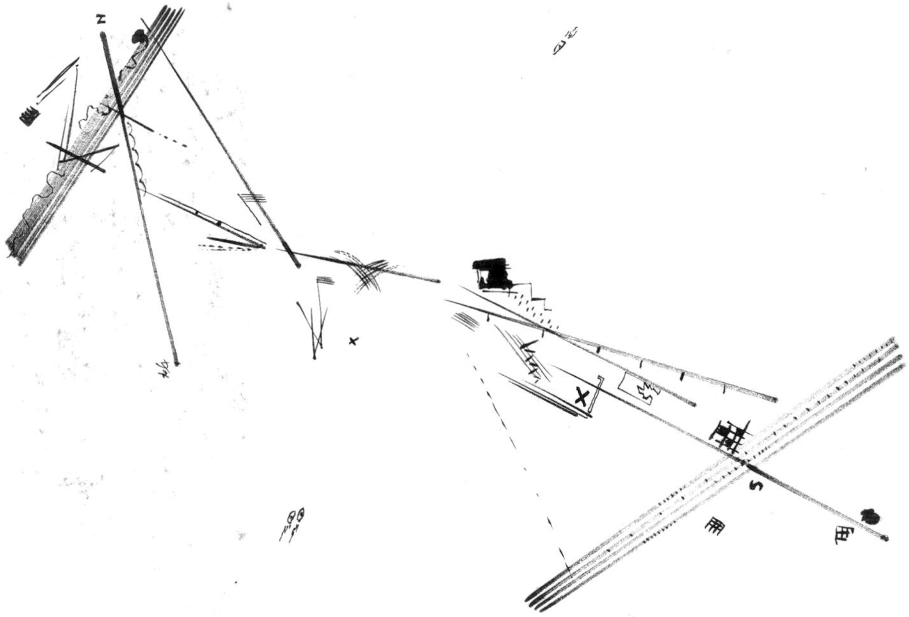

Model

Concept drawing

Concept Matrix

Between the Lines

The Berlin Museum with the Jewish Museum

The official name of the project is 'Extension of the Berlin Museum with the Jewish Museum Department', but I have called it 'Between the Lines.' I call it this because it is a project about two lines of thought, organization and relationship. One is a straight line, but broken into many fragments; the other is a tortuous line, but continuing infinitely. These two lines develop architecturally and programmatically through a limited but definite dialogue. They also fall apart, become disengaged and are seen as separated. In this way, they expose a void which runs through this museum, a discontinuous void.

The site is at Lindenstrasse, near the Rondel, once a famous Baroque intersection of Wilhelmstrasse, Friedrichstrasse and Lindenstrasse, and next to the distinguished Collegienhaus. The physical trace of Berlin is not the only trace, however. There is an invisible matrix or anamnesis of connections in relationship. I found this connection between figures of Germans and Jews.

I felt that certain people, particularly certain writers, composers, artists and poets, formed the link between Jewish tradition and German culture. So I found this connection and plotted an irrational matrix in the form of a system of intertwining triangles that would yield some reference to the emblem of a compressed and distorted star: the yellow star which was so frequently worn on this very site. I looked for the addresses at which these people had lived or worked. For example, someone like Rachel Varnhagen I connected to Friedrich Schleiermacher, and Paul Celan to someone like Mies van der Rohe and so on, and I was quite surprised that it was not so difficult to hear and plot the impact these people made: they formed a particular urban and cultural constellation of Universal History. So that is one aspect of the project.

Another aspect was Arnold Schönberg. I was always interested in the music of Schönberg, in particular his period in Berlin. His greatest work is an opera called *Moses and Aaron* which he could not complete. For some reason, the logic of the text, which hinged upon the relationship between Moses and Aaron, between, one can say, the revealed, unimaginable truth and the spoken, mass-produced people's truth, led to an impasse in which the music—the text written by Schönberg—could not be completed.

In the end, Moses doesn't sing, he just speaks 'Oh word, thou word', and one can understand this as a text as opposed to a normal opera whose performance usually obliterates the text. When there is singing, one cannot understand the words, but when there is no more singing, one can clearly understand the missing word uttered by Moses: the call for the Word. So that is the second aspect of this project.

The third aspect of the work is my interest in the names of those people who were deported from Berlin during the fatal years, the Holocaust, which one now knows only historically. I received from Bonn two very large volumes called *Gedenkbuch*. They are incredibly impressive because all they contain are names, just names, dates of birth, dates of deportation and presumed places where these people were murdered. So I looked for the names of the Berliners and where they had died—in Riga, in Lodz, in all the concentration camps.

The fourth aspect of the project is formed by Walter Benjamin's *One Way Street.* This aspect is incorporated into the continuous sequence of sixty sections along the zigzag, each of which represents one of the 'Stations of the Star' described in the text of Benjamin's apocalypse of Berlin.

In specific terms, the building measures more than 10,000 square meters. The building goes under the existing building, criss-crosses underground and materializes independently on the outside. The existing building is tied to the extension underground, preserving the contradictory autonomy of both the old building and the new building on the surface, while binding the two together in depth, underground.

With its special emphasis on housing the Jewish Museum, it is an attempt to give a voice to a common fate—the inevitable integration of Jewish/Berlin history despite the contradictions of the ordered and disordered, the chosen and not chosen, the vocal and silent, the living and dead.

So the new extension is conceived as an emblem in which the invisible, the Void, makes itself apparent as such. The Void and the invisible are the structural features that have been gathered in the space of Berlin and exposed in an architecture in which the unnamed remains in the names which keep silent.

To put it simply, the museum is a zigzag with a structural rib, which is the Void of the Jewish Museum running across it. And this Void is something which every participant in the museum will experience as his or her own absent presence.

That's basically a summary of how the building works. It's not a collage or a collision or a simple dialectic, but a new type of organization which is organized around a center which is not, around what is not visible. And what is not visible is the richness of the Jewish heritage in Berlin, which is today reduced to archival and archaeological material, since physically it has disappeared.

I believe this scheme joins architecture to questions which are now relevant to all humanity. What I've tried to say is that the Jewish history of Berlin is not separable from the history of Modernity, from the destiny of this incineration of history; they are bound together. But not bound by means of any obvious forms, rather through faith; through an absence of meaning and an absence of artefacts. Absence therefore serves as a way of binding in depth, and in a totally different manner, the shared hopes of people. This is a conception which does not reduce the museum or architecture to a detached memorial or memorable detachment. It is, instead, a conception which re-integrates Jewish/Berlin history through the unhealable wound of faith, which in the words of Hebrews 11:2 is the 'substance of things hoped-for; proof of things invisible.'

View of Facade 0

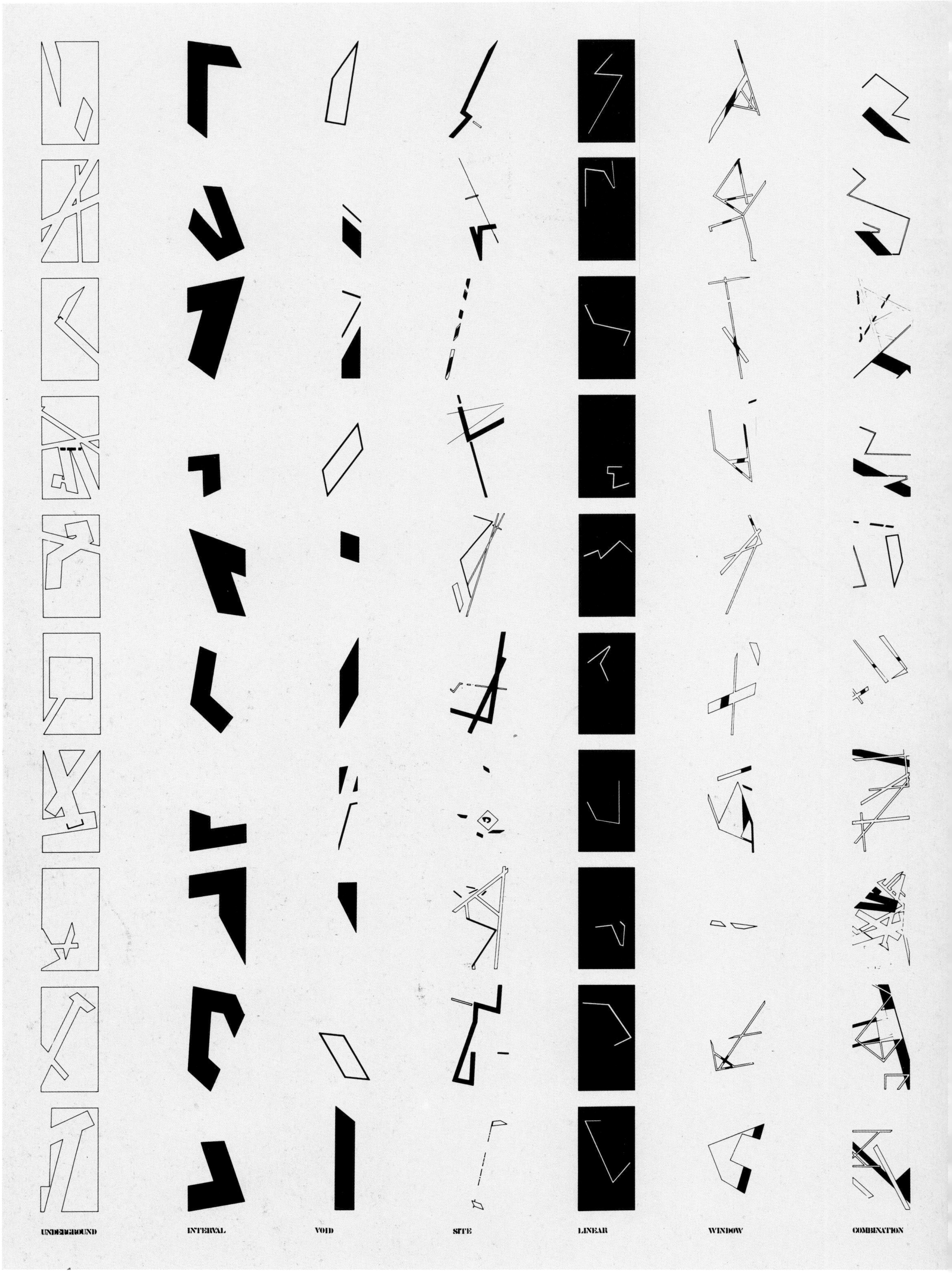
UNDERGROUND
INTERVAL
VOID
SITE
LINEAR
WINDOW
COMBINATION

"The Alphabet"

"Names" model

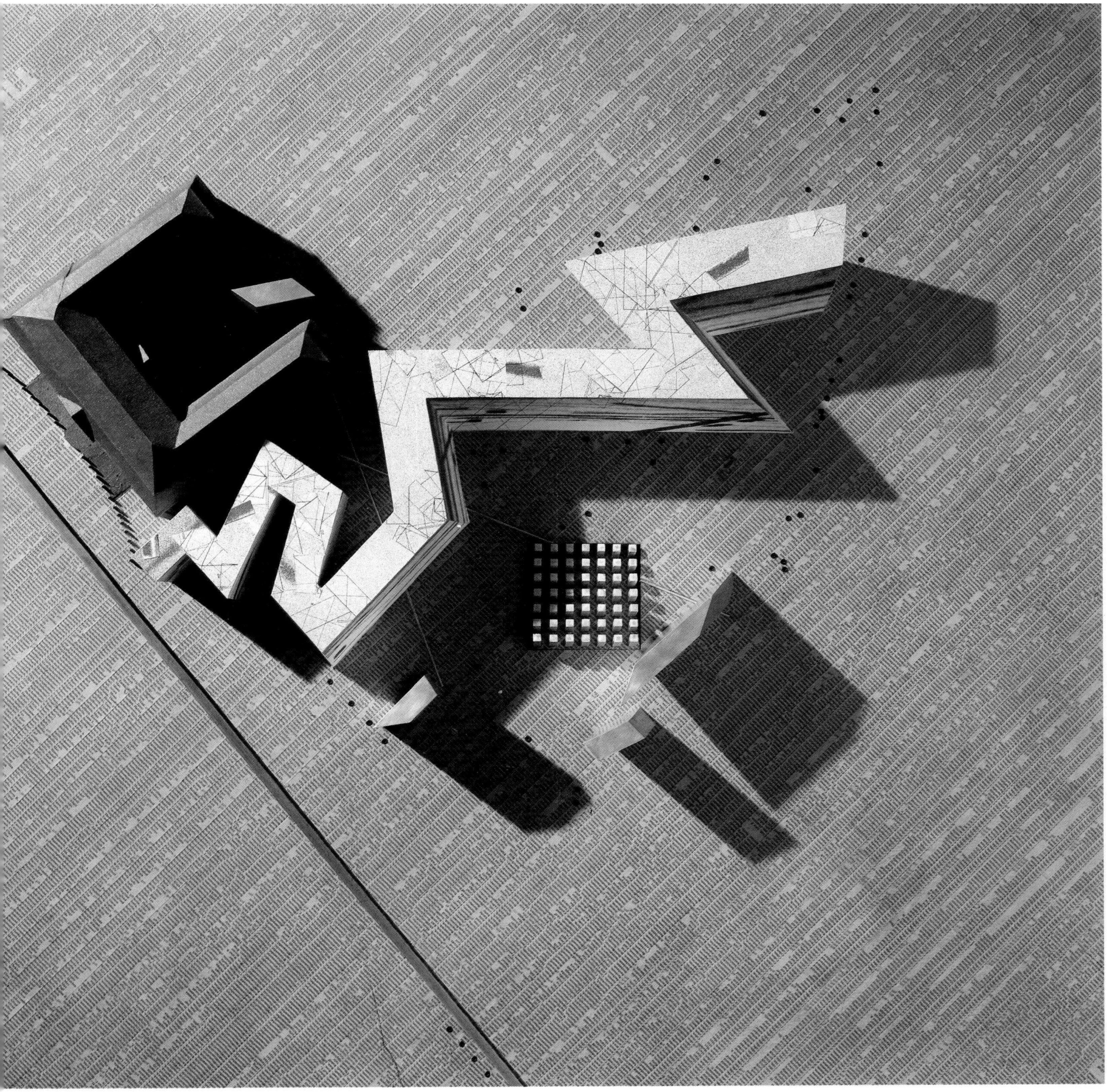

Site plan, competition stage

View from Lindenstrasse

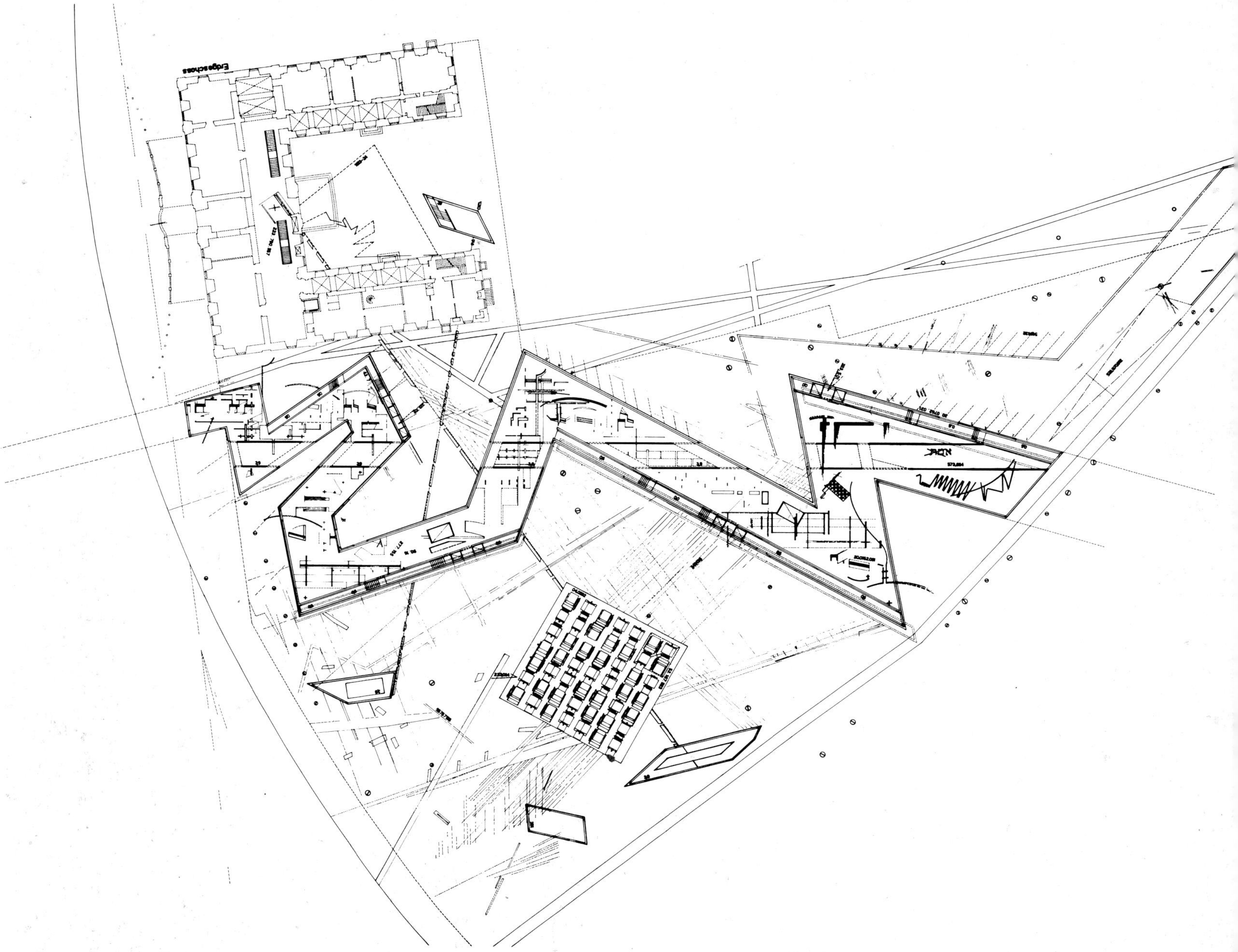

2 Stunden
Di - So
10-18 h
Chuck Berry
Jerry Lee Lewis
Little Richard
13. Juni bis 7. September • Berlin
Die Dinosaurier
sind zurück!

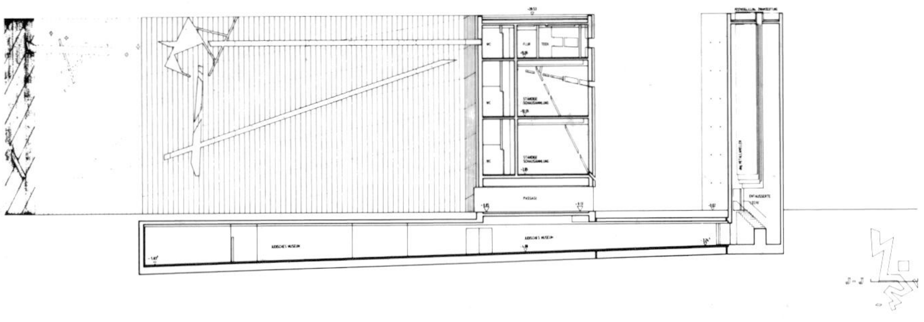

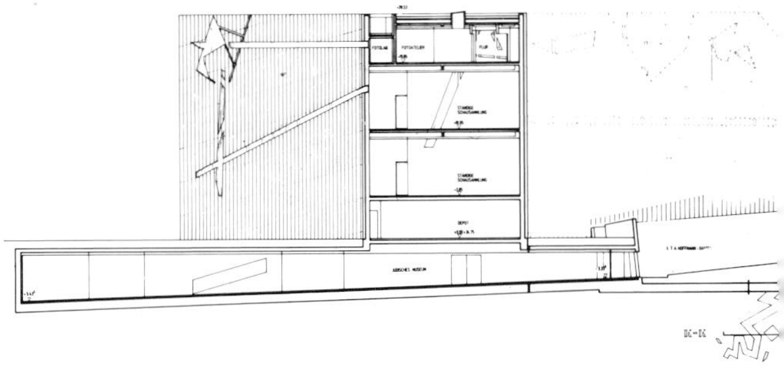

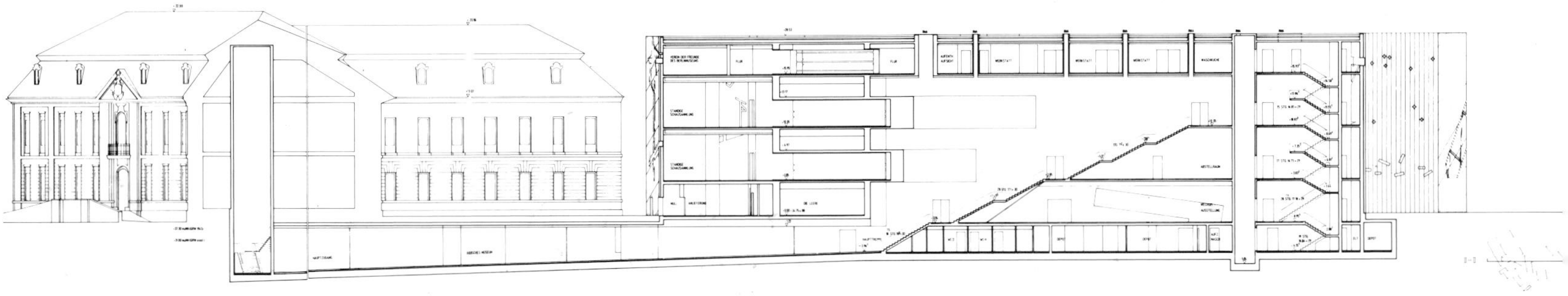

Section through main stair and Holocaust Void

View from South

Facade coordinates

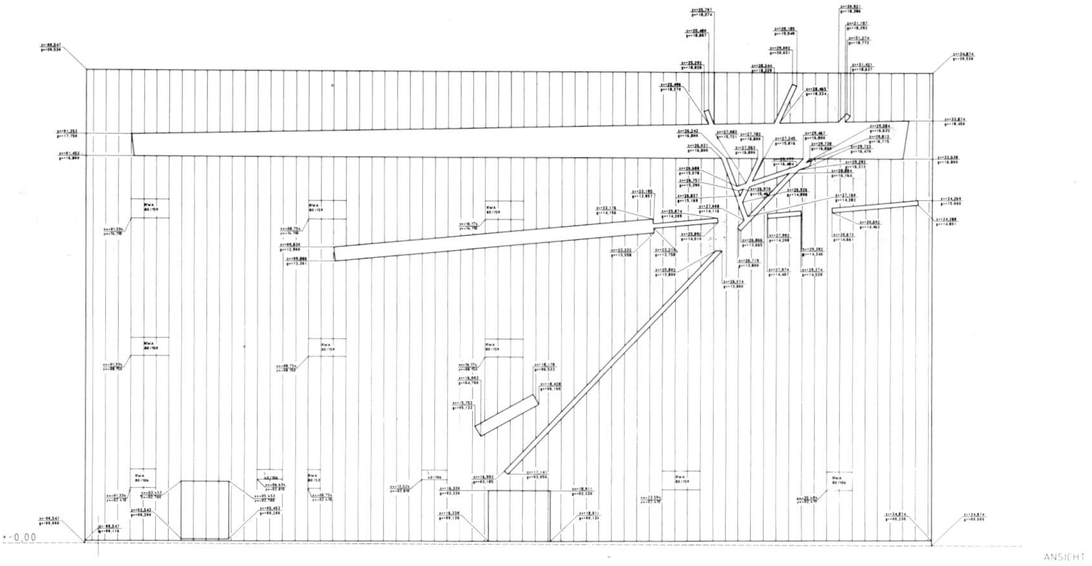
+-0,00
ANSICHT

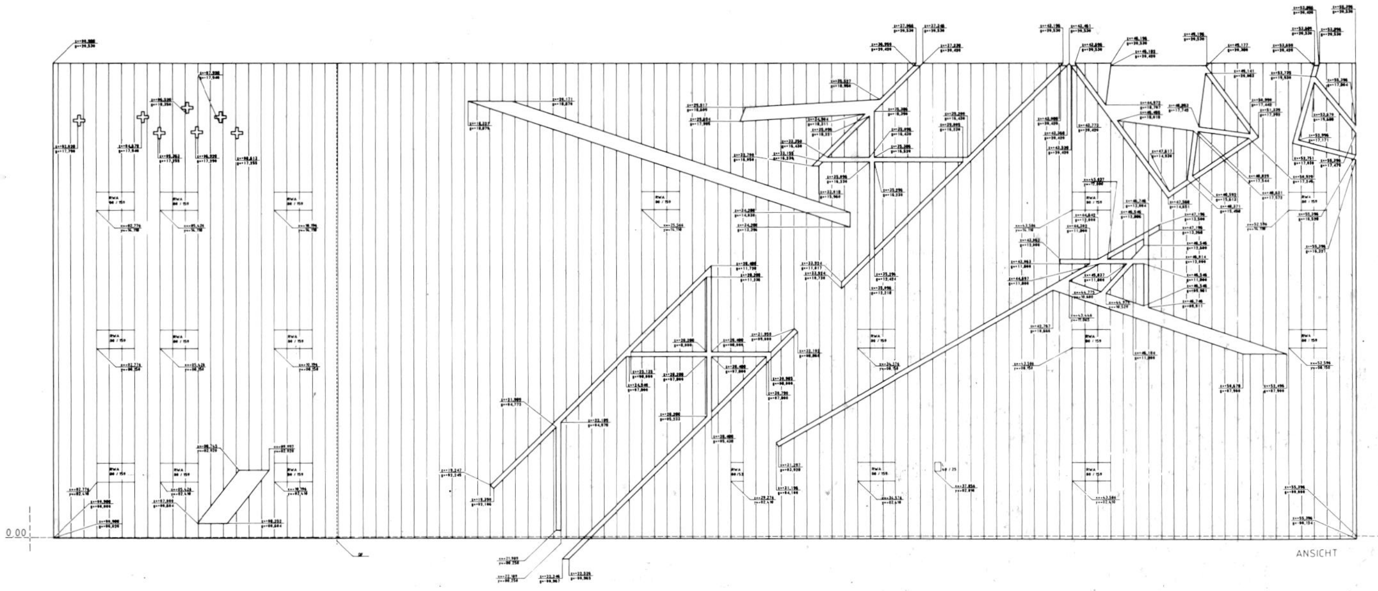
0,00
ANSICHT

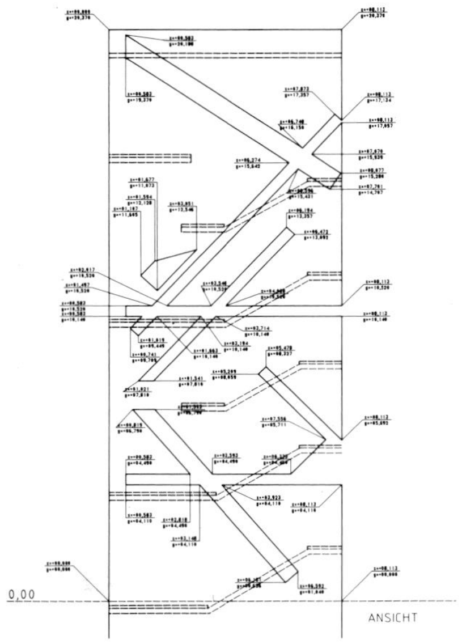
0,00
ANSICHT

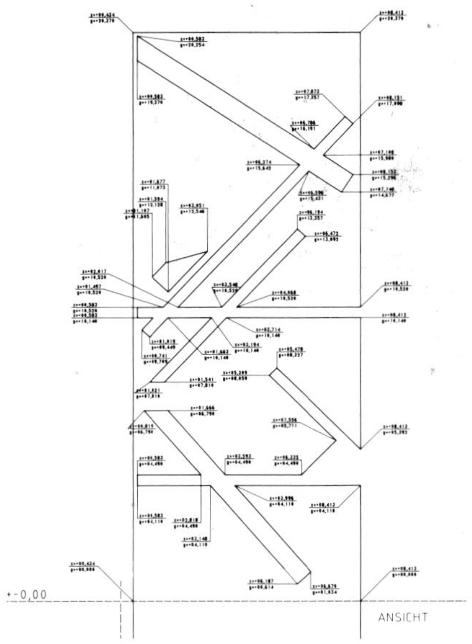
+-0,00
ANSICHT

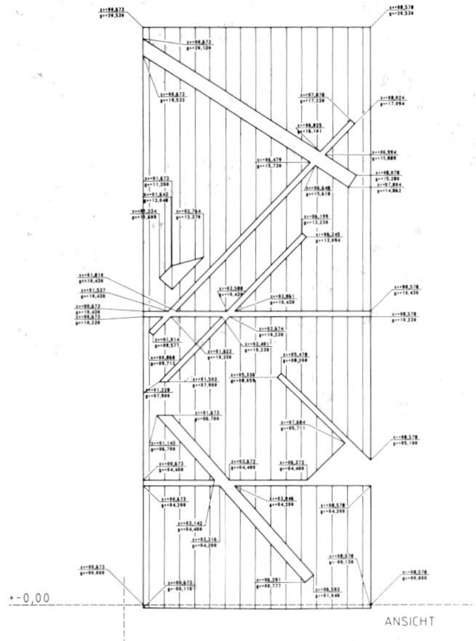
+-0,00
ANSICHT

Underground model showing "three roads", Voids and ETA Hoffmann Garden

Facade, Structural calculation plan

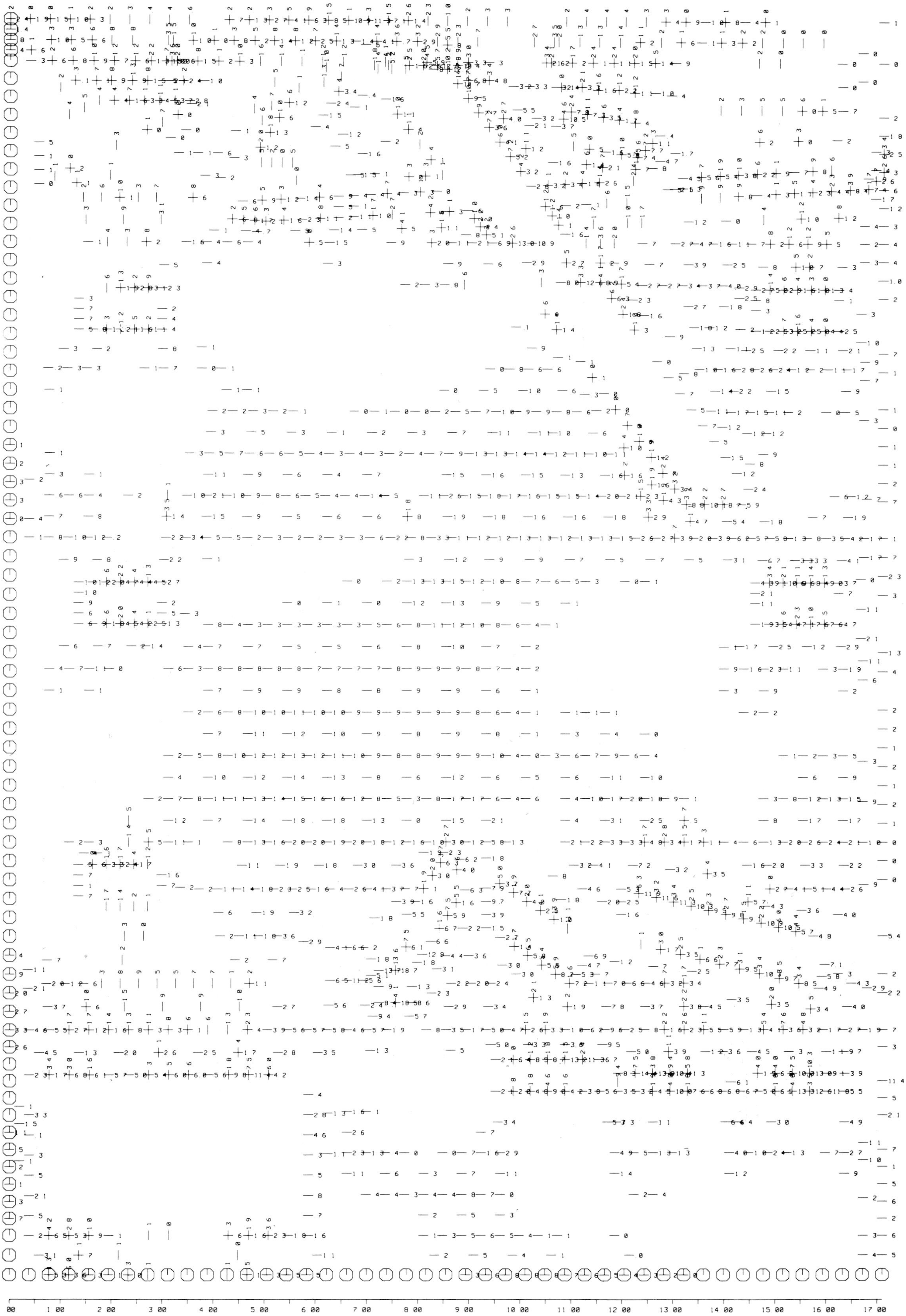
00
1 00
2 00
3 00
4 00
5 00
6 00
7 00
8 00
9 00
10 00
11 00
12 00
13 00
14 00
15 00
16 00
17 00

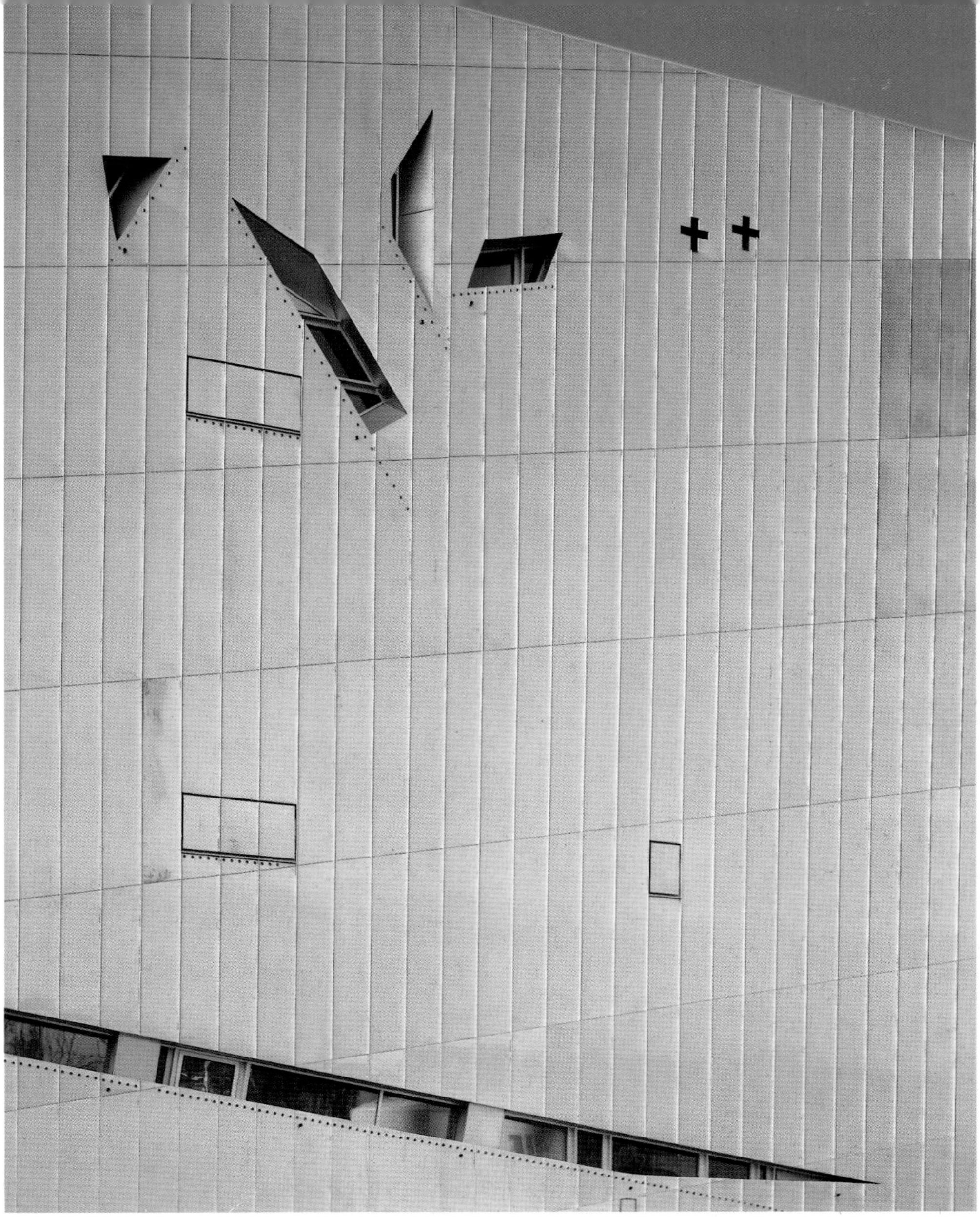

Paul Celan Hof

Facade details

View of Void Six with Bridges

Void One

Void space

Main stair with structural beams

Main stair

Garden of Exile

View from within

Open doorway to the garden

View of interior exhibition space

Interior of front stair

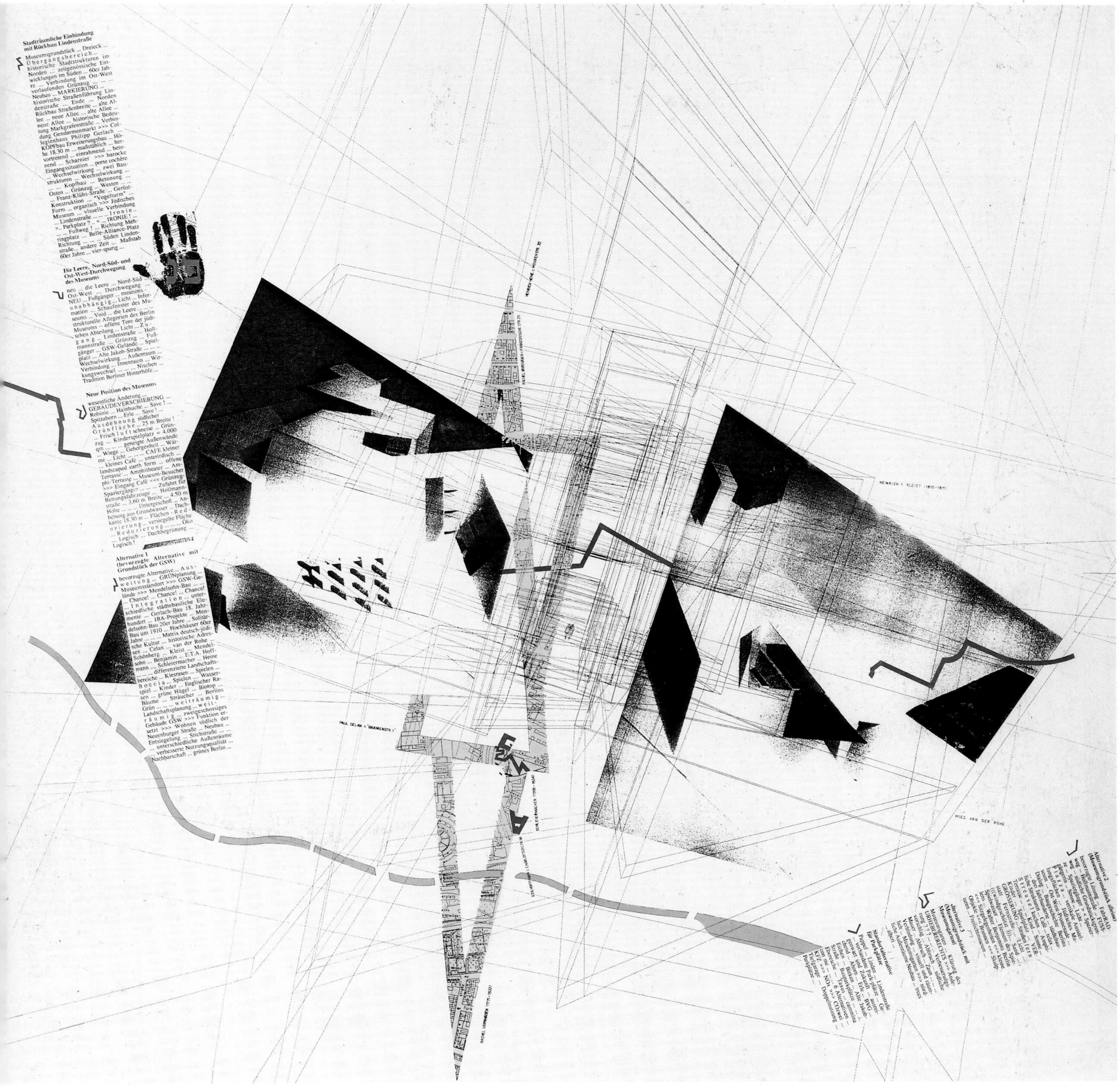

View of Holocaust Void looking up

Star Matrix

Museum without Exit: Felix Nussbaum Museum, Osnabrück

Development model showing entrance with old Swedish Bridge

It's only by a fortuitous accident and the determined will of the town of Osnabrück that the name and works of Felix Nussbaum have emerged from amongst the millions of erased Jewish names and lost works. The task of building a museum to house the artistic remnants of Nussbaum's life raises issues which are not merely architectural, but moral. I therefore believe that the destruction of Jewish culture by the Third Reich must not be dealt with solely in memorial terms. The remaining witnesses to the annihilation of European Jewry are now dying out. The paintings of Nussbaum are more than paintings—they are ever-living documents which, placed in a new context of participation and witness, elevate the narration of history as art into the emblem of the very survival of the Jewish people and of European civilization. Every element of the spatial organization, geometry and programmatic content of this scheme refers to the paradigmatic destiny of Nussbaum: his prize in Rome removed by the Nazis; the time in Berlin; the consequences of his exile from Osnabrück; the futility of escape routes through France and Belgium; his deportation and murder in Auschwitz. And yet all this tragic destiny is placed in the context of Nussbaum's abiding hope in ulitmate justice, which this proposed scheme seeks to fulfill.

It is part of the mission of this design to house the Nussbaum collection in a new museum complex, as well as to transform the entire historical ensemble of buildings into yet another whole. Expressive of permanent absence, the Museum of the Unwitnessed and Unfulfilled is a museum resonant of the fatality as well as the significance of the unrepresentable abyss of the Holocaust. The museum has a particular task: to avoid a sentimental moment in order the thematize the existing historical context of Osnabrück through the disclosure of new cultural values. The different components of the new complex are seen as connecting and composing an integral structure while at the same time exposing a permanent horizon of disconnection which paradoxically links significant places to the town, substantial points of history to spatial memory. The new building therefore does not seek to dominate as a new form, but rather retreats to form a background of hope for the existing Historical Museum and the Villa containing the folk-art collection. These buildings are treated as familiar, yet solitary everyday figures, while the entire site is reorganized around the nexus of a new topography which connects the town back onto itself. The Nussbaum Museum becomes the link to a lost history. It transmits the mysterious irreversibililty of time and destiny.

The visitor enters laterally into the Nussbaum Pathway, which is cut open in order to record and define the importance of entering the 'Museum without Exit.' The exterior of the Nussbaum Pathway is absence itself—an empty canvas of Nussbaum's martyred life—referring to the absoluteness of the crime and the importance of the public site, bequeathing a sense of openness and incompleteness necessary for the interpretation of Nussbaum's oeuvre. Within the Nussbaum Pathway there are traces of the vitality of the former Jewish life of Osnabrück. Once visitors are inside this compressed space illuminated by triangular skylights, they are confronted with a displaced volume containing the vertical entrance volume and its attendant functions. The Nussbaum Pathway makes the musuem complex visible as well as inscribing the invisible incinerated synagogue. The visitor is placed in the precarious equilibrium between the collected and the uncollectable, the recollected and the unrecordable. The Nussbaum Pathway leads the visitor through the compressed geomtery of the double cone of vision, which (forwards and backwards in time) gives the visual and kinetic embodiment of the Star of David which Nussbaum chose as his final birth and death-mark.

This trajectory through the museum makes the visitor aware of the interplay between the lost shadows of the synagogue and the light of an anticipated future. The visitor moves towards the open space of the temporary exhibitions glimpsing the narrow vertical horizon which opens at the completion of the route into the second-story connection. The temporary exhibitions of the town with the lecture hall and the activities of the day make a relevant introduction to the second level, which contains the necessary space for the unfolding of Nussbaum's work. The design suggests the importance of integrating the historical collections of Osnabrück, at least emblematically, into the context of Nussbaum's work in order to place the Nussbaum collection back in context with the Historical Museum's collection.

At the completion of the second-floor exhibits, the visitor becomes aware of the collapsed spatiality of Nussbaum's works, whose pathos lies in the double recognition of the political futility of escape and the spiritual resistance of art in the face of inhuman oppression. The second floor's unfinishable gallery is a timecut which signifies the oblique and wrenched segment: a suspended connection to the existing museum. This suspension indicates the finality of the 1944 paintings testifying to the indomitable spirit of Nussbaum and the universality of art. The volume of this critical segment is equal and reciprocal to the geometry of the cut and disconnected Nussbaum Museum.

The floating connection to the existing museum leads to an exhibition area which suggests transformations of part of the second floor of the city's Historical Museum. The scheme indicates the necessity of integrating the new and the old beyond appearances—the actual connection between the Historical and the Aesthetic. The integration of the existing and the new museums is the key task which must be accomplished so that the memory of the past will be active in the present and part of an ongoing narrative.

Thus the key structural feature of the plan suggests that the Nussbaum Museum, though separated from both of the existing museum buildings, is, by virtue of its form and function, profoundly related to them. The Folk-Art Museum, which in 1933 was the headquarters of the Nazi party, and the main Historical Museum are reattached and absorbed in a conscious and deliberate manner to the polyphonic composition. The whole represents an architectural hinge which prevents the entire site from isolating historical facts and making them banal and homogeneous. The visitor becomes aware that the work of Nussbaum, and particularly its relationship to the cultural, historical and physical identity of Osnabrück, requires extraordinary spiritual differentiation. Thus the import of public space (both internal and external) and the relation between the ecosystem and the architecture are clear.

The Nussbaum Museum thus becomes a profound place for the encounter between the future and the past, not simply a testament to an impossible fate. The unpainted paintings of Felix Nussbaum demand nothing less than to become visible to the contemplative eye.

Competition drawing – Sections through Nussbaum-Gang and Nussbaum-Haus

Construction photo – View down Nussbaum-Gang

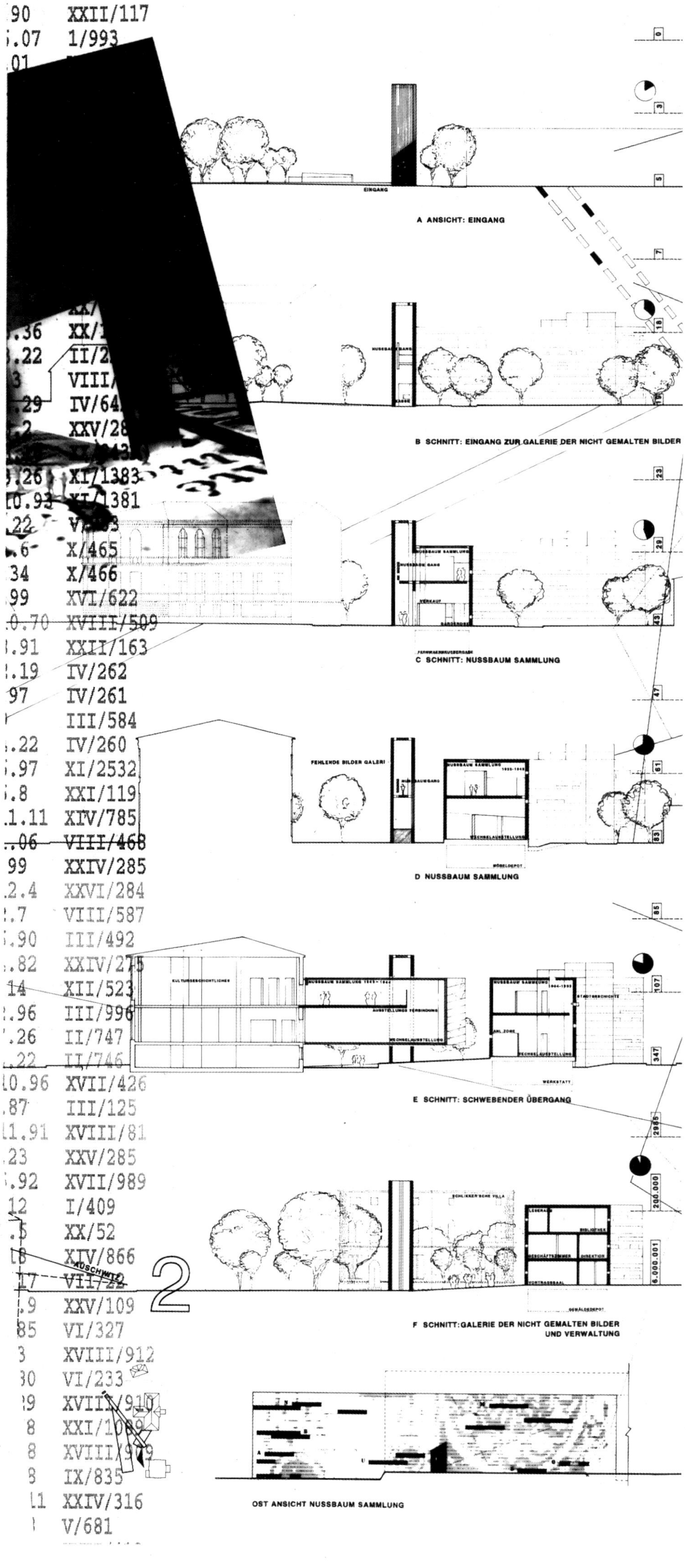

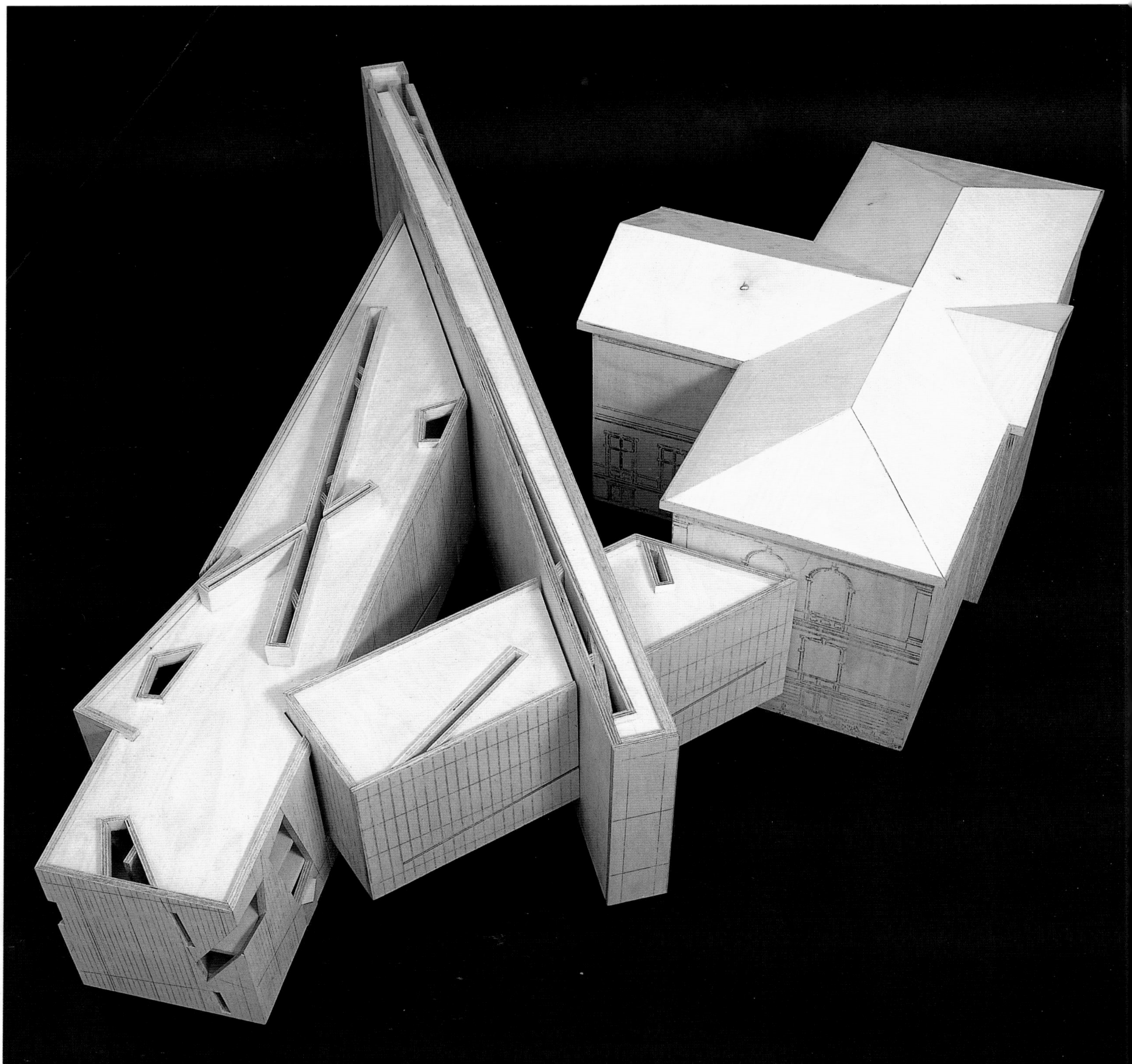

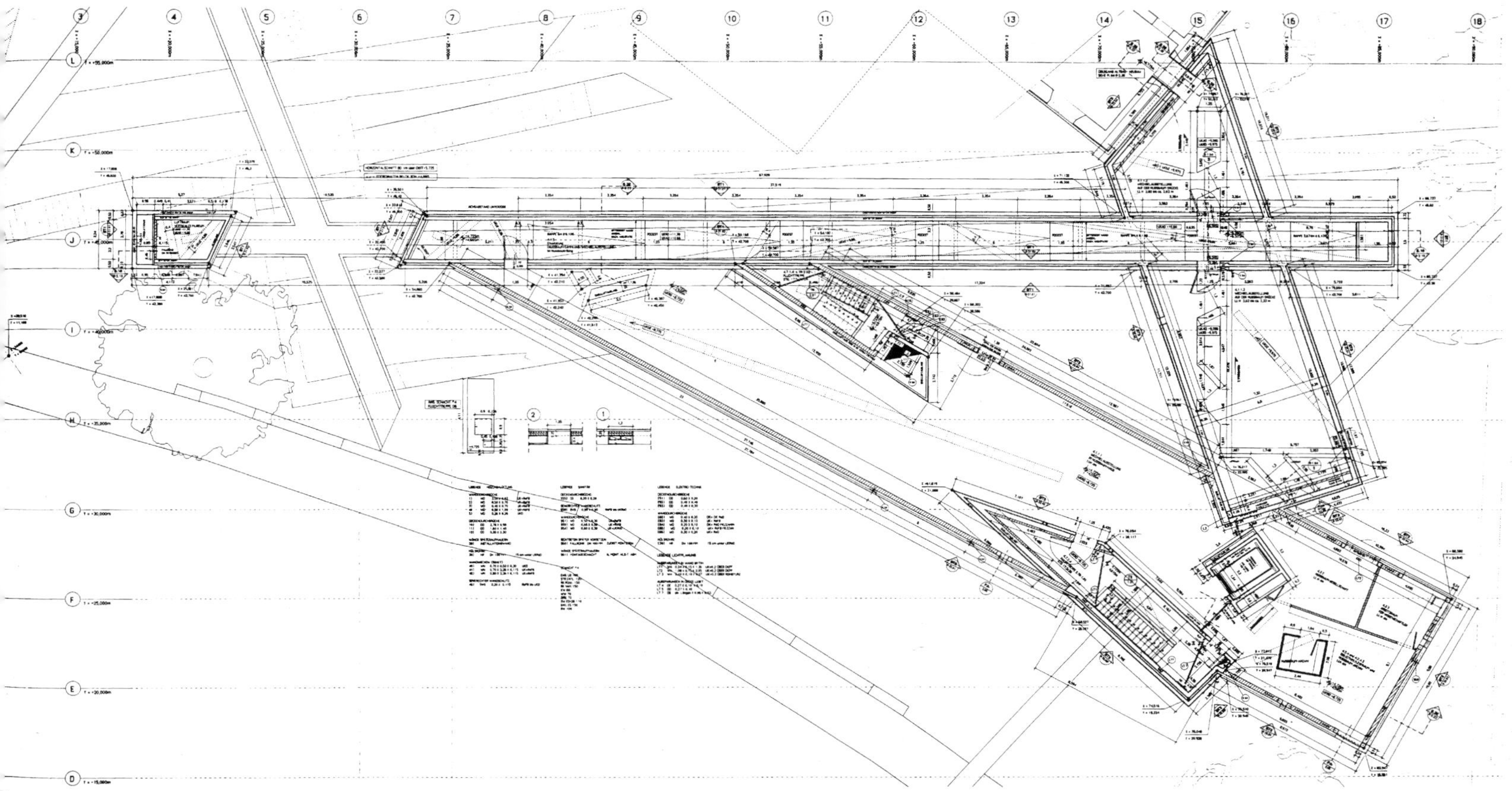

lan

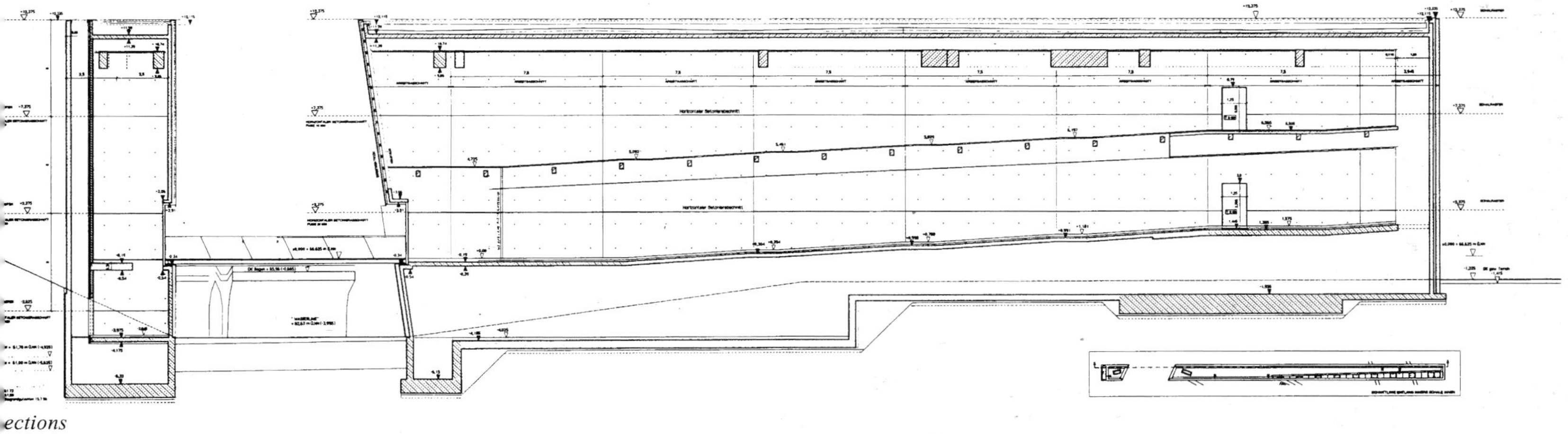

ections

Development model

Groundfloor plan and section through the Nussbaum-Gang

View of Nussbaum-Haus, ground floor and mezzanine levels

View of Nussbaum-Haus, ground floor and mezzanine levels

Competition drawing – "Museum ohne Ausgang"

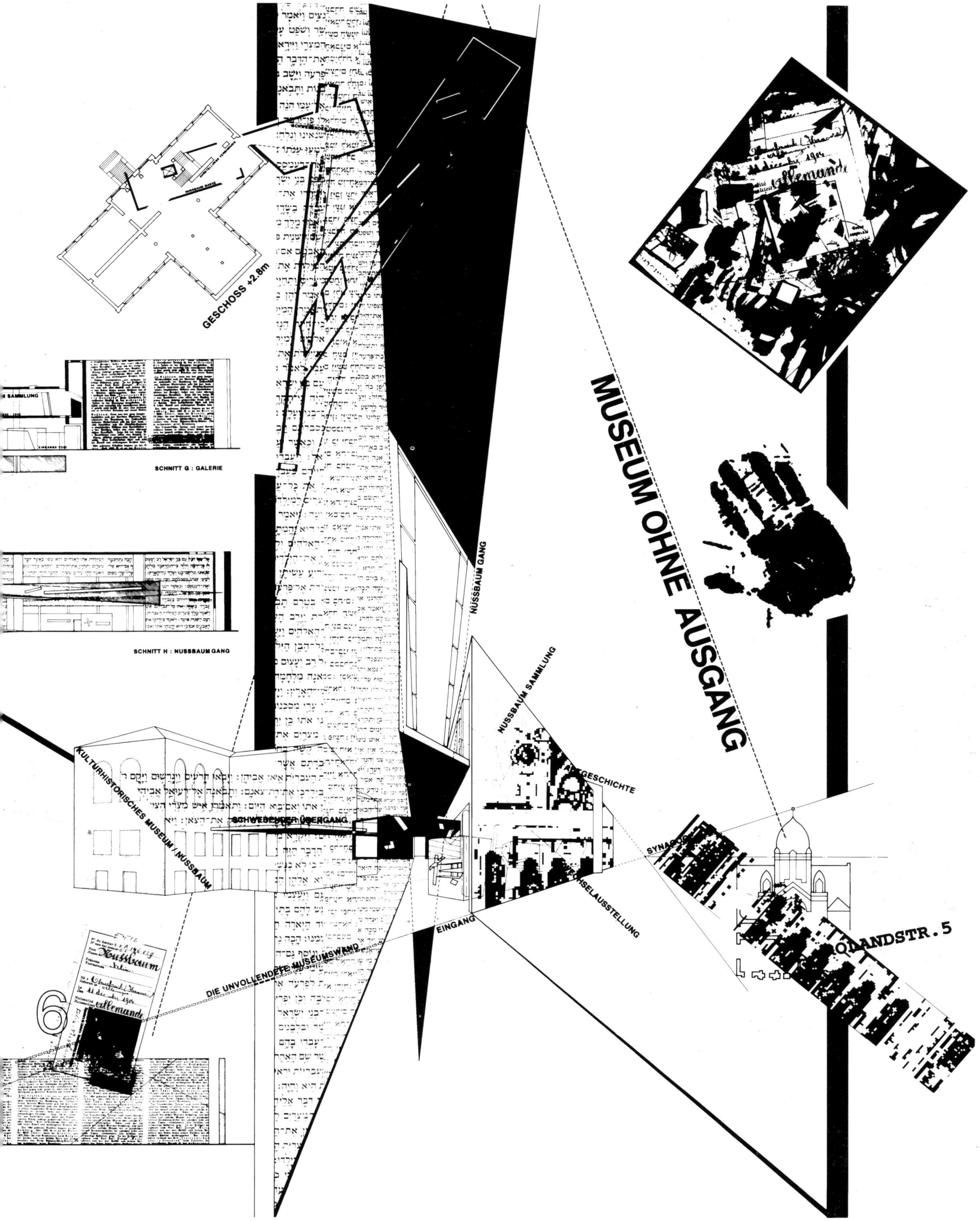

GESCHOSS +2.8m
SCHNITT G : GALERIE
SCHNITT H : NUSSBAUM GANG
MUSEUM OHNE AUSGANG
NUSSBAUM GANG
NUSSBAUM SAMMLUNG
KULTURHISTORISCHES MUSEUM / NUSSBAUM
SCHWEBENDER ÜBERGANG
EINGANG
WECHSELAUSSTELLUNG
DIE UNVOLLENDETE MUSEUMSWAND
LANDSTR. 5
Nussbaum
allemande
6

Three Lessons in Architecture

Architecture Intermundium

Lesson A: Reading Architecture = Reading Machine
Lesson B: Remembering Architecture = Memory Machine
Lesson C: Writing Architecture = Writing Machine

This Bienalle proposal deals with all ten projects and takes the form of participatory engagement with three large machines. Thus the public itself is involved with creating and interpreting Architecture in its broad social, cultural and historical perspective.

The three 'machines' propose a fundamental recollection and a retrieval of the historical destiny of Architecture, a singular, if unexpected, homecoming. These mechanisms constitute a single project and are mutually interdependent: each forms a starting point for the understanding and functioning of the others. Together they form a hermeneutic cycle in which the ten Bienalle projects are seen, explicated and overcome.

As metaphysical equipment, the three machines and their respective architectures seek to release each of the future sites unto themselves—thus letting the present remain a given, even as it moves towards its own past.

Lesson A

teaches an almost forgotten (medieval) process of building—a process which is in its own way not yet fully unfolded in Architecture. Like the medieval monastery out of which the Reading Machine[1] emerged, the method of construction and the technique of understanding bring about a revolution of architecture's *techne* that coincides with the movement of the text that it propels.

As a place of intersection between archaeological reconstruction (Ramelli, Palmanova, military engineering) and the will to power that it discloses (metaphysics, monasticism ideology), the Reading Machine reveals the tautological reality of the architectural text. The eight books—each a single word uttered by the forgetfulness of Being that resolves itself by turning back in order to come forward—lie on eight shelves. The books come and go for a comparison not only with each other but with the weight of their support. Light as they are, the weight of the seven last words of Metaphysics crushes the gears and axles, whose relation to the reader is always the same—though often this relation is inaccessible from the reading position.

The wheel revolves and in completing a revolution returns to its starting point while exposing its own uselessness and kinetic beauty.

Executed in a 'medieval' manner, with glueless joints and using no energy of a contemporary kind, this machine represents the triumph of spirit over matter, of candle-light over darkness. It is made solely from wood, as are the books.

1 dedicated to Petrarch

Reading Machine

consists of that which can still be remembered in Architecture. As a historical program the ten Bienalle sites have been filtered through Giulio Camillo's Memory Theater. As a precise inter-weaving of the memory tradition with the agony of a 'Deus ex machina', this theater represents the workings of a Renaissance Mind and shows its internal equipment and the arrangement it reveals.

The Memory Machine[2] consists of the backstage only—the spectacle takes place wholly outside it. As a mechanism for projection, concealment and illusion, this prosthetic piece of equipment exposes and also hides the Venetian projects.

Since the process of its construction remains in the classical arena (imagination, measurement, idea), the subversive element of mechanics (Teatro Farnese vs. Teatro Olympico) enters in only those places where memory has succeeded in retaining its surrogate authority.

As a ghost of Humanism's cosmic hubris, the Memory Machine seeks to disengage the ten Bienalle sites from the earth in order to return them to their original, destined loci: Joyce's Dublin and Tatlin's Moscow.

Done in 'renaissance' style, the Memory Machine abounds in the kind of inventiveness and caprice that we associate with the Odradek.

It is executed in wood and retains in its structure the 'hanging papers' seen by the King. This project represents the stage of Architecture's appearance and is a testament to its own manifestation. Also made of wood are the eighteen subordinate spectacles, which include the Cloud Machine and the Wave Machine, as well as the 'schizophrenic forum.' Colorless: the bloody red illuminates the shiny exterior of an inner sanctum dedicated to what remains nameless. Metal is used exclusively for non-structural reasons, related as it is to light itself.

Memory Machine

2 dedicated to Erasmus

Lesson C

teaches the artless and science-less making of Architecture. As a fully engaged project, this machine industrialises the poetic of Architecture and offers it as a sacrifice to its own possibilities of making a text. Architecture, like shoemaking, becomes a problem of putting the nail in the right place.

Since this Writing Machine[3] processes both memory and reading material, it takes the ten Bienalle projects into exact account. Not only the City itself (Palmanova), but all places written into the book of Culture are here collected and disposed.

Through an Enlightened vision, the random mosaic of knowledge is gathered together into 7 x 7 faces, each mirrored in a quadripartite realm. The totality of Architecture is shattered by the reciprocal foursome of earth, sky, mortals and gods and lies open to contemporary stocktaking.

The four sides of this 'Orphic' calculator or probability computer prognosticate the written destiny of Architecture, whose oblivion is closely associated with Victor Hugo's prophecy. The four-sided cubes work in the following Swiftian manner:

Side 1) The City as a Star of Redemption is refracted and congeals into a 'boogie-woogie'- like constellation.
Side 2) is a metallic reflection which shatters and disrupts the spatial-mathematical order of the 49 x 4 sides.
Side 3) consists of a geometric sign which points to a graphic omen or architectural horoscope.
Side 4) enumerates the 49 saints who accompany the detached pilgrim in order to care for his unerasable vulnerability.

Thus the oppositions and complementary reciprocities which glide through the whole constitute a 'destabilized technology' which would break up the mechanism instantly if the computerized controls (twenty-eight handles) weren't there to keep it stable. The Writing Machine is the first totally unstable text. As opposed to 'stable' architectural texts, which fly best in a straight line of myth and resist the pilot's effort to climb, bank or dive, this 'unstable' prototype is extremely agile—having no natural flight path. It jumps around the text's sky and is guided by an 'active control system' which can perhaps never again disclose its starting position (see position at the opening of Bienalle; see position at the end).

The Writing Machine is a contribution to Roussel Scholarship: it links Africa and the Impressions of Italy through those miraculous figures whose presence is both inevitable and contingent: Angelica, with a grid, burnt on a grid; St Donatella, or Mossem, killed by burning of text onto feet, killed by burning Iambic text onto forehead, St Theodore of Constantinople. By rotating the 'foursome', the arrangements appear, ready for interpretation. These seemingly random relationships are generated by an extremely sophisticated system which consists of 2,662 parts, most of them mobile. All are involved in an unpredictable rationalization of place, name, person. Once in motion, the stockpiling and accounting of places, cities, types of buildings, gods, signs, saints, imaginary beings, forgotten realities will present almost unsurmountable difficulties through the revolutionary discipline of this turn towards a Buddhism of Action.

The machine is made of wood, graphite and metal and contains:

1. Complex gear-shaft-driven systems which rotate.
2. 49 cubes which revolve at various speed ratios.
3. faces which show: a) Euro-African City; b) Saints who have emerged from the Bienalle and who return to Roussel's *Book of Saints*. c) the empty Sky; d) divined graphic configurations based on horoscopes and omens.

Synopsis of Bienalle Projects

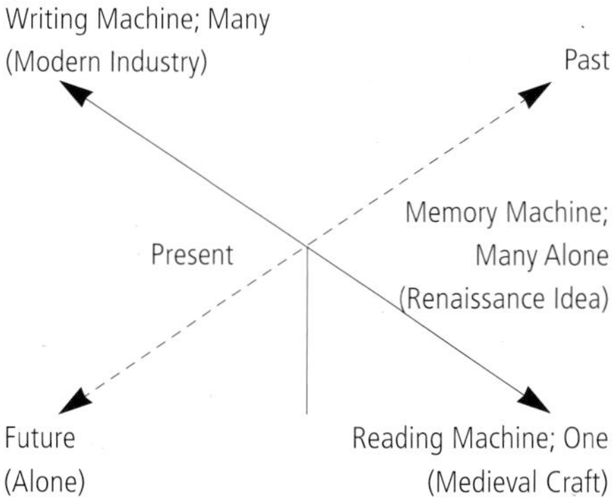

The Bienalle Projects are situated along the intersection between the Axis of Architecture (Time) and the Axis of Technology (Soul).

The Bienalle Projects generate the crossing of manifestation and oblivion, throwing technique into relief and drawing the veil over Architecture.

3 which is black and throws a gleam.
dedicated to Voltaire

Writing Machine

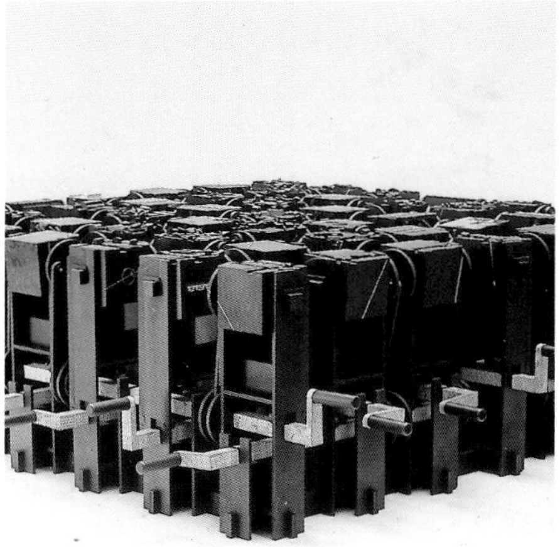

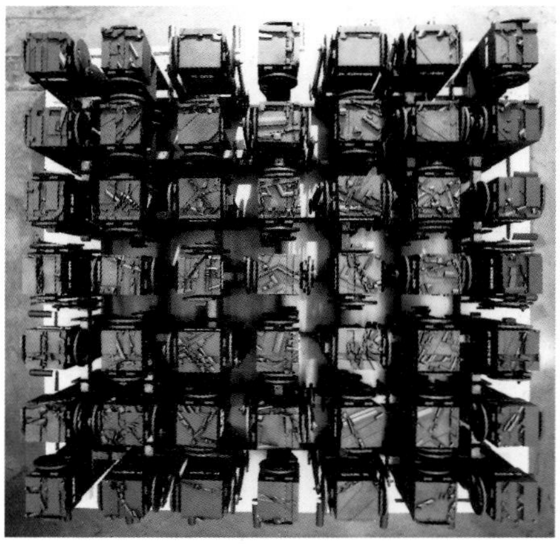

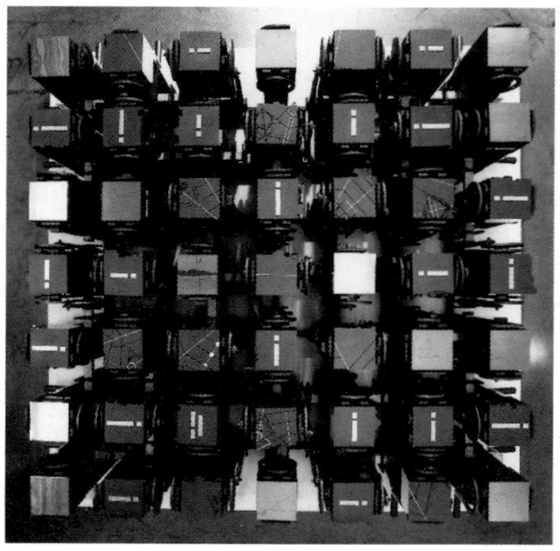

Musicon Bremen

Philarmonic Hall, Bremen

It is a great challenge to build a major regional music center in an historically sensitive context. This fact, together with the necessity of responding to new cultural trends of performance, audience participation and urban revitalization, makes the Musicon Bremen a project of prime significance. But these two factors have to be seen in the context of a new ecological response to the use of the building and the rhythm of the city.

Fundamental idea

To create a new and significant urban space and a major concert hall for Bremen adequate to the overture of the 21st century. By providing dynamic and flexible public spaces both inside and outside the Musicon Bremen, a new idea of Musical / Urban / Ecological space is opened. A participatory space is created which has a wide variety of uses, multiple relations and flexible adaptations, offering a vision of the integration of musical culture, urban life and the natural environment. This project seeks to create a new place for leisure and relaxation, stimulation, culture and urbanity for Bremen.

Urban strategy

The siting and geometric configuration of Musicon Bremen are determined by an organic relationship of the buildings function to it's strategically important urban site which is both built and natural.

The urban design strategy seeks to configure the external and internal spaces of the Bremen Musicon by freeing the building to embrace such important ecological concepts as minimizing the building's footprint on the ground; making a strong connection between nature and pedestrian movement; extending areas associated with the park both on the ground plane and within the green connector; taking advantage of the sun, water and earth in the public spaces.

It is important to integrate the building into the fabric of Bremen by avoiding the all-too-frequent and negative disconnection and destruction of urban spaces at ground level which such large spaces command. The success of Musicon Bremen does not depend merely on a discreet public building, but on the re-interpretation of invisible, eroded and ever-present lines of communication connecting the city of Bremen and Northern Europe.

Urban design

Musicon Bremen is an urban fulcrum responding to the twenty-four hour pulse of the city. It is conceived as an open urban matrix which brings together different and historically heterogeneous areas of Bremen into a vital and imaginative whole. The site is created by the permeability of passage and access of both implied and existing places and promenades which exist between the four elements: Bürgerpark (east), the railway station (south), Bürgerweide (west) and the Stadthalle and park (north). In this way, the entire building becomes an urban foyer which extends and re-invents the image of Bremen.

The siting emphatically re-establishes the importance of the northern side of the railway station by transforming this vague zone of the city into a balanced area corresponding to the historical city of Bremen. The importance of reconstituting the long-eroded historical developments along the virtual north-south vector is key to the reintegration of the railway station, Stadtwald, the Bürgerpark, the Stadthalle and the Bürgerweide into a rich and multi-dimensional field for the people of Bremen.

In order to harness energy, both human and ecological, the project establishes the importance of pedestrian circulation, the importance of places and their openness, and music as a whole. Musicon Bremen becomes the cornerstone articulating different spatial sectors, becoming a permeable gateway which connects pedestrian space along an uninterrupted horizontal plane.

Open space

Open space extends the park zone towards the station on one side and the university on the other by the creation of a yin/yang field between the parabola of the Klangbogen and the parabola of the Gustav Deetjen Allee. This area—bracketed by the Musicon Bremen and the Stadthalle (diagonally) and by the station and the Park Hotel with its pool (orthogonally)—is activated by a series of small-scale interventions which include new green areas, the unsealing of the presently sealed ground, walkways, promenades, a pavilion, bicycle paths, a fountain and a children's play area. The texture of these accents connects the pedestrian and tram movement from the city with the activity of the Bürgerpark, the Bürgerweide and the Hauptbahnhof by bringing to visibility the variable musical keys of Bremen.

There is a strong corner established by Gustav-Deetjen-Allee and Theodore-Heuss-Allee on the south-eastern side. The building opens towards the recently completed arcade building to the south and signifies a welcoming zone to passengers arriving by rail not only to the music hall but to the beautiful parks lying to the north and north-east.

This strong corner is a reception zone along the important route of Gustav-Deetjen-Allee. To the west, a connection is made between the Musicon Bremen and the Bürgerweide by addressing the nature of open space and the events which have traditionally taken place there. To the north-west a connection is made to the Stadthalle and the park by creating a correspondence and an intensification of activities between these two zones.

In summary, the urban design re-integrates contradictory functional areas of the city (station and park, public and private, new and old) by weaving gently through the weft and warp of Bremen.

Building typology

The typology of Musicon Bremen is determined by:

a. the central importance of musical performances;
b. public participation in the building without necessarily going to a concert;
c. the interrelationship between the Musicon Bremen, the Stadthalle and the Bürgerweide;
d. the creation of magnetic connections between the historical city and the park and
e. the intertwining of the past and the future.

The building is fundamentally a box enclosing and articulating significant public spaces and functional connections. This articulation specifically defines in plan:

1. the shops and the public entrances on the ground level;
2. the diagonal green lobby which opens onto the park with its restaurant at the tip;
3. delivery and retail areas which are themselves conceived of as part of the spectacle of performance and
4. the floating volume of the auditorium opening up the ground plane and at the same time creating a roof for public festivities.

Circulation and connections

The entire circulation system is a continuous diffusion of public space towards the discreet and specific spaces of performance.

Musicon Bremen is structured by an open ground plane with multiple entrances and identifiable public spaces in order to make the building fully accessible, visible and transparent to the public. The intermediate vertical level continues the ground plane through the organization of lobbies, bookshops, children's spaces, exhibition spaces, musicians' spaces, recital hall and the floating green bar with its restaurant. On the upper level, one finds the auditorium and its related functions.

Care has been taken to provide full accessibility and the same sequence of spaces to the handicapped and those who are not, to those who are musicians and those who are not.

Concept of performance

Spatial and functional requirements are organized around the following themes:
a. heterogeneous, simultaneous and variable performances and audiences;
b. the centrality of the stage and the ease and speed of servicing it and
c. the need for identity and qualitative character of each performance and the seating requirement.

The Musicon Bremen is configured to respond to its specific functional program by providing seating for an audience of twenty-five hundred people for classical performances and thirty-two hundred people in standing/seating configuration. A number of alternative and low-tech solutions for the transformations of seating and use configurations are possible. The Musicon Bremen is open to a number of future transformations of musical use based on stable functional and acoustical principles.

Construction, materials and realization

The building is a low-tech structure (based on traditional flexible seating systems) with energy-saving dimensions. The building materials are inexpensive local materials which include lightweight cladding, stone and economic finishes. The intention is to create a building for all people which has a tactile and colorful quality in its external and internal finishes. There is no glazing associated with the building as such. The green bar alone allows a dramatic movement of light, which plays an essential part in the creation of an 'ecological garden' (green lobby).

The large unopened areas of the facade are to be articulated with strong geometric and material compositions. These facades are newly envisioned through the projection of images as well as by the imprints referring to the history and music of Bremen. The multi-faceted interior reflects the most advanced research in acoustics, while the exterior refers to the clear dynamics of the city of Bremen.

The concert hall can provide unusually responsive acoustics for the performance of classical music. It is able to offer other functional arrangements for musical events which range from modern music through rock music, dance, lectures and sport-theatrical events. The particular spatial and tectonic form of the building is able to capture the musical events in spaces of intimacy and difference by creating a close rapport between the identity of each seating arrangement and its particular stage. It is an alternative to the banal boxes which thematize technology and speed rather than the magic and specific spatial form of each performance.

Functional sectors

The entire building is coherently held together through public activities such as the sale of tickets, boutiques, city information offices, retail spaces, workshops, cafes and the diagonal green lobby. The green bar (which allows for the possibility of being connected to and extended) is an essential spatial and ecological unit connecting the horizontal and vertical functions of the building.

An important dimension of this project is the dissemination of public lobbies in such a manner that groups of different intensity, size and function can find the appropriate building scale which defines them. These lobbies are indeed extensions and mediations of both performance and public space.

Retail facilities, workshops and administrative offices have their independent entrances while tying into the life of the building as a whole.

The musicians' entrance and parking area form a separate 'world within a world' with their own internal circulation independent of the public at large.

The depots, workrooms and delivery spaces are separated from the main public spaces while contributing through their visibility (elevators, hoisting mechanisms, work) to the overall festivity of events in the future.

The varying elements of function (B-A-C-H) constitute a fugal counterpoint to the monolithic seating of almost three thousand people at each performance.

Acoustic diagrams

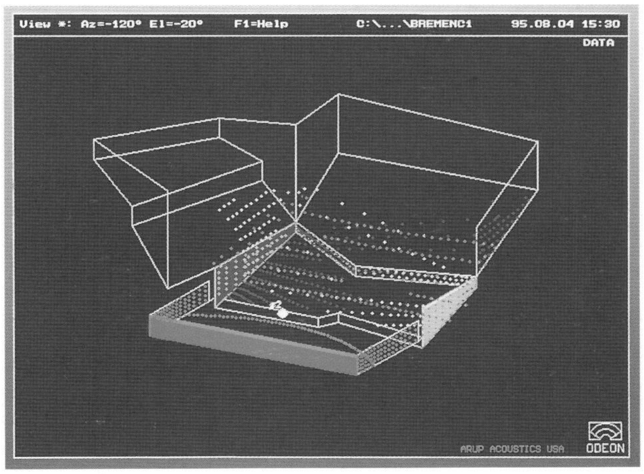

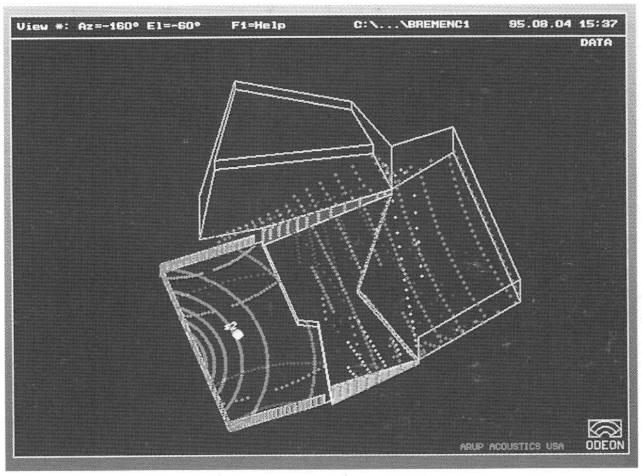

Site model, view looking North

Site plan

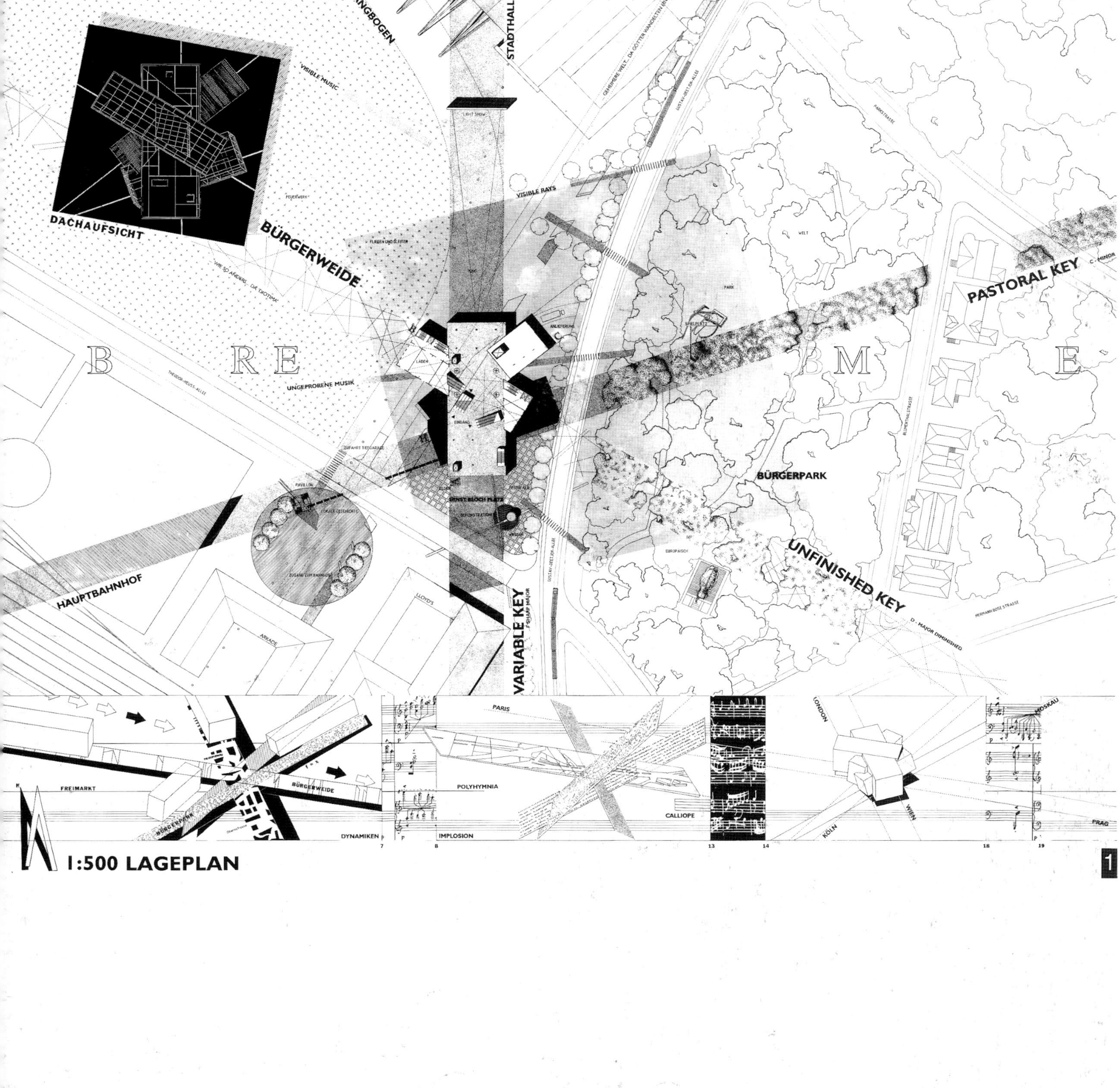

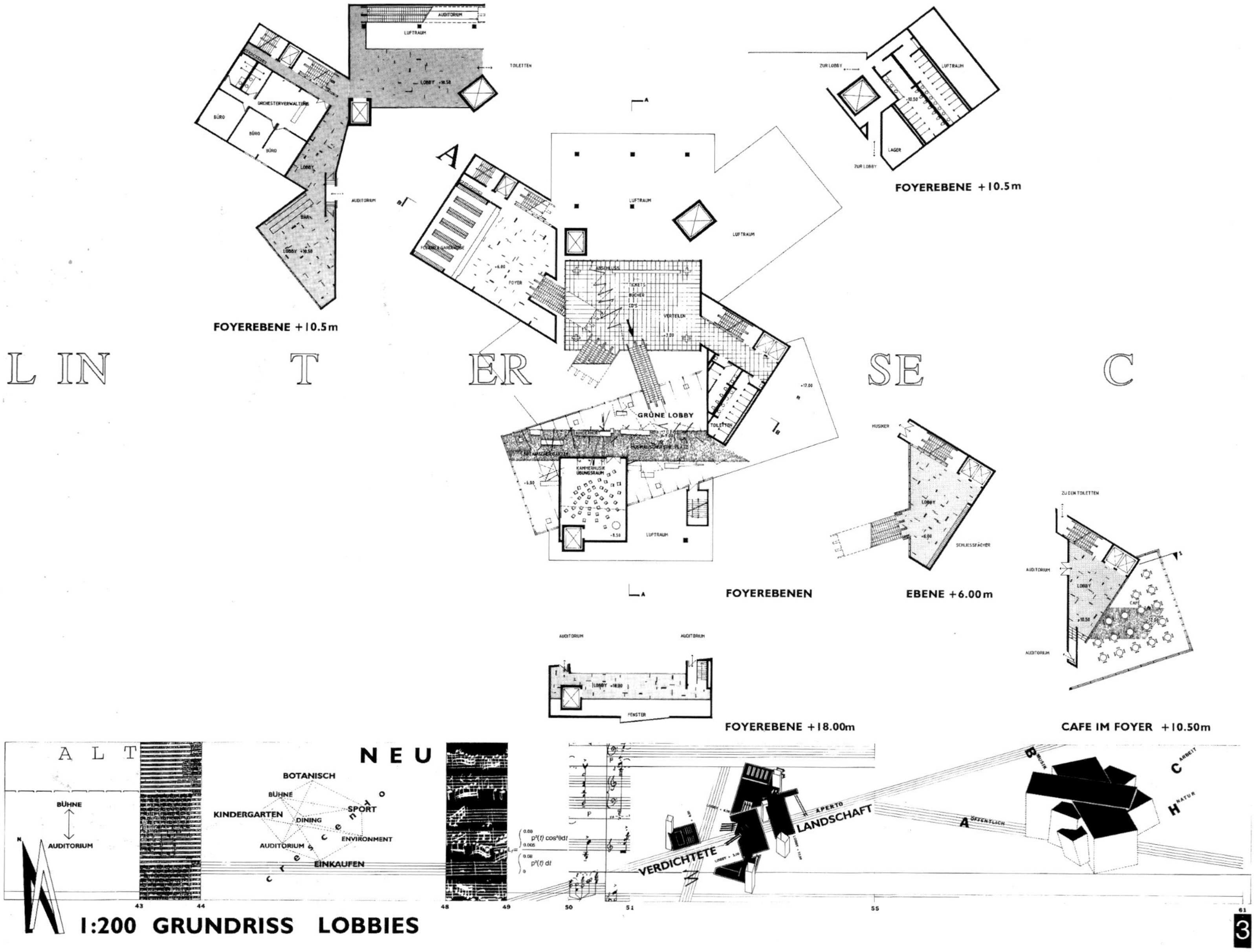
FOYEREBENE +10.5m
FOYEREBENE +10.5m
L IN T ER SE C
GRÜNE LOBBY
FOYEREBENEN
EBENE +6.00m
FOYEREBENE +18.00m
CAFE IM FOYER +10.50m
ALT
NEU
BÜHNE
AUDITORIUM
BOTANISCH
KINDERGARTEN
DINING
SPORT
ENVIRONMENT
EINKAUFEN
VERDICHTETE
LANDSCHAFT
1:200 GRUNDRISS LOBBIES
3

Plan of lobbies

Plan of auditorium

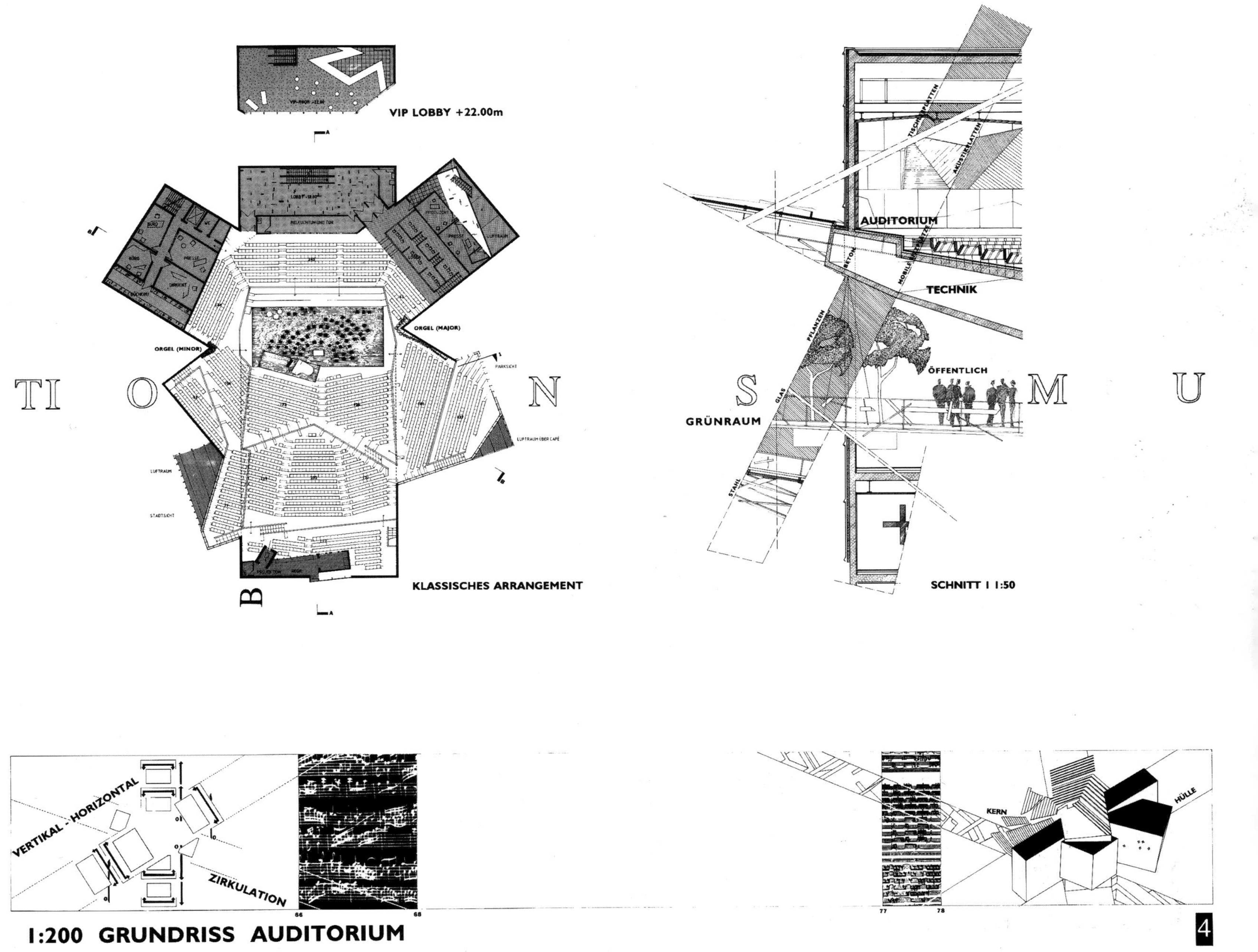

East elevation

Section through auditorium

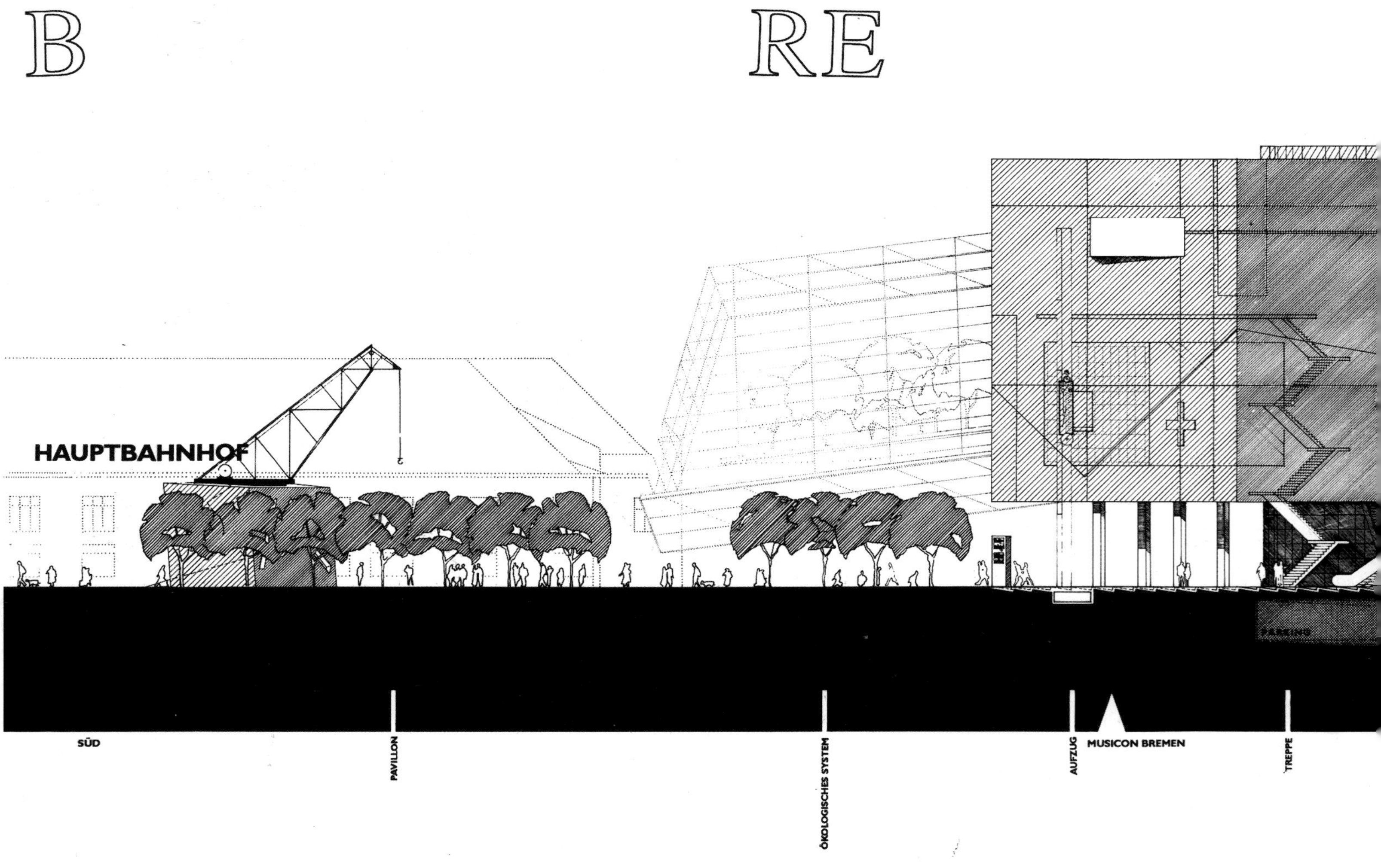

N TE R S EC

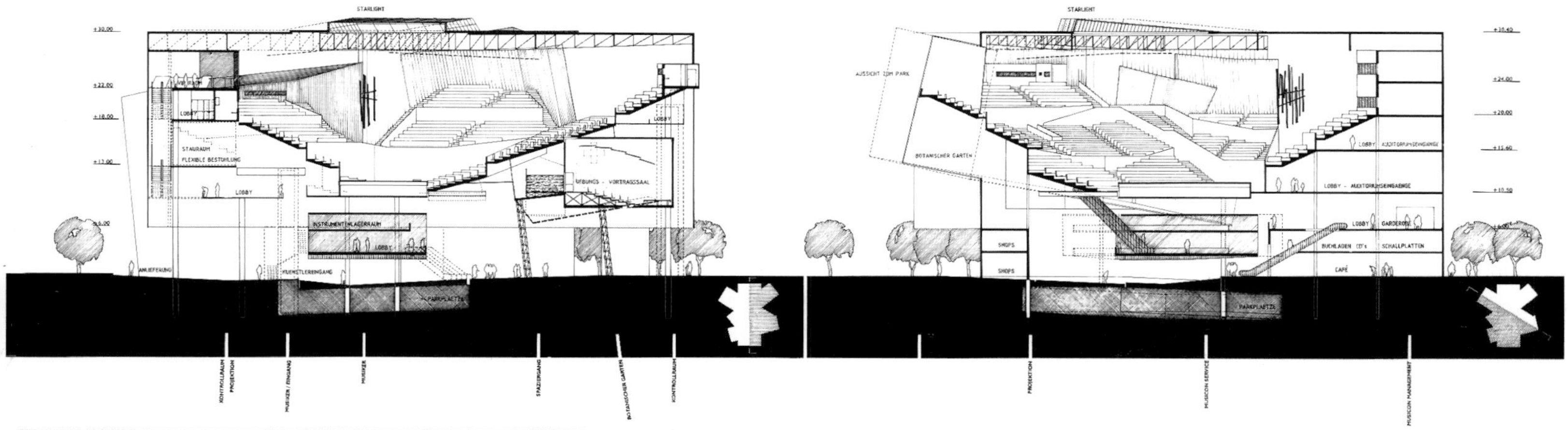

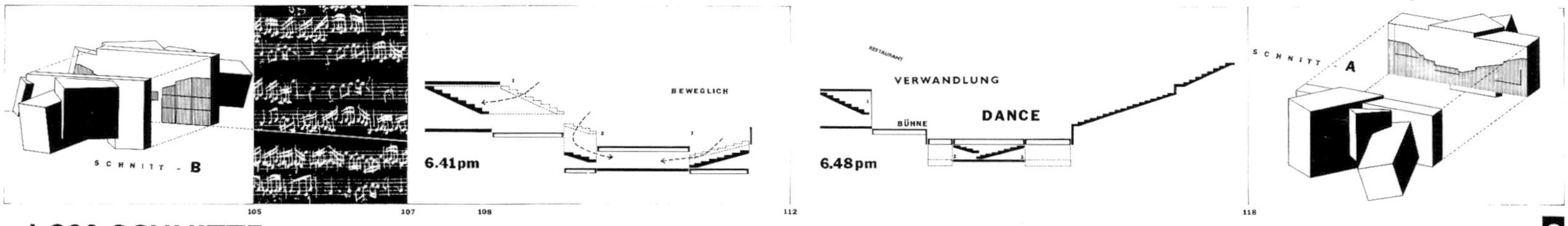

1:200 SCHNITTE

6

M EN

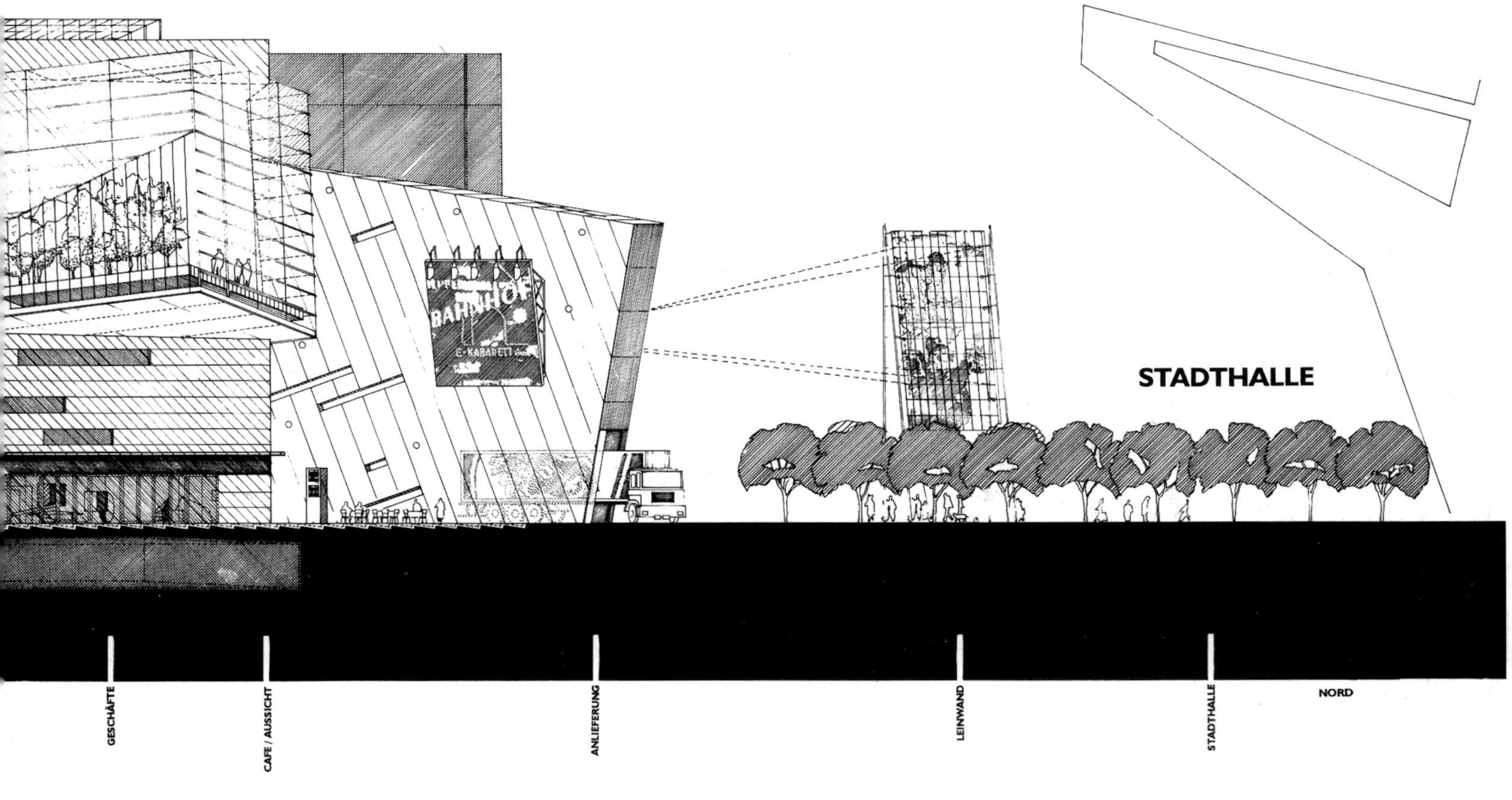

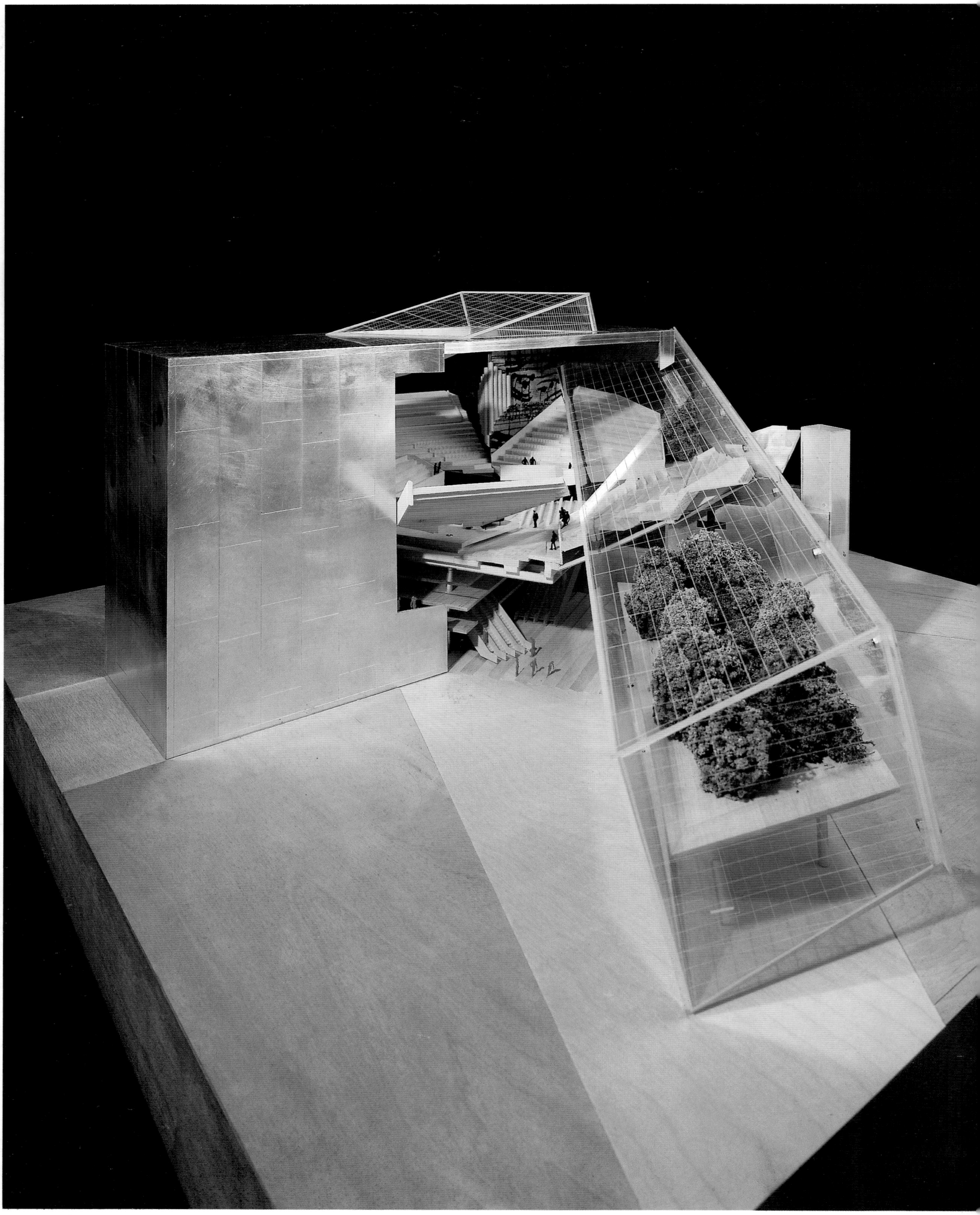

The Botanical Garden

South facade of Botanical Garden

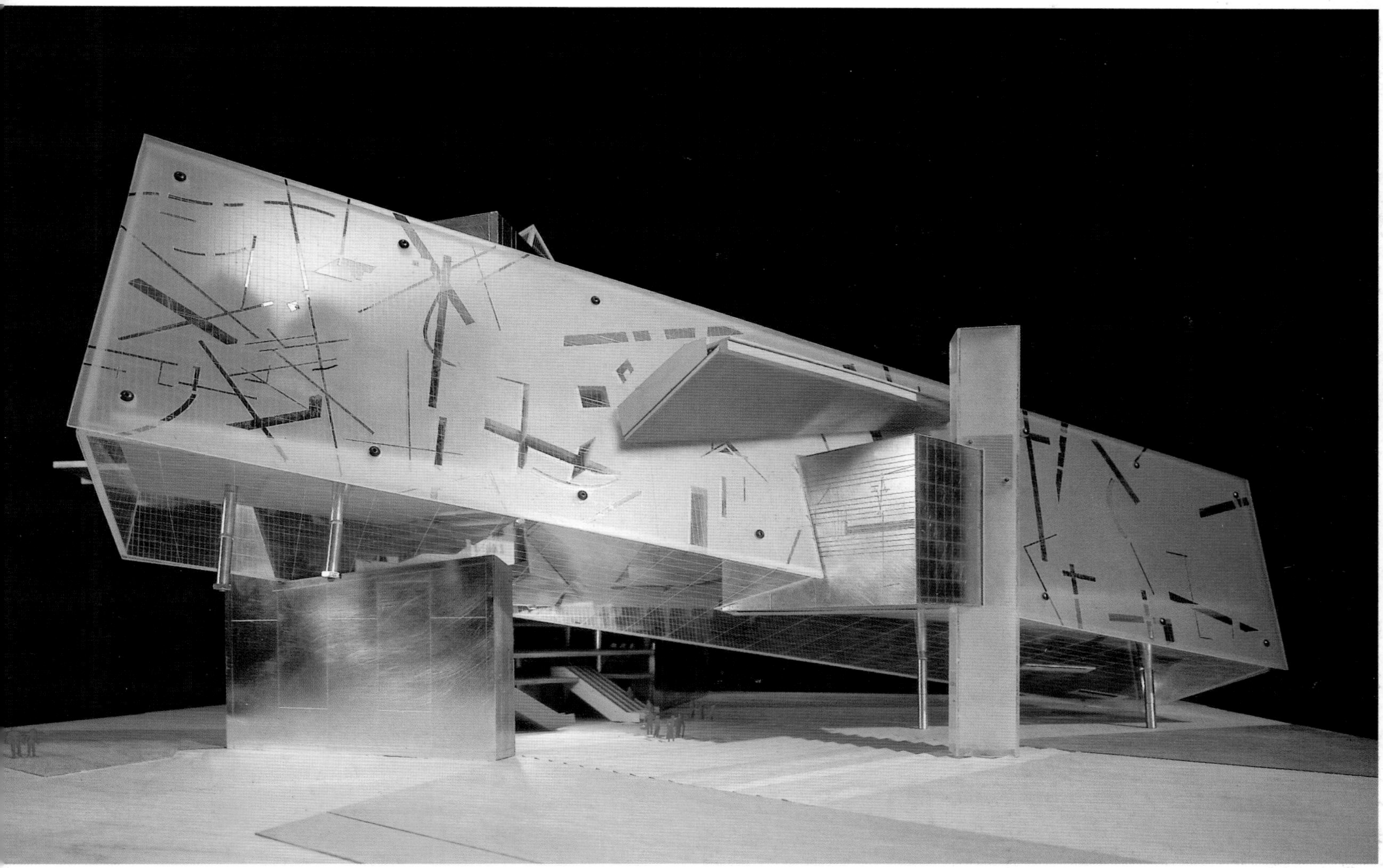

BECK'S

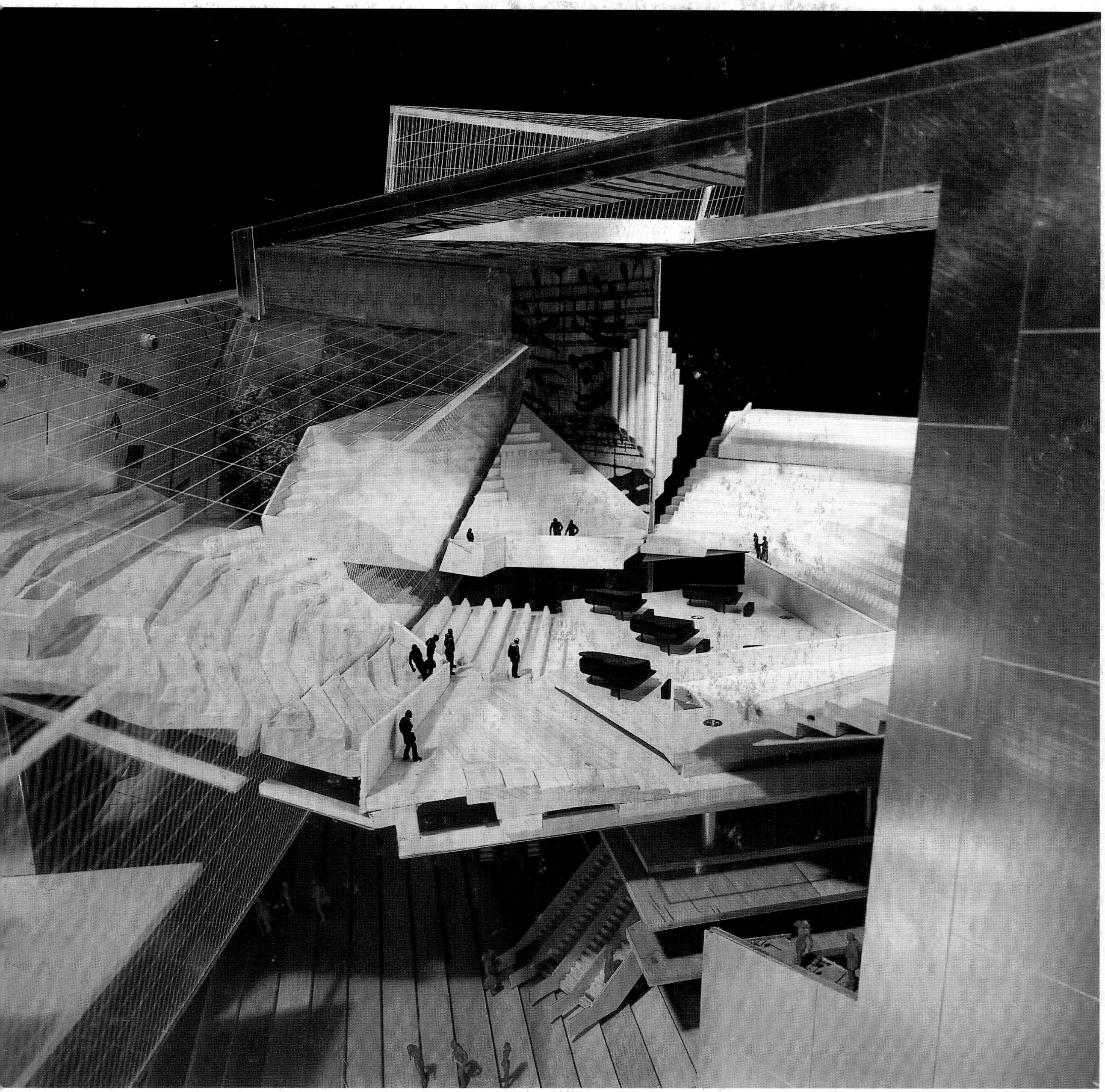

Model photo Plaza/Entrance

Delivery zone and illuminated lobby

Model detail, auditiorium

The Spiral: Extension to the Victoria and Albert Museum, London

When facing the main entrance to the Victoria and Albert Museum, one is confronted by two words to the left and right: 'Imagination' and 'Knowledge'. This dialectic describing the inspirational force, or muse, within the idea of the museum has recently come to involve the integration of new interactive methods of learning and dialogical forms of understanding as means to develop the imagination and knowledge of the visitor.

The V & A has taken up this radical agenda in its proposition to build a new extension on Exhibition Road. By creating a second main entrance to the museum, pluralizing the experience of its vast collections and proposing a program involving an integrated mixture of exhibition spaces, educational facilities and new methods of interpretation, the extension engages contemporary ideas about alternative organizations which open the experience of the visitor to new possibilities of using a museum.

The V&A's mission to provide a gateway to the 21st century via its own collections requires a vision which on the one hand goes beyond the purely institutional relation of the public to the arts, and on the other goes beyond the museum conceived in the image of the past. To design such a museum, one must orient the visitor's imagination both to the possibilities of the distant future and to the rediscovery of a new past, which can only be satisfied by unexpected interactions and new kinds of experiences of the collections.

This project addresses this challenge through a bold response to the historical context emerging out of the tradition of John Soane and Nicholas Hawksmoor. Like Soane's own house, it is through the interpretation of the museum as a mirror of the human mind, at once taxonomic system and rational labyrinth, that a reciprocity is established between the archaeology of history and the adventures of the eye and mind. The new extension positively engages the existing museum complex, without obfuscating its own newness.

The design is structured around three dimensions:

the eternal spiral of art and history;
the interlocking of inside and outside;
the labyrinth of discovery.

The design takes these dimensions and translates them into a sophisticated ensemble of functionally related spaces.

The eternal spiral of art and history manifests itself in the overall form of the entrance building and in its circulation system. The enclosure of the new building and its internal spaces are created out of a continuous wall, whose total length is that of the perimeter walls of the entire V&A block, spiraling upon itself around a virtual, rising axis. Upon entering, visitors follow this spiral movement as they circulate through the galleries. This movement also informs the distribution of people to the rest of the museum. The form of the building, the relationship of its spaces and the circulation of people evoke the spiral movement of the stars, archaic towers and temples, and the unexpected unfolding of spirals in modern mathematics, genetics and construction.

The precise winding together of the spiral to create an interlocking of the inside and the outside of the new building brings the visitor into close relation with history and the present, the city and the museum, experiencing directly an interpenetration of views and histories. Through this interconnection, a variety of specific and dramatic natural lighting conditions are created throughout the museum's diverse and dynamic exhibition spaces, which make the new building a beacon of light and energy to the surrounding areas from both inside and outside.

The labyrinth of discovery is the organizational leitmotiv which mediates between the specificity of the unwinding spiral and the functional distribution of the museum's new programmatic requirements. This image of the labyrinth is not a chaotic form, but rather a rational diagram incorporating a heterogeneous system of organization for the artefacts and exhibitions.

This three-dimensional structure offers an alternative vision for the visitor of reinterpretation and rediscovery through which wholly new kinds of relationships can be established to the historical buildings and collections. Visitors are respected by not being treated as moving particles in a neutral space or as passive voyeurs of the past, but as participants in a visceral, intellectual and spiritual experience, an ongoing discovery of the unfolding drama of art and its history.

The form of the new building is derived from archaic traditions and rituals and from contemporary advancements in our knowledge about art and the cosmos. It infuses these seemingly irreconcilable aspects together in its organization and urban image into an emblem articulating the cross-cultural collections of the V&A, the multi-cultural profile of its visitors and the fusion of the arts, technology and history.

Its structure mirrors the multifaceted order of the museum as a whole, which is a gateway to the history of the decorative arts. The new building, then, as a gateway to this gateway, offers the visitor a distilled view of the collections of the past and future. With a total circulation of one tenth that of the entire museum, the extension is therefore in scale, form and relationship a microcosm of the whole. It is not different from the rest, but finds its place within the overall matrix of networks, paths and anticipations, reorganizing access and orientation to the mass of the existing galleries without flattening the visitor's experience. Through the interlocking spiral form, clear functional distribution and numerous linkages to various parts of the rest of the museum, the new extension is the visible externalization of the whole, making it the Ariadne's thread within the labyrinth of treasures making up the collections.

We believe that the visitor should not enter the museum through a barrier, but that the new entrance should be open and inviting, an exhilarating emblem of the dynamics of the museum's diverse exhibitions. We propose, therefore, that this drama be achieved through a new garden at a level lower than the street, out of which the form of the building grows. The visitor enters the museum via bridges over this garden. We propose that the Webb Screen be lowered and made to face the new garden, becoming the frame for an outdoor exhibition space visible from the lower levels of the new extension. In this way it will be given its own new significance—no longer a screen, but a frame for activity.

The new building is itself divided into two parts:

❑ In the levels of the extension below street level, a modern laboratory for temporary exhibitions, educational facilities, performance, theater, lectures, films, etc. is organized within a rigorous functional system designed for maximum flexibility.

❑ On the upper levels of the new building, an interactive field continuum of traditional and non-Cartesian spaces is enclosed within the folds of the spiral. These floors house the new galleries for the permanent collections and the orientation center. The exhibition galleries are lifted out of the anonymity with which such spaces are often presented, and instead articulate a new figure responding to the tension between spatial relation and programmatic field. With their special qualities of light and space, they function together with a system of movable partitions to create specific and interesting spaces which can at the same time accommodate a wide variety of potential exhibition methods, from traditional exhibits to installations emerging out of new media forms.

As a concept for the structure and cladding of the facades of the new building, we propose the idea of the fractile, a new kind of tile pattern whose economy allows a multiform language to emerge out of an elementary geometric piece interpreted in a variety of different ways. As a strategy towards the surface, the fractile bridges the gap between the wondrous tiles of Granada, Isfahan and Beijing and the tile technology used on the space shuttles, bringing decorative arts onto the surface of the building. It offers endless variations in formal articulation and the relationship between surface and structure within the economy of building construction. We envisage that the development of the motifs and patterns for the facades could be developed in connection with the educational activities of the museum via an interactive citizens' participation program so that the building surface could become an expression of an ongoing decorative surface of unpredictable yet controlled interactions.

The new museum for the V&A on its last available site is like the last chord of a symphony. Only when this chord is played do the first notes acquire the form of their fulfillment. Our vision for this project is to provide a center which does not totalise and a displacement which does not disorient. It is a chord which does not bring the rest to a static form, but which reorients towards the reinterpretation of the entire museum in a new and open way. This last chord does not end the music of the museum, but extends it towards unknown and future horizons of the mind and of space.

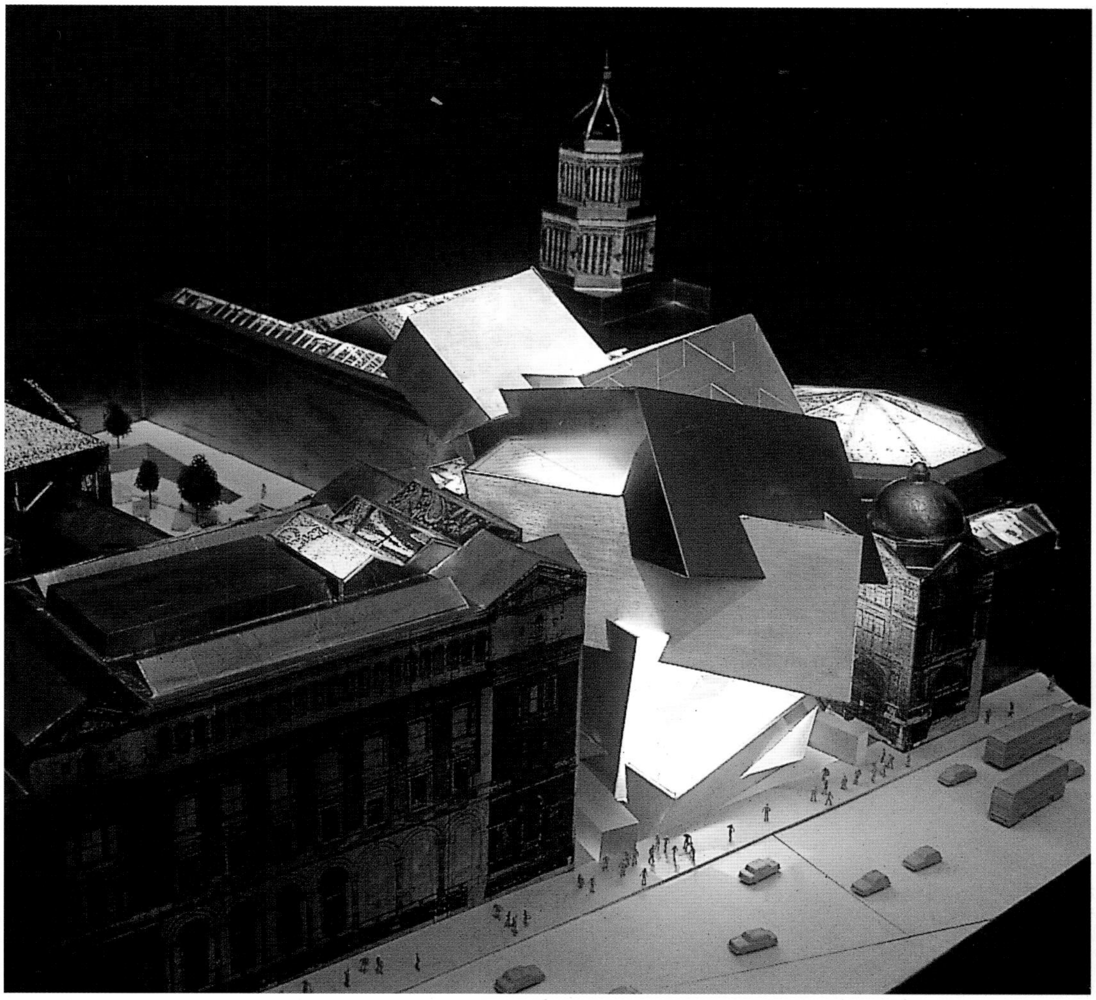

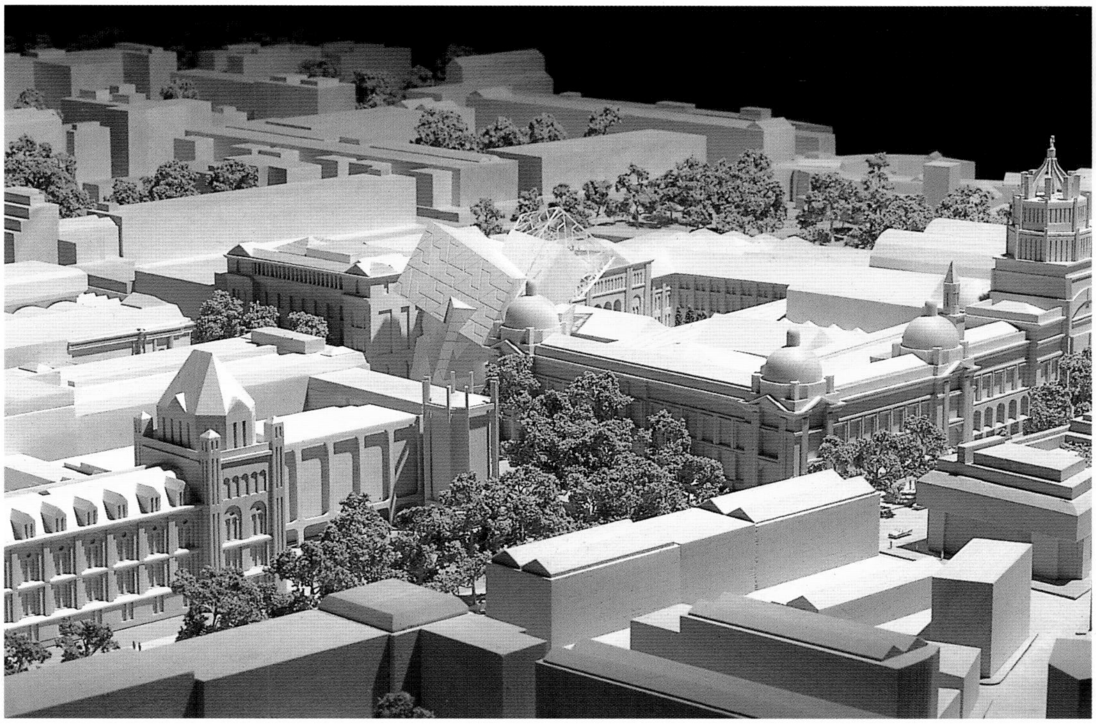

Competition model, Exhibition Road at night

The Spiral in the context of V & A, Natural History and Science Museums

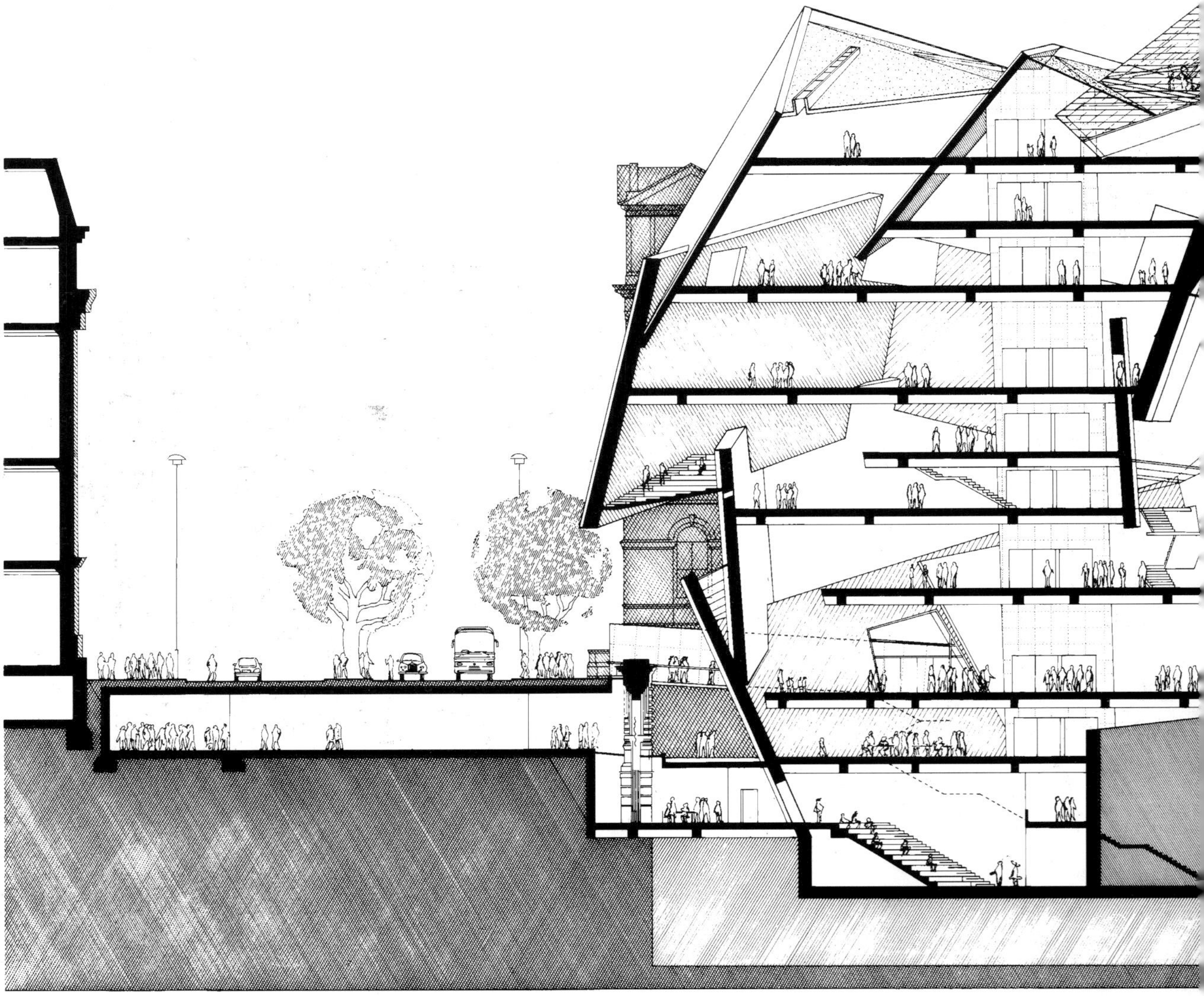

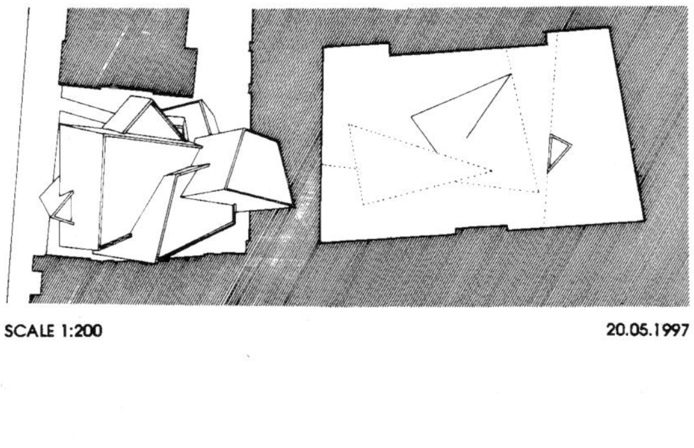

SCALE 1:200 20.05.1997

EAST-WEST-SECTION

East/West section through Extension and Garden

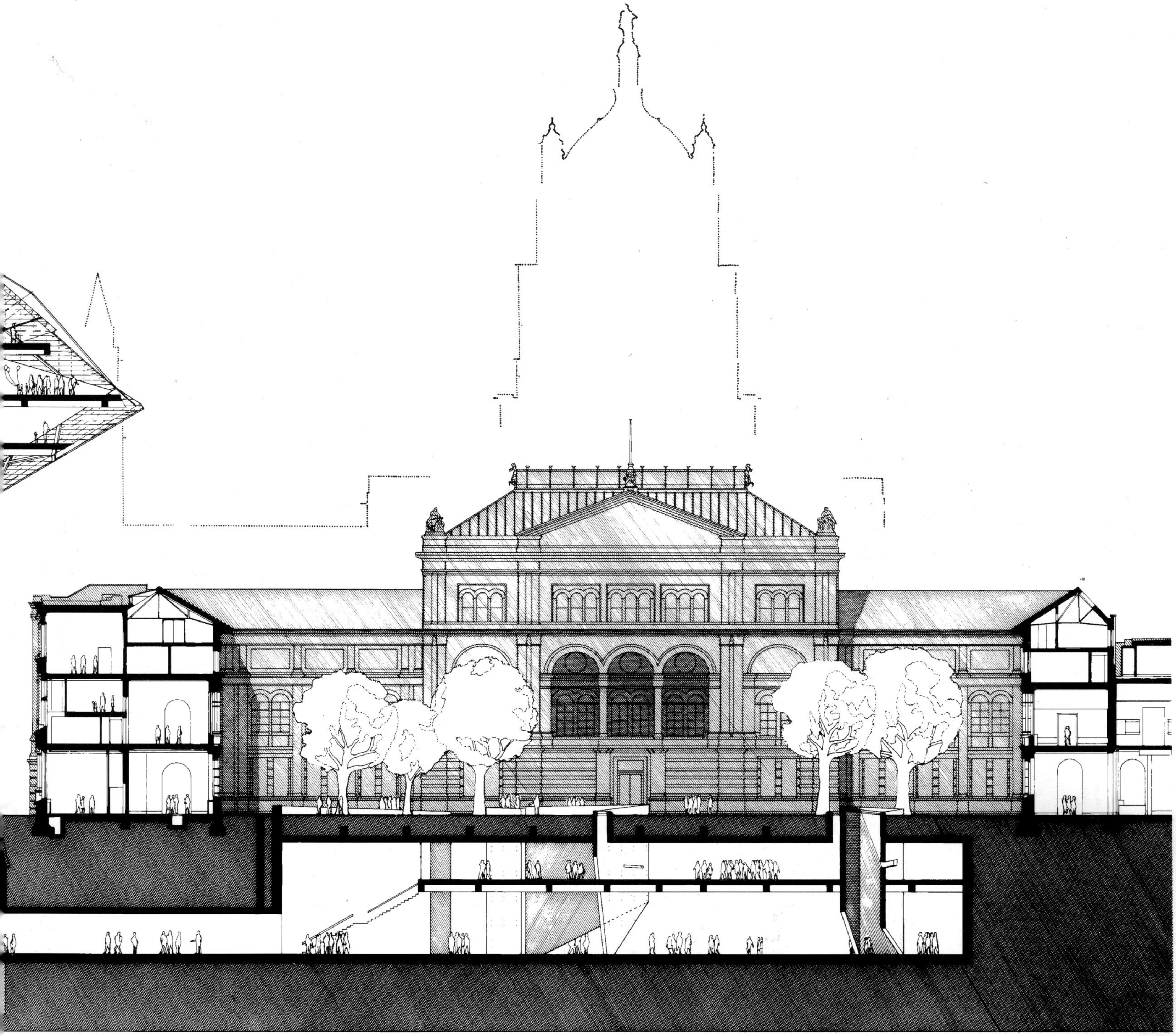

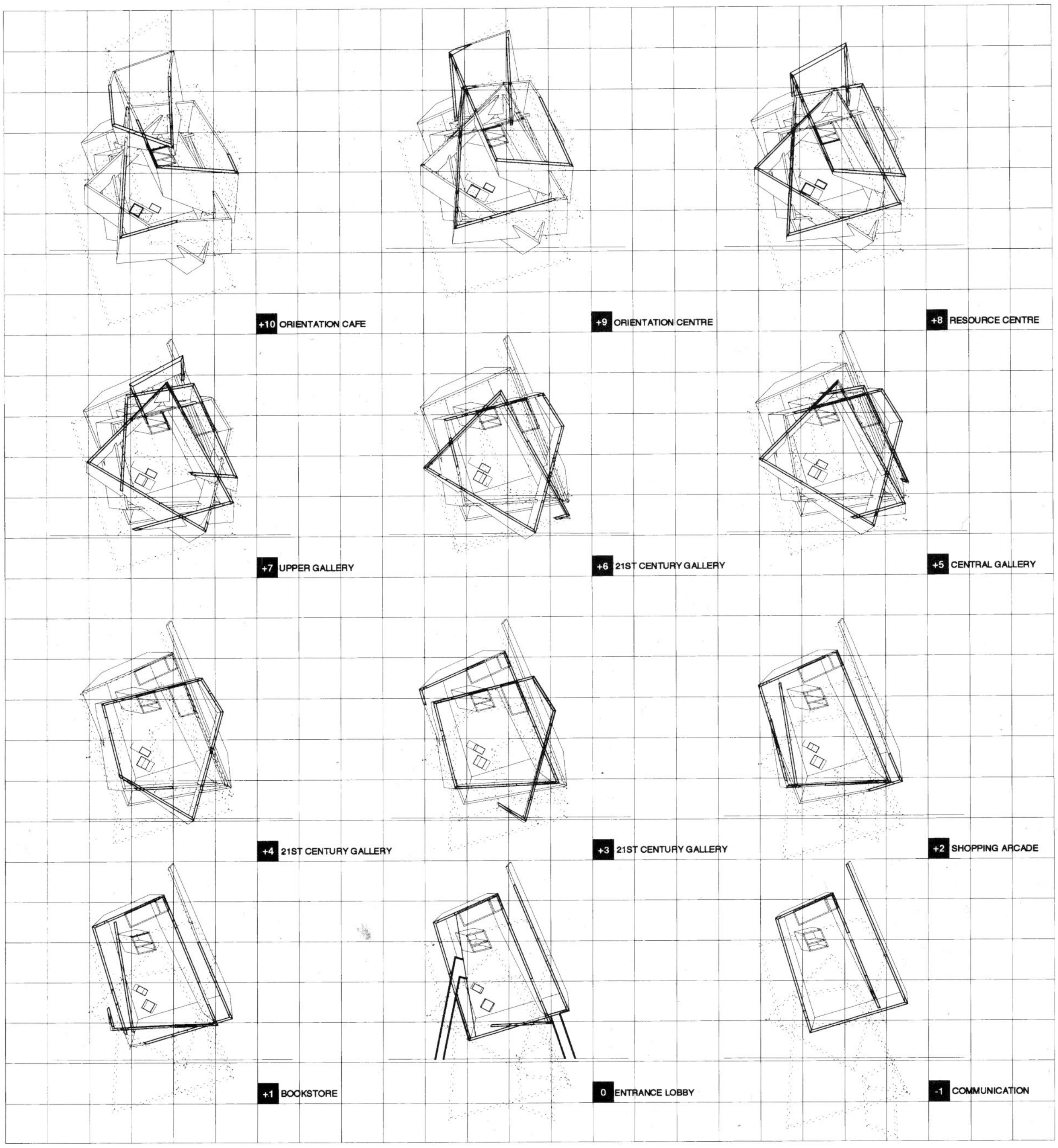

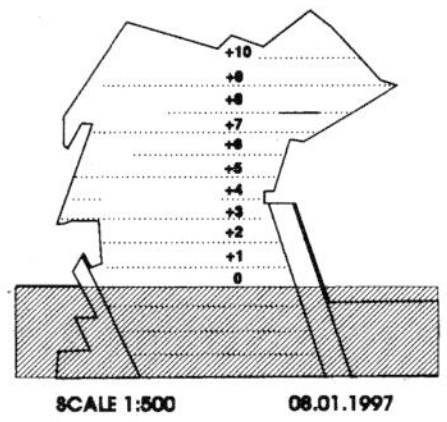

SPIRAL DEVELOPMENT

Spiral development diagrams

Perspective view of interior

View of Pirelli Garden and
Observatory from above

Competition model,
view of extension from East

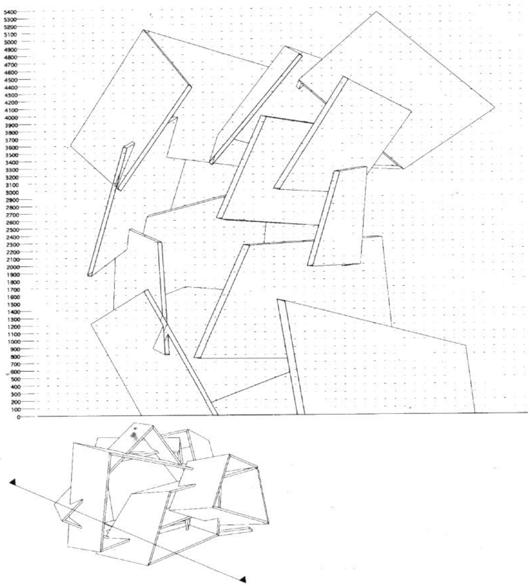

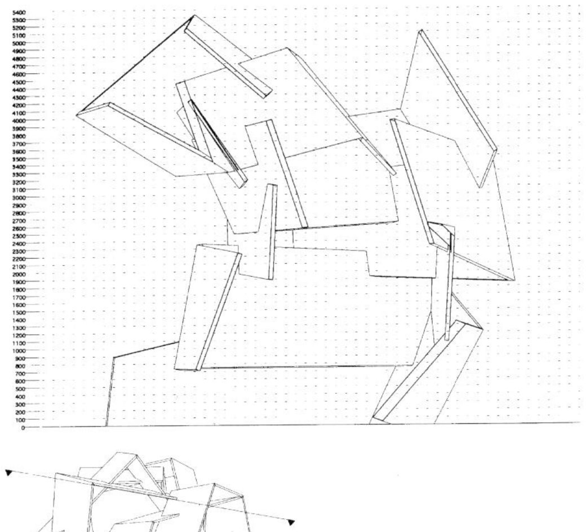

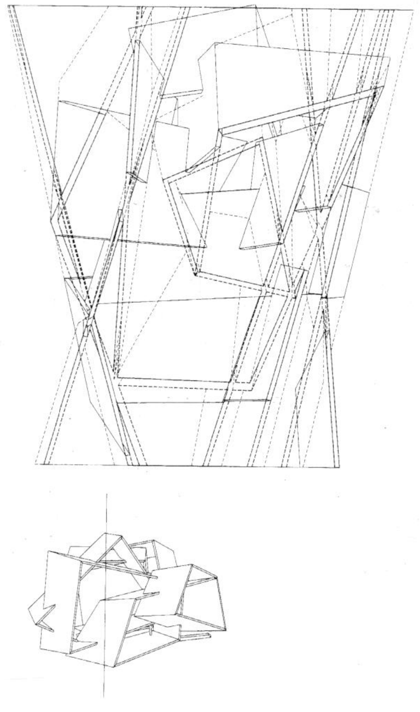

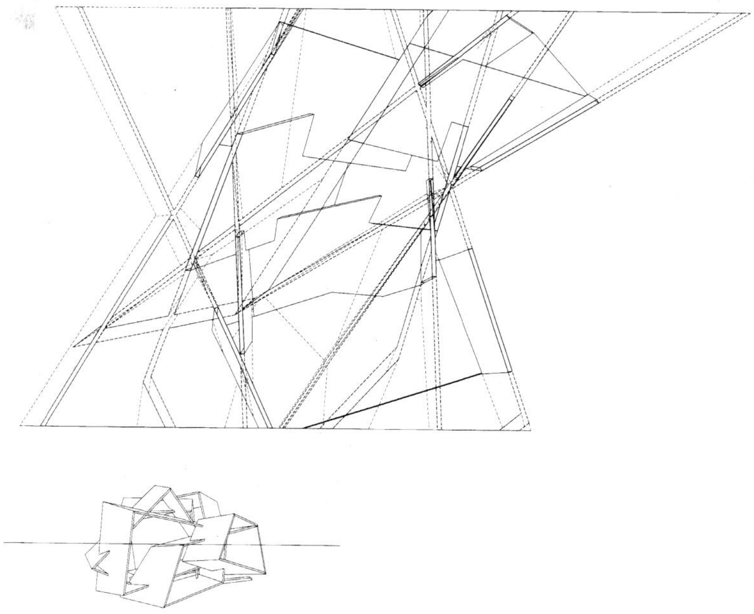

Sections of Spiral walls
Extruded walls diagram

Model, view from Exhibition Road

The Tenth Muse

Wiesbaden-Gerstengewann Office Complex

The office complex for the 21st century must not only meet highly advanced energy, ecological and technological requirements but must also radically reformulate the very philosophy of the 'work-day.'

The architectural ensemble must offer a new spatial, visual and symbolic interpretation of the office world and its environment.

The office crystals, with their autonomous character, are distributed in a free and dynamic configuration constituting an openess in which the interior quality of space, the roof and nature on the ground offer a true place-to-be.

Muse Lines cut across old boundaries which used to divide routine from leisure, private from public, and work from pleasure. They thus tie together multiple diverse images across the spectrum of the mind.

These Muse Lines, dedicated to the musical rememberance of *work as play and play as work,* seek to rearticulate new desires generated by technological organization along the path of Imagination, Invention and Individuality. These structures, in association with more traditional functions, offer new materials for inspiration and work.

The Urban-Roof-Nature is no longer the boundary where buildings end, but extends the social life of employees by offering a changed relation to the City and to Nature which is generated intensely at the foot of the building. The landscape grid decomposes progressively, giving way by the end of the century to the forest: redressing the existing ecological imbalance.

The Tenth Muse — the Unexpected — leads the chorus of pure crystals condensing the post-contemporary city.

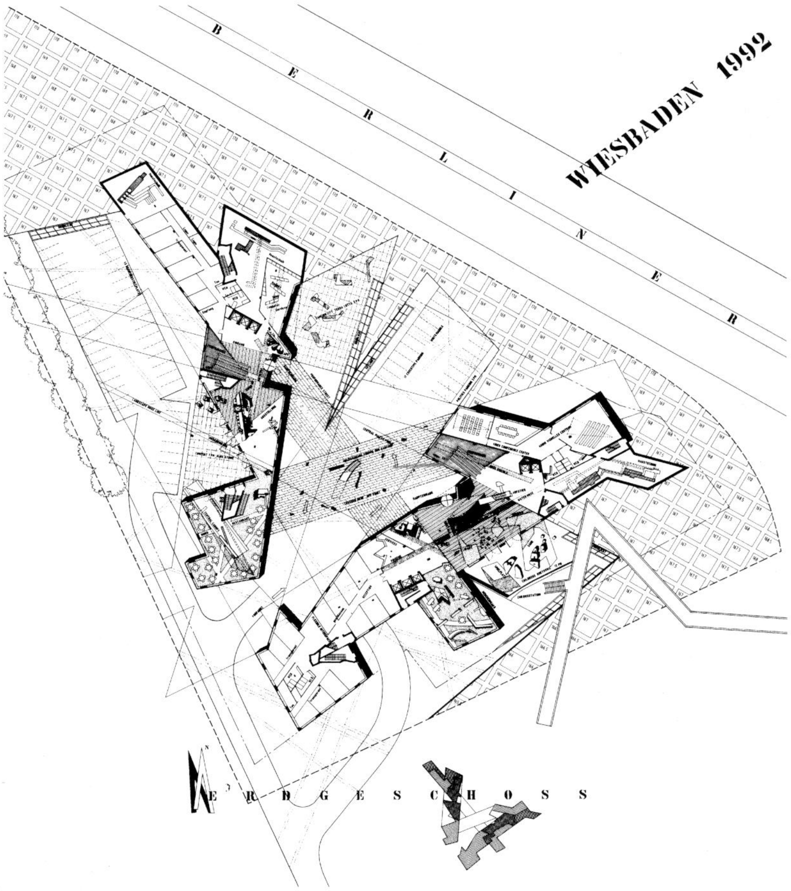

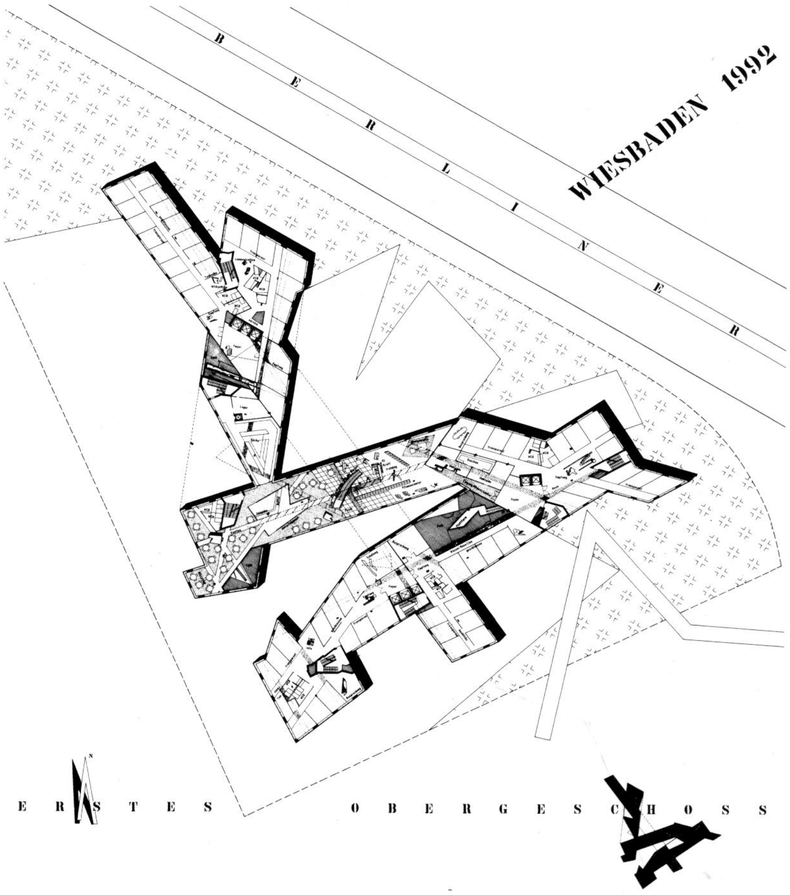

Ground floor plan

Second floor plan

Axonometric

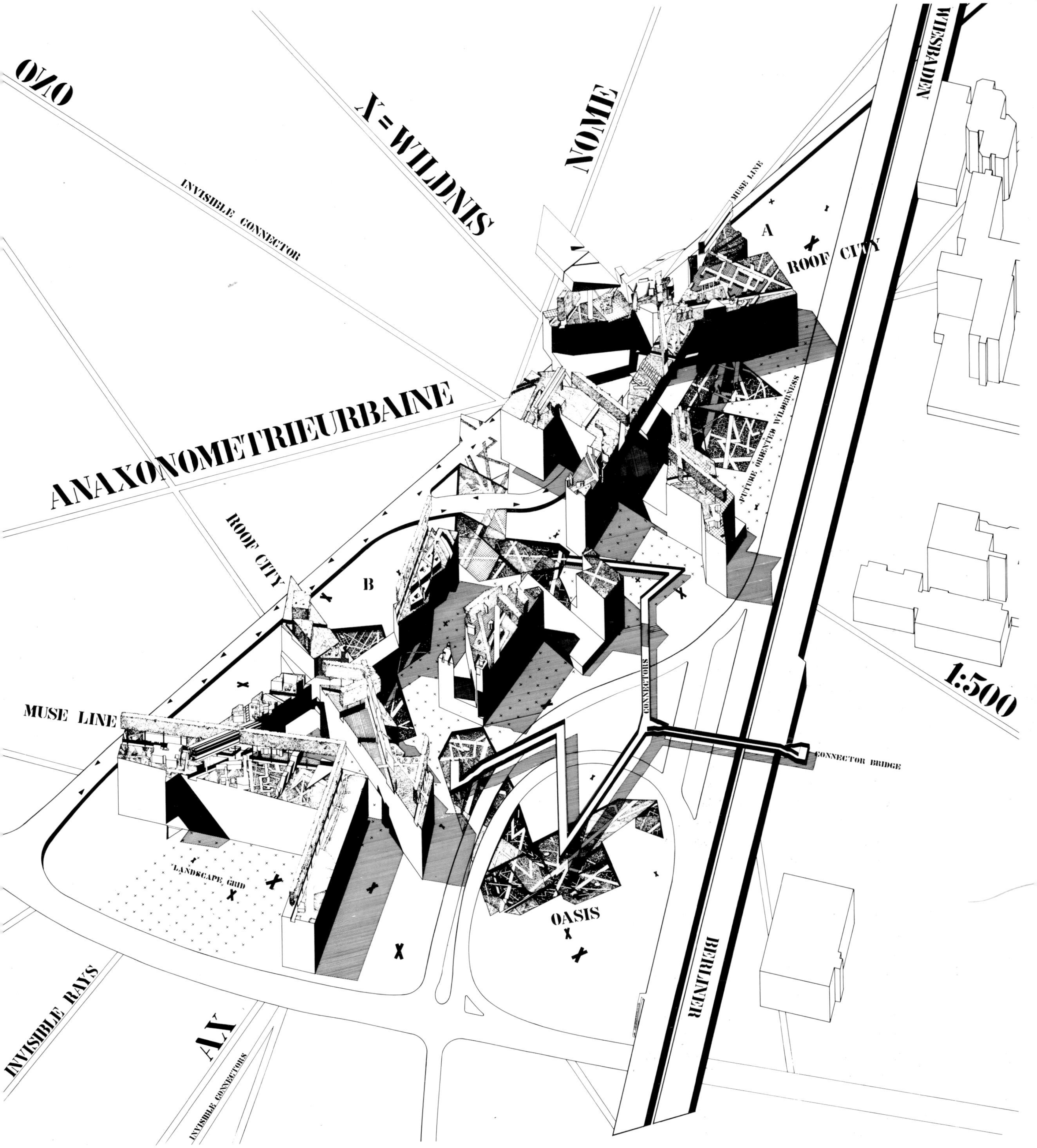
OZO
X=WILDNIS
NOME
WIESBADEN
INVISIBLE CONNECTOR
MUSE LINE
A
ROOF CITY
FUTURE ORIENTED WILDERNESS
ANAXONOMETRIEURBAINE
ROOF CITY
B
CONNECTIONS
1:500
MUSE LINE
CONNECTOR BRIDGE
LANDSCAPE GRID
OASIS
BERLINER
INVISIBLE RAYS
AX
INVISIBLE CONNECTORS

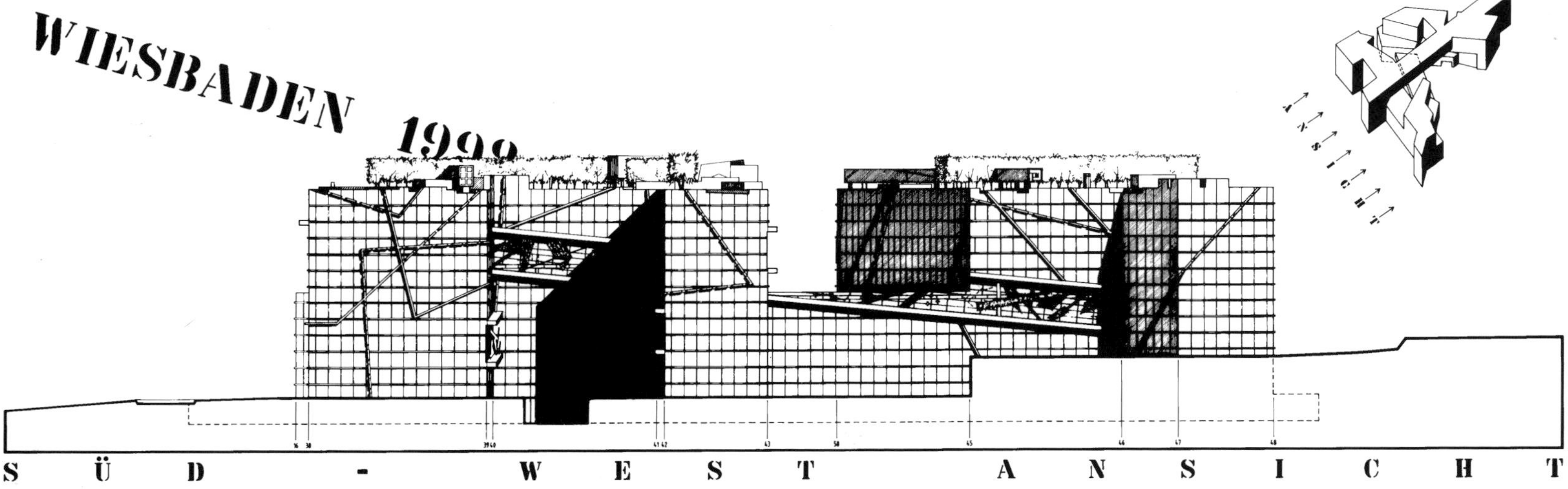

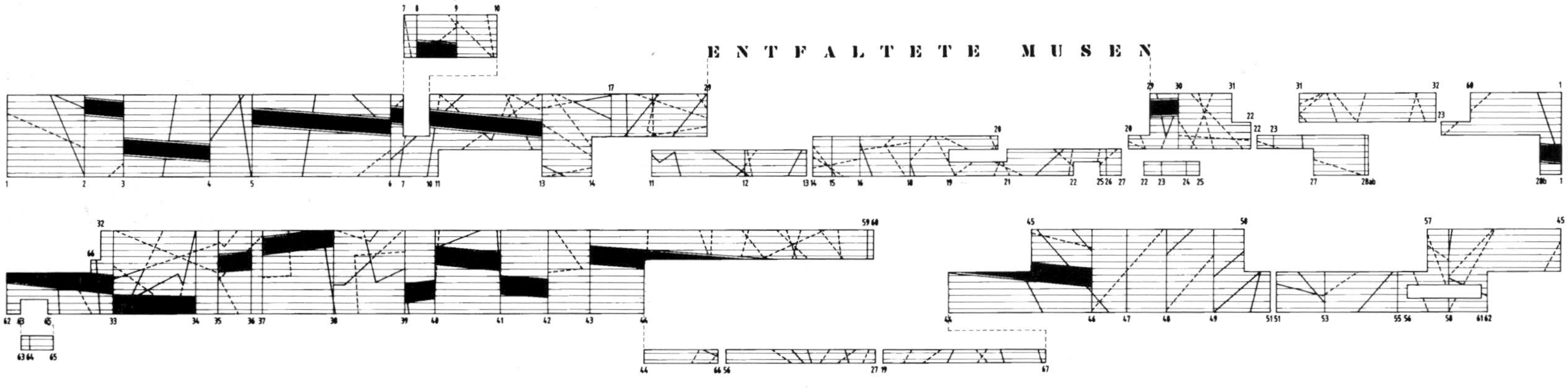

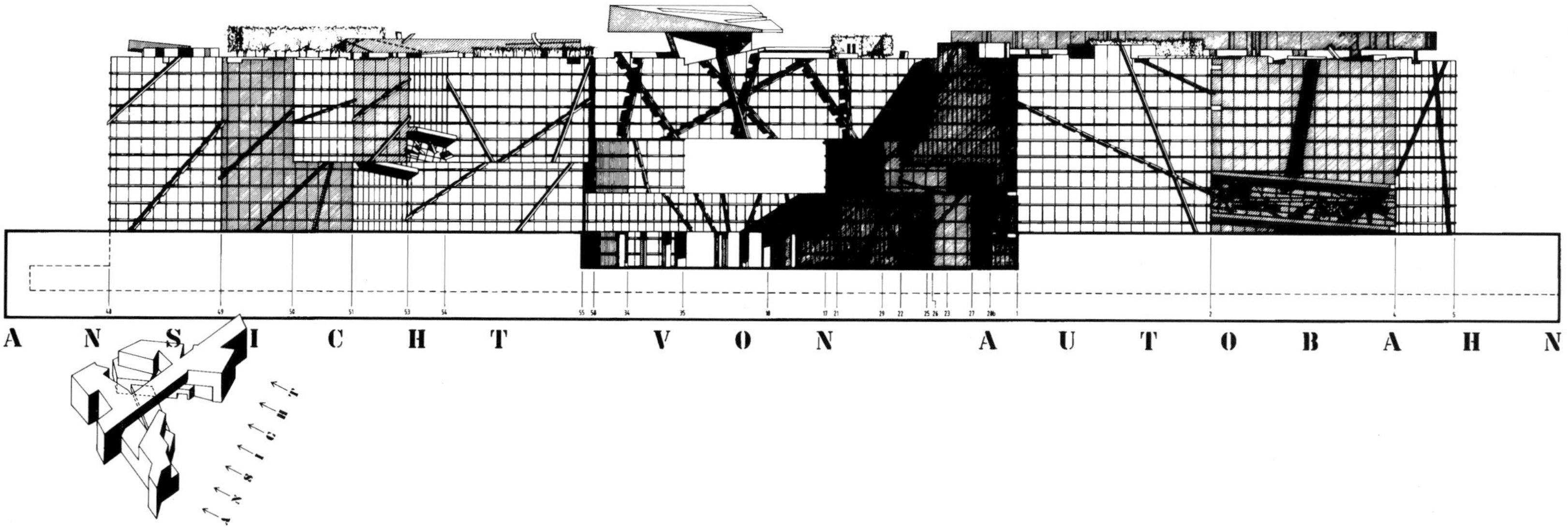

Facade studies

Model, facades with 'Muse Lines'

Über den Linden

The future development of Berlin depends on the spirit of Creative Imagination whose substance is hope and whose proof is ethical conviction. This substance is faith in the city and its culture rather than the manipulation of economic/political variables for short-sighted gains under the cover of 'planning'. It is exploration, not exploitation, which is paramount; invention, not calculation, which is necessary.

The *Über den Linden* project seeks to substantiate the image of the historical center of Berlin in scale, function and character through transformation of buildings, streets and former lines of division. To revitalize the historical East-West thoroughfare, it is necessary to bring it into the dynamics of the 21st century both functionally and urbanistically. Only by breaking through the barriers of 19th century planning and thought will the dam which separated East and West (even before its political division) be breached, allowing the energies of Berlin to flood back freely into everyday life.

A new architecture is appropriate to the new Berlin. It is not by increasing income while living on the same old capital and the same stock of inherited architecture that Berlin can grow.

A radical, less certain and more vital enterprise is necessary, probing the depths of the spirit of Berlin from which its intellectual and social character takes sustenance. In this way, an open architectural vision will become the reality of a new capital yielding new dividends and not just a 'one-time sum,' spent and forgotten.

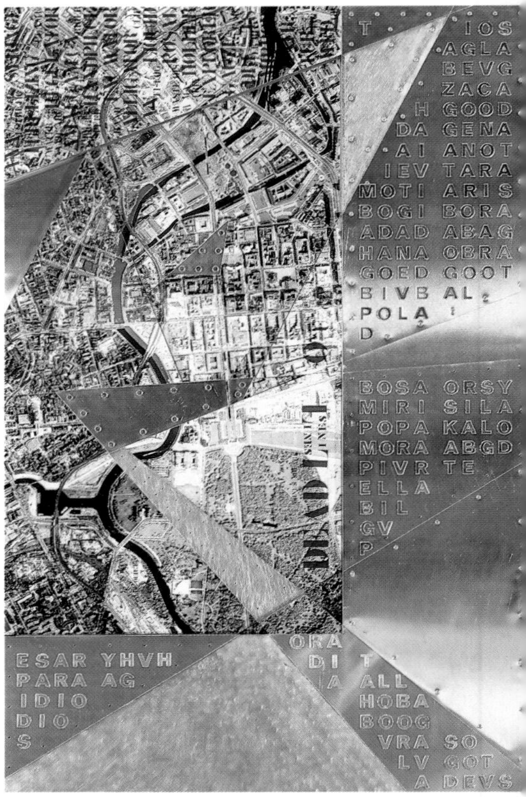

"Machine for Producing Gods"

Model

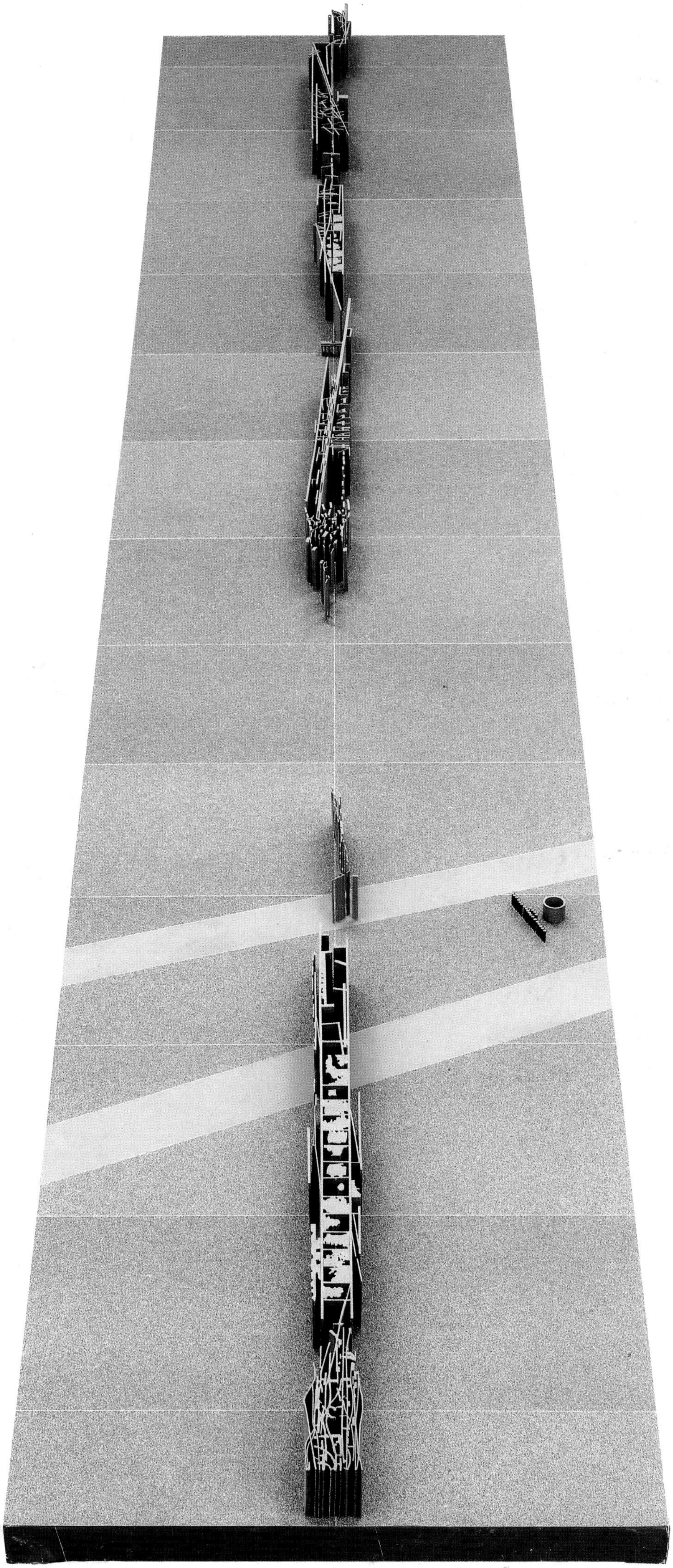

The Aleph Before the Beit
Jewish Community Center and Synagogue, Duisburg

Rabbi Elazar bar Abina said in Rabbi Aha's name: For 26 generations the Aleph complained before G-d: I am the first of the letters yet you didn't create Your world with me! Don't worry, said G-d, the world and all its fullness were created for the Torah alone. Tomorrow when I come to give my Torah at Sinai the first word I say will begin with you.

The Aleph before the House. The Aleph represents the unity of Israel — the unity of G-d. The Aleph stands for more than a letter, more than an emblem, more than the fiery beginning from which the, ברשי stems. The Aleph gives substance and connection to the four letters of the tetragrammaton: Yud (י), Heh (ה) and Vav (ו) — the ineffable and unpronouncable Name. These letters have their seat and are given form in the One. The structure of the Aleph is related to the Book in which it appears. Therefore the Book and the Aleph together represent the spiritual and cultural identity of the Jewish people. The Aleph and the Book are the twin elements used to organize and structure the urban, architectural and functional dimensions of the project.

The letter Aleph, is the beginning. Like all Hebrew letters it has the structure of the body. It is structured in three dimensions of Unity: the head, signifying the teacher; the body, standing for the Community; the supporting leg, representing children's education.

To continue the Jewish tradition across the desert of assimilation and annihilation is to return to the living sources of Jewish space and symbolism so that a community can be renewed. The new synagogue today should reflect an optimism and independence of Jewish culture amidst its neighbors. In this way, the project continues the short-lived tradition in Germany of synagogue building which began with Erich Mendelsohn — a tradition which does not model the synagogue after the typology of a Christian church.

Urbanistically, the project is sited and aligned to the historically prominent features in the city of Duisburg. The building stands with the vertical hinge of the Book facing the river and the main entrance to the complex facing the promenade which is the focal point of the new city development. The Book opens in two directions: a solid–colored tiled page and the Star of David looking towards the city; a vertical scaffolded page interwoven with greenery looking towards the East, towards the light of Jerusalem. The extended wall of the Book shields the school and echoes the old city wall. On the eastern side there is a proposal for a large landscape park with children's playground. There is also a special festival entrance for groups and large functions accessible from the inner court at Springwall. The main body of the synagogue and community center is located centrally between the foot (school and administration), the book, and the head (foyer and apartments).

The synagogue is conceived as a central gathering place for service, worship and study. The Torah is contained in a Tablet Wall whose movable structure allows for a diversity of services and their varying relationship to the community center. The movable wall is a functioning symbol of the fact that worship is not frozen in space or in objects and that "since the Exodus, freedom has spoken with a Hebrew accent". (Heine)

The configuration of seating allows for flexible arrangements, and unites the community in service while respecting Orthodox rules. The wooden ceiling refers to the no-longer existing Polish synagogues and articulates their forms. The two *Heh* skylights represent two poles of light, the secular and the religious, whose intensity differs though their size remains the same. The synagogue is part of a bigger social space which includes community activities such as eating, studying and gatherings. This space contains a kosher kitchen with its own direct delivery access. In this way, worship and community are integrated into a fluid relationship reflecting life. The facades of the synagogue building are structured around windows which bring the text of light through the intricate patterns of the Talmudic page. The synagogue building is constructed of wood.

The School is an articulated part of the complex and is connected to the synagogue and community space by the courtyard. This inner courtyard, filled with the laughter of playing children is part of the everyday atmosphere of the synagogue. The school is embraced by an outer wall which responds to the city wall across the street. It is constructed of concrete with colored tiles which in their polychromatic quality clad the building and extend its surface towards the standing page of the Book. The inner wall of the school is light and opens toward the court. This building also contains the administrative offices.

The 'head' of the letter contains the main entrance and the foyer. From this point the community members kinetically trace out the Aleph in circulating through the building. On the uppers levels of this building are the apartments of the Rabbi and the circumciser. This building is constructed out of concrete with windows and patterned reliefs relating to the tiling system.

The entire Aleph configuration is expressed in the verticality of the 'Open Book'; the lineaments of the buildings held organically together by the functional relations of schooling, meeting and worship. Learning and the interpretation of the Book constitute the visible structure of reality. They are the external and internal form of this architecture which positions, unites and articulates the building in the historical and urban space of the city of Duisburg.

The scheme celebrates a true rebirth of the Jewish community in a building which accomodates a complex program and which is itself part of the open and eternal tradition of Intellect and Faith.

Model of 'Aleph'

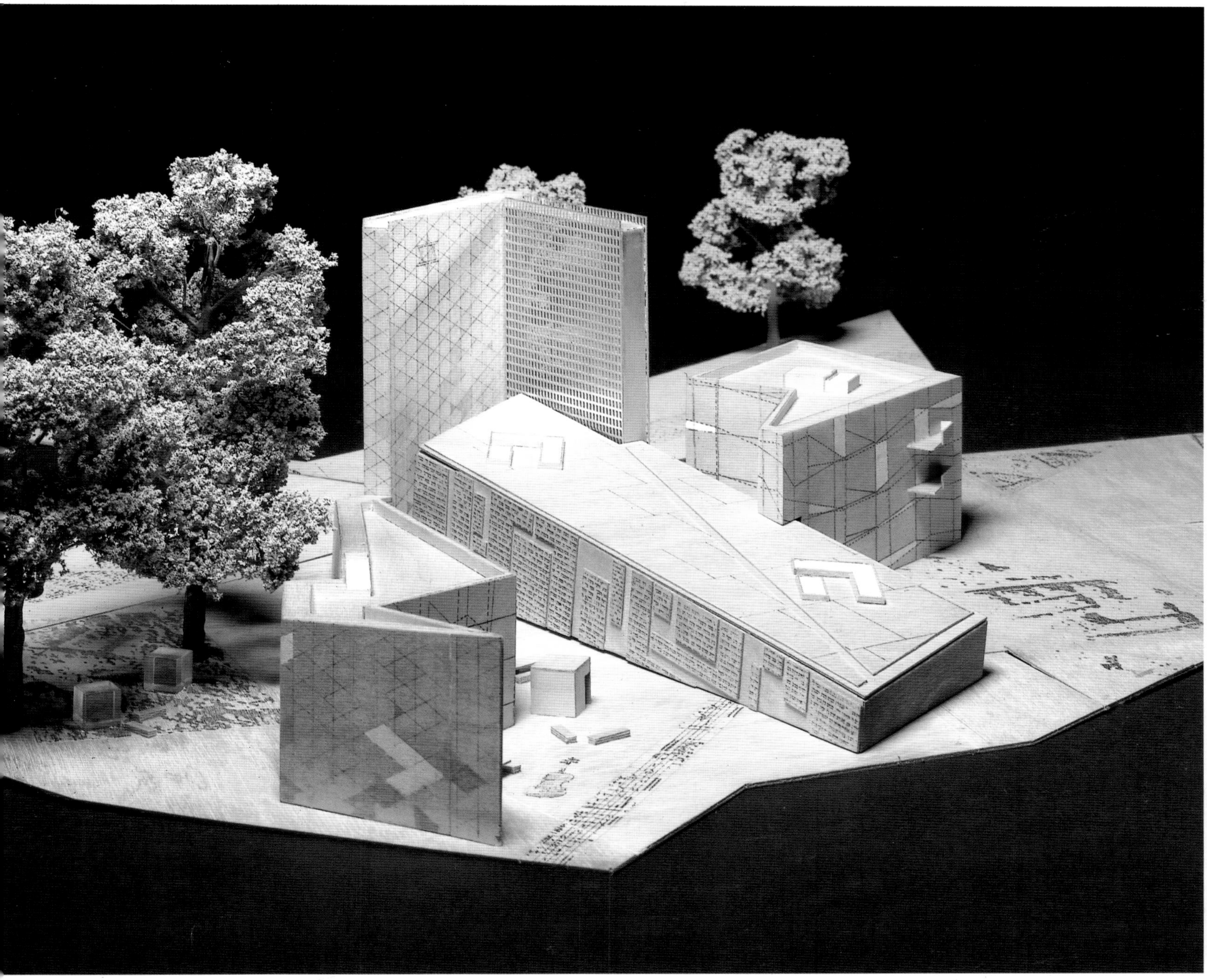

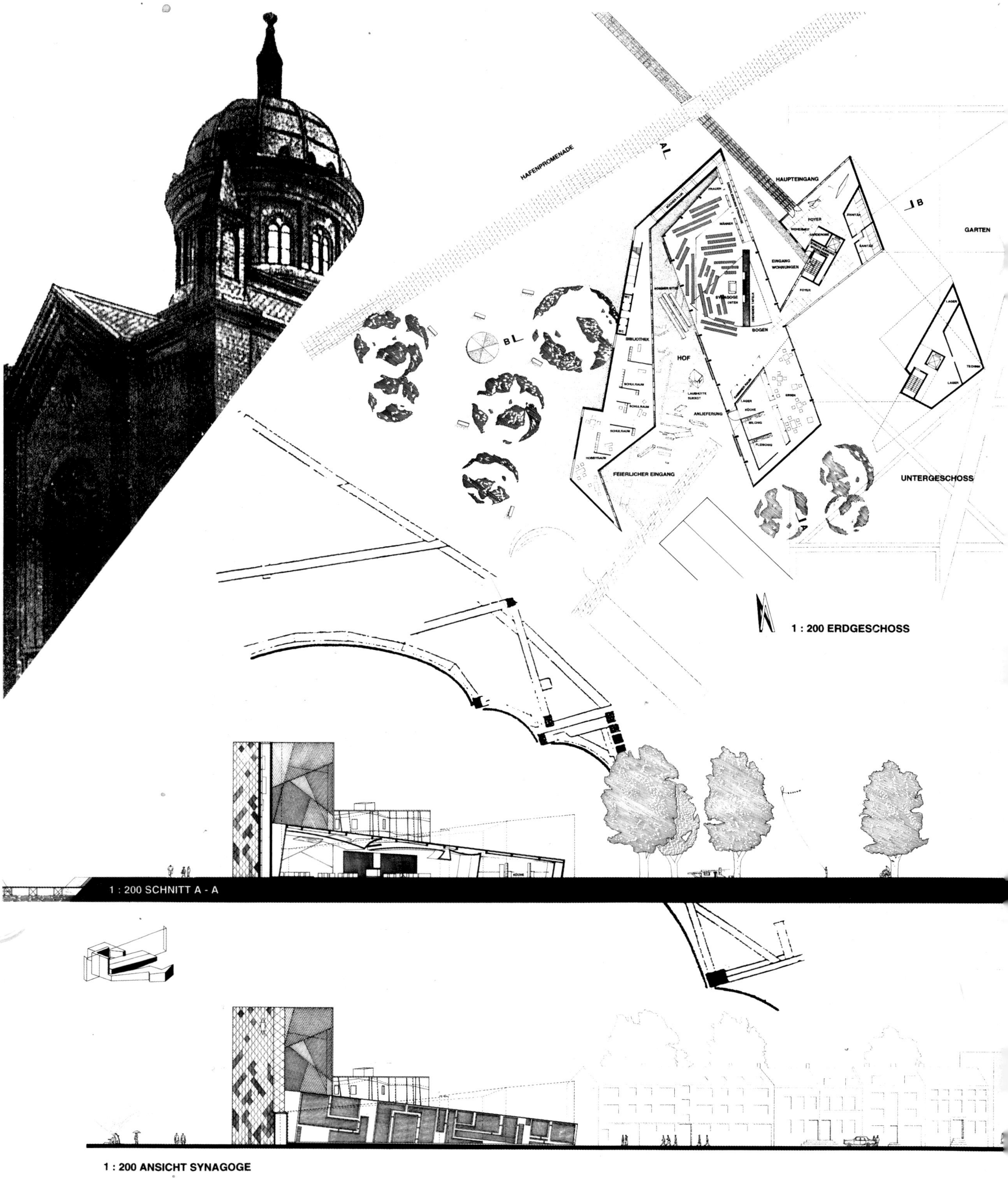

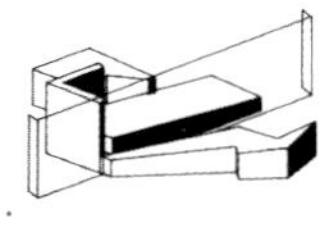

Competition drawing – Groundfloor plan, section, elevation

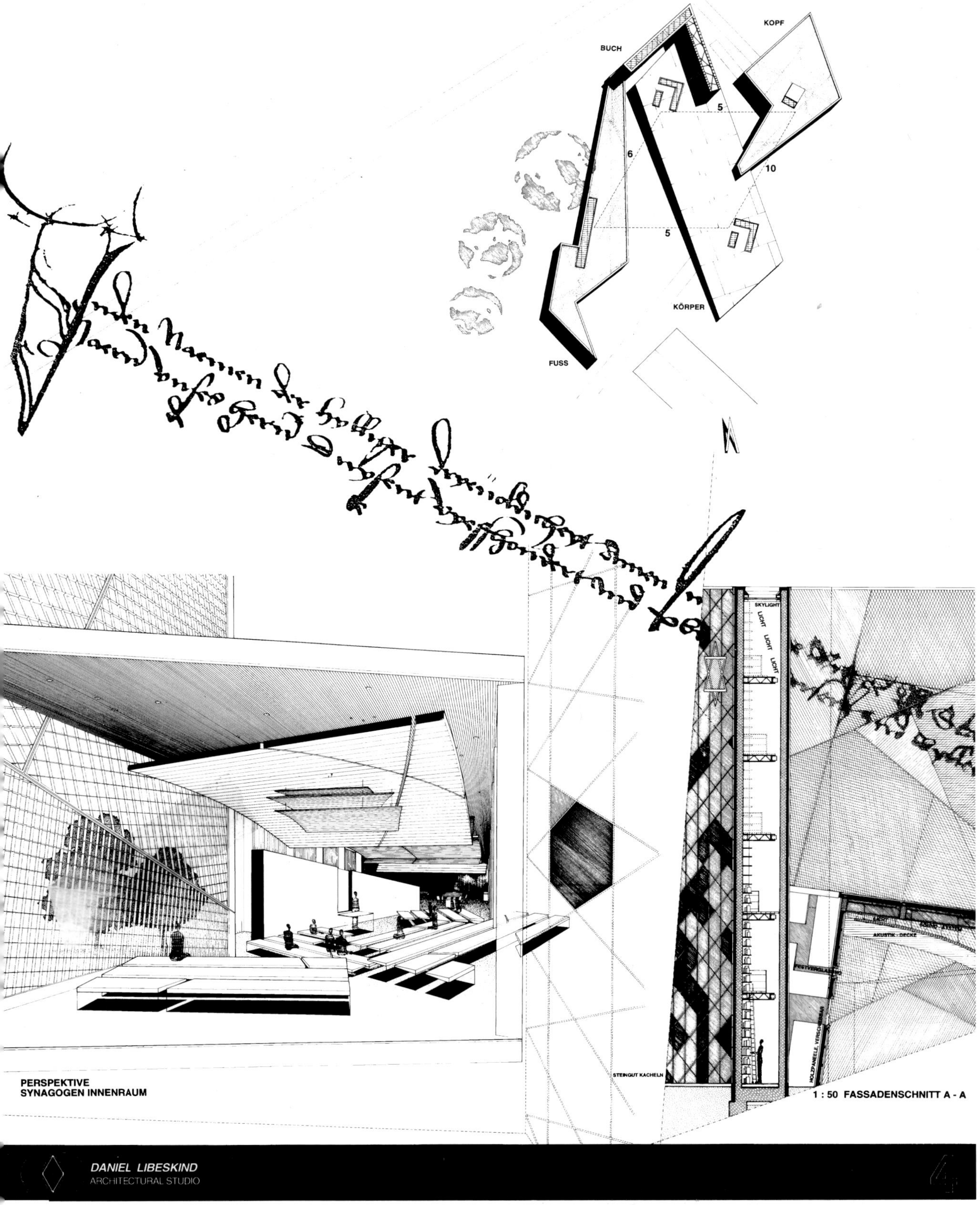

Competition drawing - Interior of synagogue, section through facade

Mo~~u~~rning
Sachsenhausen, Oranienburg

Some time ago, I was invited to a competition that called for the urbanization of the former SS-lands adjacent to the Sachsenhausen Concentration camp. I decided to ignore deliberately the suggested program and take the issue of urbanizing these lands in another manner altogether, proposing an alternative to the requested thousands of units of housing. I proposed an alternative which, because I did not follow the brief, resulted in my disqualification from the competition. I was, however, awarded an Honorary prize for reminding the jury that this site had history

Many of the citizens of the city of Oranienburg and others in the State of Brandenburg believed that the first prize scheme which provided housing was not the answer to these lands and subsequent to the decision of the jury, I was invited back by the Mayor of the City to address the issue and present my scheme to the elected members of the Building Committee. It has been an interesting political process for the last four to five years. We traveled regularly to Oranienburg to speak with officials, to address committees; once in a while, newspaper articles would appear, television programs would be shown. I am pleased to say that the citizens of Oranienburg, and the government of Oranienburg and Land of Brandenburg have asked me now to proceed with a design prepared for a new type of plan and building on this semi-profane site.

The task of urbanizing the territories formerly connected with the Sachsenhausen concentration camp raises the most fundamental political, cultural and spiritual issues of the 20th century. What must be faced in any endeavour to recreate and redevelop such an area is the need to mourn an irretrievable destiny, in the hope that this mo~~u~~rning will affect the connection between the political program, the area's topography and its social use.

The paradoxical challenge of the work is to retain a strong memory for generations to come and at the same time to formulate a response which provides new possibilities, new activities and new images of a hopeful future. The site is no longer organized along the former monumental central axis of the concentration camp, which celebrated the triumph of inhumanity. As a result of this difference, the site is split into two areas treated in wholly different ways, in order to displace the imagery of the past and to reconsecrate the land.

After discussion with the mayor of Oranienburg and concerned officials in the State of Brandenburg, I altered my scheme. For reasons of cost, I eliminated the lake I had first proposed, and in its stead built canals which criss-cross this part of the site, while providing some kind of ground cover to augment to the decay and ruin of the SS buildings.

The adjacent site is heavily planted with local species of trees, forms a new stratum for vegetation and provides a natural habitat of an especially intense kind. Within this wooded sanctuary, there is a clearing which, in a controlled and deliberate manner, structures a future development for this area.

I proposed for the building and urbanization of the site a program which is responsive to the critical nature of this historical area. I have called this development area the 'Hope Incision' because it contains public and private facilities for a new economic, social and cultural infrastructure. The building program provides space for retraining facilities for the unemployed, for the underemployed and for the young. There is a dense development of buildings which provide facilities for private computer schools, industrial retraining programs and private service-sector training, as well as offices for physical and mental health clinics and other forms of therapy. It is my intention that foundations be invited to sponsor social, cultural and political societies which can rent offices and rooms for research and discussion.

Space is provided for a library, archive, museum and ecumenical chapel. The free space outside the built area can be used for growing plants and flowers and for the development of horticulture.

Finally, as a reflection of the need to create and recollect on this particular site, there is a plan for space which can accommodate small companies which are just starting up. Various disciplines connected to cultural production, such as instrument makers, furniture restorers or ceramists are invited to found their companies at this site.

This proposal quite emphatically rejects trivializing the site with any plan for placing housing on it or otherwise domesticating it. Instead it suggests a land use which combines ecological intervention and invention with an economic base for the city of Oranienburg. Its aim is to bring people to this place, to reveal, disclose and remember. At the same, time this must be a place for hope, a place where those who are trying to rebuild Germany can find a workplace, a working future, new growth, contemplative quiet, physical and mental rehabilitation: the dawn of a new Mo~~u~~rning .

Site model

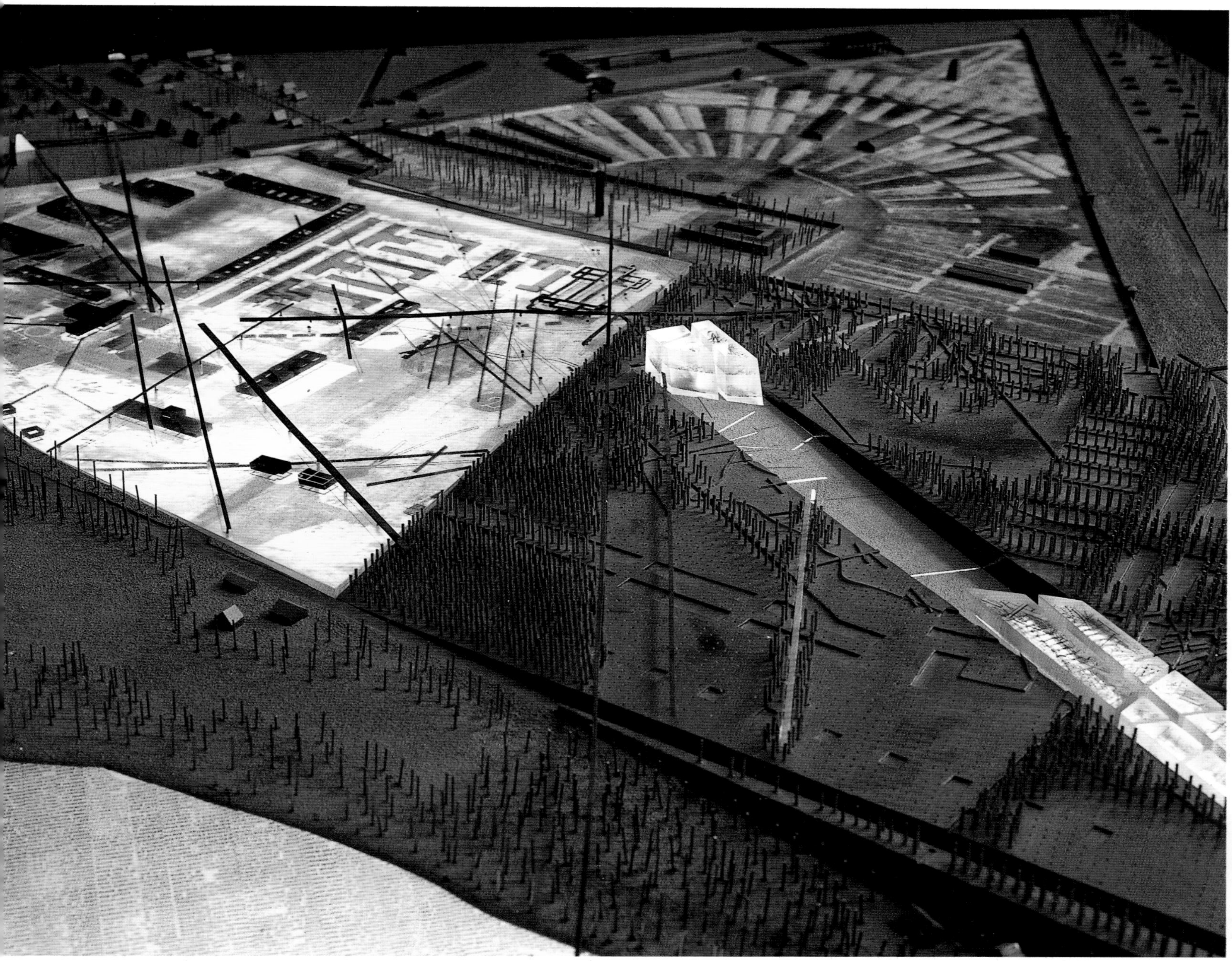

Model detail with raised pathways

Model detail with 'Hope Incision'

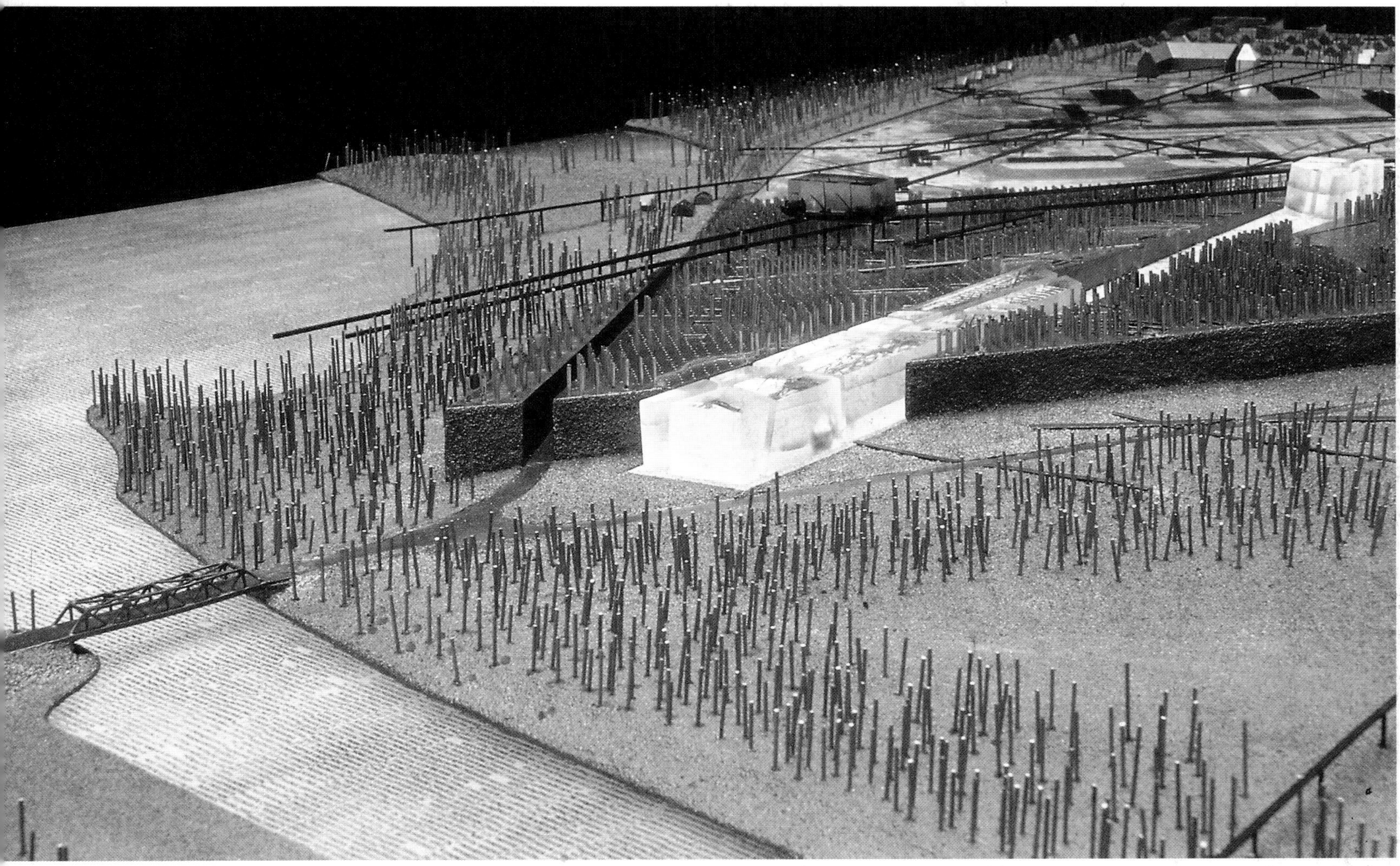

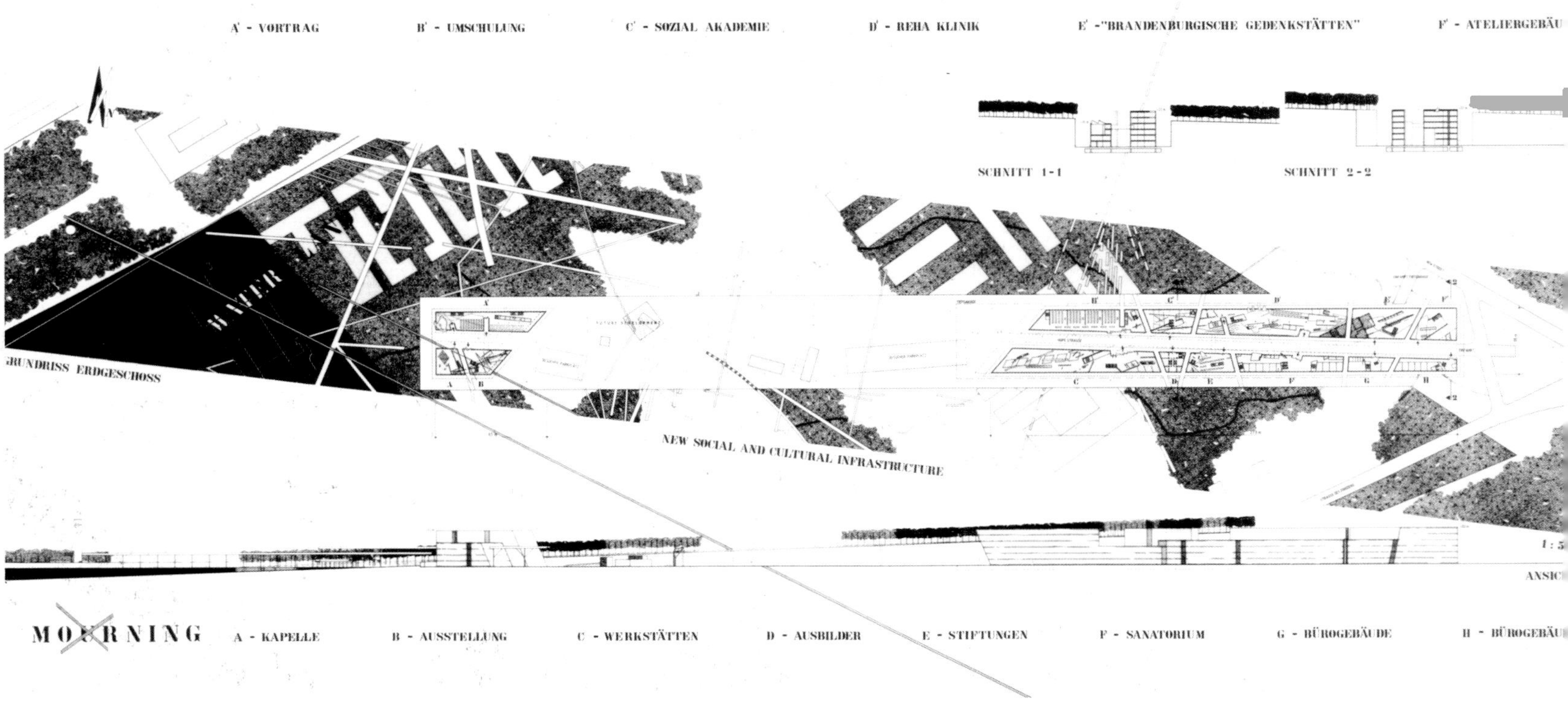
A' - VORTRAG
B' - UMSCHULUNG
C' - SOZIAL AKADEMIE
D' - REHA KLINIK
E' - "BRANDENBURGISCHE GEDENKSTÄTTEN"
F' - ATELIERGEBÄU
SCHNITT 1-1
SCHNITT 2-2
GRUNDRISS ERDGESCHOSS
NEW SOCIAL AND CULTURAL INFRASTRUCTURE
ANSIC
MOURNING
A - KAPELLE
B - AUSSTELLUNG
C - WERKSTÄTTEN
D - AUSBILDER
E - STIFTUNGEN
F - SANATORIUM
G - BÜROGEBÄUDE
H - BÜROGEBÄU

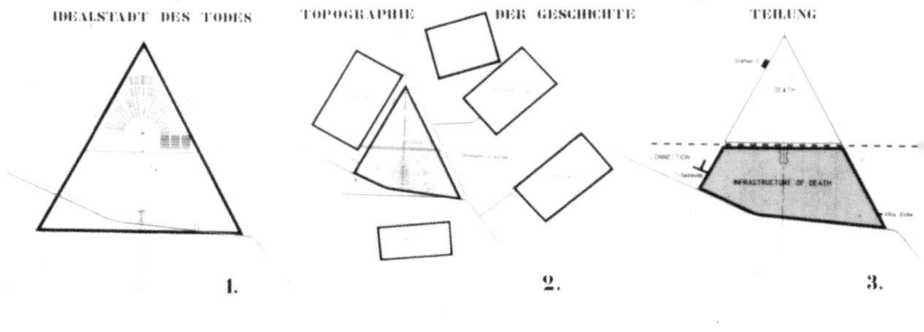
IDEALSTADT DES TODES
TOPOGRAPHIE DER GESCHICHTE
TEILUNG
INFRASTRUCTURE OF DEATH
DEATH
1.
2.
3.

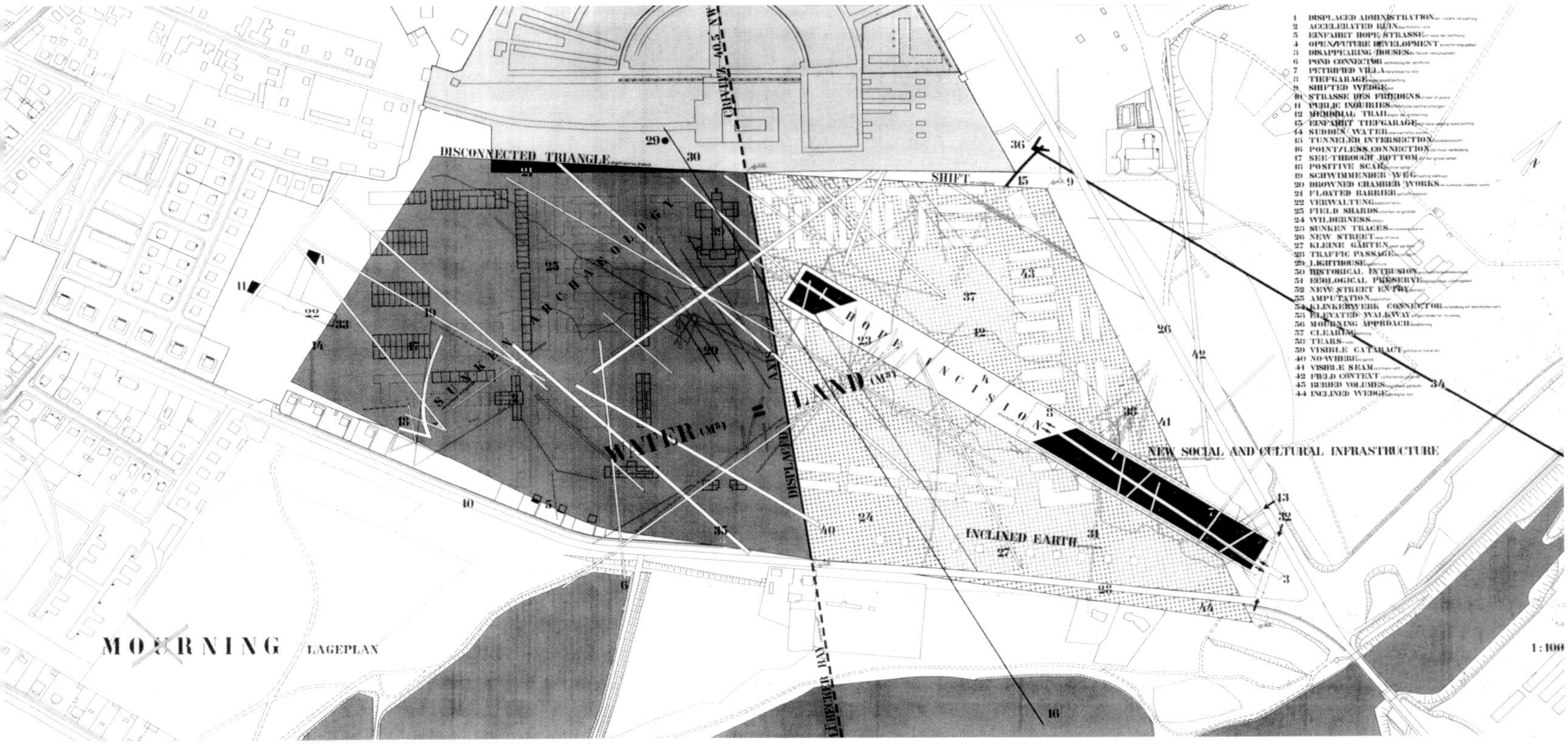
DISCONNECTED TRIANGLE
SHIFT
SUNKEN ARCHAEOLOGY
HOPE INCISION
WATER (M³)
LAND (M³)
DISPLACED AXIS
INCLINED EARTH
NEW SOCIAL AND CULTURAL INFRASTRUCTURE
MOXRNING LAGEPLAN
1:100
1 DISPLACED ADMINISTRATION
2 ACCELERATED RUIN
3 EINFAHRT HOPE STRASSE
4 OPEN/FUTURE DEVELOPMENT
5 DISAPPEARING HOUSES
6 POND CONNECTOR
7 PETRIFIED VILLA
8 TIEFGARAGE
9 SHIFTED WEDGE
10 STRASSE DES FRIEDENS
11 PUBLIC INQUIRIES
12 MEMORIAL TRAIL
13 EINFAHRT TIEFGARAGE
14 SUDDEN WATER
15 TUNNELED INTERSECTION
16 POINT/LESS CONNECTION
17 SEE-THROUGH BOTTOM
18 POSITIVE SCAR
19 SCHWIMMENDER WEG
20 DROWNED CHAMBER WORKS
21 FLOATED BARRIER
22 VERWALTUNG
23 FIELD SHARDS
24 WILDERNESS
25 SUNKEN TRACES
26 NEW STREET
27 KLEINE GÄRTEN
28 TRAFFIC PASSAGE
29 LIGHTHOUSE
30 HISTORICAL INTRUSION
31 ECOLOGICAL PRESERVE
32 NEW STREET ENTRY
33 AMPUTATION
34 KLINKERWERK CONNECTOR
35 ELEVATED WALKWAY
36 MOURNING APPROACH
37 CLEARING
38 TEARS
39 VISIBLE CATARACT
40 NO-WHERE
41 VISIBLE SEAM
42 FIELD CONTENT
43 BURIED VOLUMES
44 INCLINED WEDGE

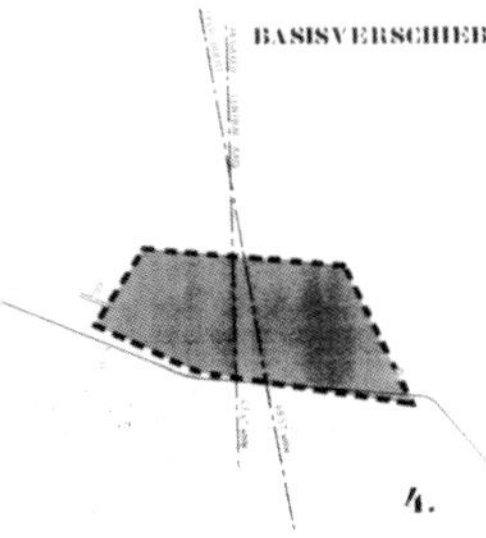
BASISVERSCHIEBUNG
4.

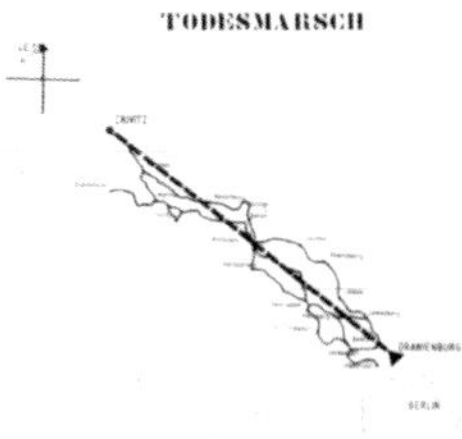
TODESMARSCH
5.

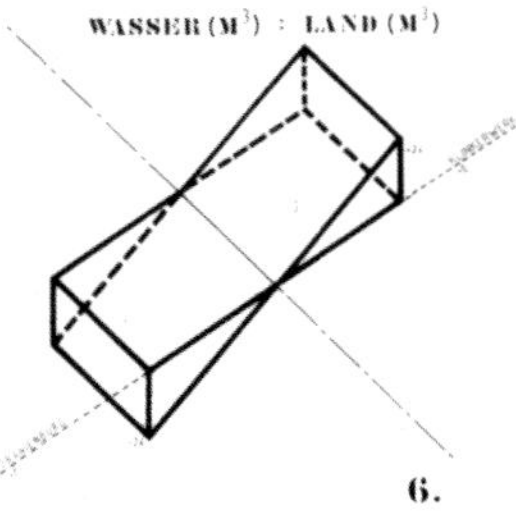
WASSER (M³) : LAND (M³)
6.

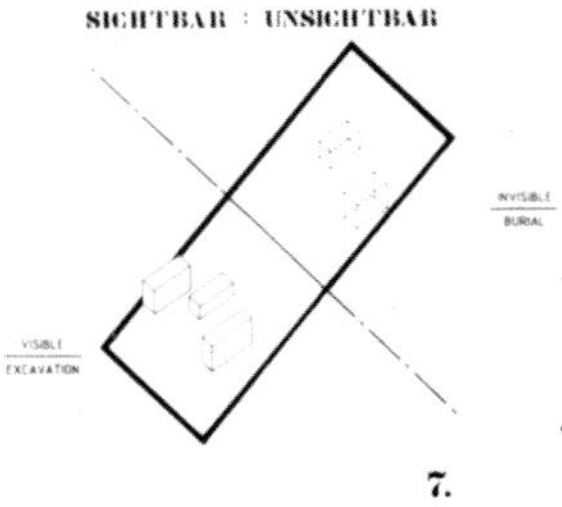
SICHTBAR : UNSICHTBAR
INVISIBLE
BURIAL
VISIBLE
EXCAVATION
7.

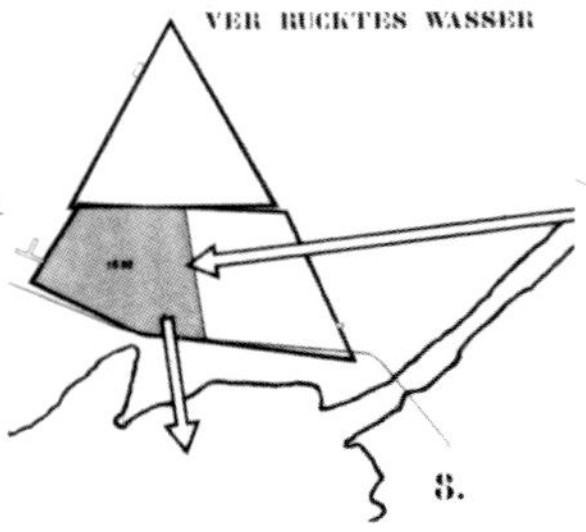
VER RUCKTES WASSER
INVISIBLE
BURIAL
8.

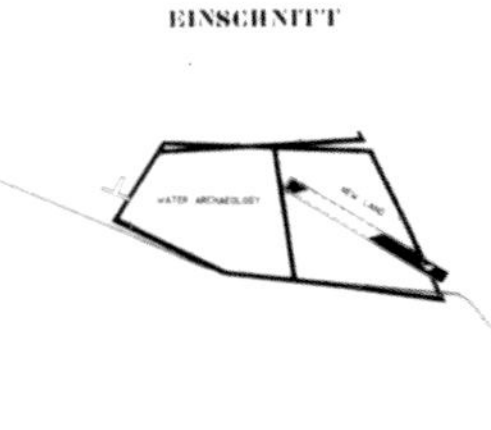
EINSCHNITT
9.

ESSAYS

Jacques Derrida
École des Hautes-Études en Sciences Sociales

Response to Daniel Libeskind

You know that someone — I think it was a philosopher — says 'Language is the house of being.' He meant, in some way, one's own language. You feel at home when you speak your own language. And one of the things I have to face now is to speak English, to improvise in English, and I do not feel at home at all. That is my first experience of *das Unheimliche*: improvising, after Daniel Libeskind, in English.

I have to cross, to intersect, some of the questions I had prepared and those that came to my mind while listening today. My remarks will look like a sort of wandering, an erring, and a zigzagging. And speaking of zigzag, it has just occurred to me that I have a very good friend in France, someone I much admire, who has written a wonderful book entitled Zigzag. I highly recommend it. It is a book written by Jean-Claude Lebensztein, who is an historian of art, a writer interested in music, art and so on. As a young Polish Jew, Lebenszstein lost his family in the War. He was brought up in France, in the country. I dedicated some texts to him and played with the initials of his first name — J. C. — and it works. This is my first association.

Now, how can one respond to such a presentation? It was breathtaking. The thing I discovered that surprised me was the reference to the sealed part, to the part you could not experience, which was the most expensive part to build. I have a question about the relationship between this inaccessible part of the building — sealed, silent, and most precious, filled with real secrets like tabernacles — and the question of the void. I will try to articulate a question about this, but before arriving at the question — zigzagging, wandering — let me elaborate something about this 'response'.

I have to 'respond' to you. How does one 'respond' to an architect? I think yours is an architecture of response in the sense that all the writing — everything of yours I have read — and your presentation this evening indicate that you want to have an architecture that invites participation. The visitor, better, the addressee, must respond by answering and by experiencing the building, even if, and especially, if, he or she is a nonarchitect. Somewhere you say, 'I do not make any distinction between architectural theory and the built project,' and somewhere else you mention a text that has no architectural equivalent. One of my questions will be this — it will have to do with the non-buildings in the project and in competitions.

The structure, the experience of competitions, in which you along with many other architects are involved, is the moment when the projects as such may not give place to a building. This opens the space for all the experiments with nonarchitectural possibilities — having to do with literature, with music, with paper. I would like, if you would be willing to follow me in this direction, to ask a question about the relationship between this open field of experiments for competitions — when you do not know whether the project will be built — and the discourse with which you describe or try to convince 'the other'. Not only us here, but the ones who make the decision, the ones who pay for the buildings. This is a naive and trivial question, but I am always wondering about the addressee — the people *to whom* you present. I do not mean the jury, which I suppose is composed of architects who understand your discourse, but the ones, like politicians or the powerful, who make a decision: what can they understand in such a discourse — which is already so difficult for us? That is a question I will leave suspended.

I had prepared some quotations for you, but do not want to speak long, so I will just skip them. I have instead some living memories having to do first with Celan and then the Wall.

First remark. This afternoon we heard something about the city — philosophy, architecture, and the city — not only about these but also about politics — this polis. Once we reach an epoch in history where the polis is not the ultimate unit of social space — there is a book about the post-city age or something like that — well, now, in this post-city age, the social space in which we live may no longer be organized in the form of a polis. This has a number of consequences. The very *concept* of Graeco-Western politics, which was structured by the Greek polis, is not adequate any longer to all the interconnected concepts, to everything we are discussing here. Perhaps 'politics' is not a good name for it all. Which does not mean that we are becoming apolitical. Perhaps whatever we are discussing here in terms of politics is already beyond the city, beyond polis, beyond politics. I will come back to this after speaking of Berlin and Celan.

But before that, another zigzag, if you do not mind. Some weeks ago I was in Prague. I was invited — as usual, as an incompetent outsider — to discuss the problem of the city. What are they going to do with Prague now? They want to restore and preserve the old city, which is already a layered complex of many styles and epochs. They also want to do something else: they want to escape all the hegemonies, all the investments, heading their way from Germany and the United States. They want to end this age. But how?

I gave a small speech, referring to Kafka and speaking of memory. Kafka, in Prague, spoke neither Czech nor Hebrew. Somewhere he says that language is the way we breathe and that since he speaks neither Czech nor Hebrew, he is doubly asthmatic in that city. Nevertheless, Kafka complains about the fact that for a number of complex reasons, the ghetto in Prague had been destroyed. He mentions the memory of this destroyed ghetto, and the fact that ghosts are still haunting it, even though he had not known the ghetto nor had the memory of all those Jewish people in it. We were thinking in this direction, about the way one could keep the memory of the city intact and yet build something in this post-city age. Now back to Berlin and Celan.

A few years ago I was invited to give a lecture on Celan in Berlin. It is said that only if we had been witnesses to these experiences of Celan could we understand what is encrypted in these poems. At all events, I was invited to give this lecture in a hotel that had been closed in the 1920s, located just in front of the Wall. The hotel was opened on this occasion. There was an old man who was keeping up the hotel. It was such an extraordinary experience — to give a lecture on Celan in this hotel just in front of the Wall. This led me to question the Wall and the city.

Now, you, Daniel Libeskind, build a Jewish museum in what remains a city — not merely any city, but the City of Berlin. During the process of the elaboration of the plans for your project, as everybody knows, the Wall came down. My question would be to what extent this event affected your project. Then there is the matter of reunification. What, according to you, has motivated the acceptance of your project, acceptance by whom, and under what conditions?

The other association I had has to do with what you said at the beginning of your presentation regarding the German-Jewish connection. When you explained why 'Between the Lines' refers to a discontinuous void, the first reason you gave was the history which associated Germans and Jews. I have worked on this question for some years in seminars and have tried to understand what I would call the German-Jewish *psyche*, meaning here the soul but also the French sense of 'mirror.' I tried to read in many texts from the eighteenth century until now — mainly texts by people you have mentioned, Benjamin and others — the terrible history of this specularity. I remember that there is a Berliner you did not mention, a friend of Benjamin's — Scholem. He thought that the German-Jewish tradition was a myth, a legend. When at some point Buber and Rosenzweig had translated the Bible into German — a project Buber did not finish until after the War, because Rosenzweig died in 1929 — there was a celebration in Jerusalem of this translation of the Bible into German. Scholem gave a speech in the presence of Buber. He of course congratulated Buber, and then said that it was a gift the Jews as guests (*Gastgeschenk*) wanted to give back to the Germans — but that it was too late, there had never been anything like a German Jewishness or a Jewish Germaneness. This is a myth, a legend, said Scholem; and now nobody will ever read such a Bible. So, the truth is that this couple (German-Jewish) never existed — now less than ever. I was thinking about what Scholem would have thought about this 'gift' you offer to Germany, to West Germany, to Free Berlin, and now to Germany as a whole. What do you think of this return of the museum as a gift, the gift of a ghost, a ghostly gift to this country?

I have a hypothesis about what links everything you said about Jews and Germans, about the city of Berlin, and the question of the void. If we had time, and if I were not embarrassed by my English, I would have tried to elaborate the links. First, Berlin as a city is not simply one among others — it is an exemplary city, and because of this you can articulate both the singularity of everything you have done and the universality of the meaning of your project. Why is Berlin exemplary? It is a city, has been a city, because of its split, which symbolizes all the division of the world, all the divided cities of the world — think of Jerusalem, for instance — and because the inner differences and the void precisely follow the line or the cut of this difference. Berlin could be considered a noncity, a city whose identity or unity is split along an interrupted line. To the extent that it is so divided and so nonidentical, Berlin could claim to be exemplary. It is precisely the way every nation, every people, when they affirm their own singularity, try to justify their avant-garde structure: they say, 'We are the avant-garde, because in our singularity we are witnessing universality, and we bear the responsibility for the universal, for humanity as such.' National affirmation always goes through this exemplary logic, and Germans and Jews have thought of themselves as having been responsible — for universality, for mankind, for the avant-garde. I am thinking of a terrible text by another Jewish German, Hermann Cohen, who, during the First World War, wrote a frightening text on Germaneness and Jewishness. In this text he claimed that there was a privileged alliance or symbiosis between Germans and Jews. By the time of the War he was addressing American Jews, trying to convince them to prevent America from entering the war against Germany. It is a very crazy and very elaborate text. He was a great philosopher, a neo-Kantian, a socialist, and a German Nationalist. Some say he was even a German militarist. He died before the end of World War 1, but his wife died in the camps in the late 1930s. He thought that the alliance between Germans and Jews — and he went back to the Hellenistic period of Greek history to prove it — had an absolute privilege, that Germany was the motherland for Jews all over the world.

Here the logic of exemplarity was at work. He was saying, 'We Germans and Jews, in our privileged relationship, are precisely the avant-garde, the best example of what mankind should be.' Sometimes, therefore, I am a little anxious about the language of exemplarity. When you said that Jewish culture was the avant-garde, you immediately afterward said that, of course, you were speaking metaphorically or metonymically for it is not as an empirical group that we can use Jewish culture as an example. My anxiety has something to do with this exemplarist logic, and this could well lead me to the question of the void.

I had prepared some notes while reading some of your text on the void, but need not read them here: you have said more or less the same this evening. This void which has to be made visible is not simply any void. It is a void that is historically determined or circumscribed; and it is not, for example, the indeterminate place in which everything takes place. It is a void that corresponds to an experience which somewhere else you have called the end of history — the Holocaust as the end of history. You have said, again somewhere else, that architecture should start at the 'end' of architecture. The 'end' would mean a number of things exemplified here. The end could be a limit, but also the origin. Architecture starting from the end means that it has to understand itself and its practice by coming back to precisely what is its own limit; it must go to its limit in order to start from it. The end is but the edge. The end might also be death. The void you are determining here is the void as determined by an event — the Holocaust — which is also the end of history. Everything is organized starting from this end of history and from this void — this is what makes it meaningful. It is not simply a place giving place to everything we build or enter into or experience.

I am thinking of a discussion that developed between myself and Peter Eisenman about the void and the *chora*. Each time Peter Eisenman mentioned absence in the void, it was a determined ontological void. I referred to the Platonic *chora* — in Greek this means 'place'— and in Plato's *Timaeus* there is a place that is neither divine nor human, neither intelligible nor sensible, a place that precedes history and the inscription of Forms; and it challenges every dialectic between what is and what is not, between what is sensible and what is becoming. Yet this place, which receives all the Forms and which gives place to everything that is inscribed in the Forms, is not a void. Plato insists on that. Nor is it something that gives or receives. It has not meaning, in terms of giving or receiving from or to a subject, be it human or divine. My question — and I say this in admiration and gratitude, for having been so moved by what you have to say — my *anxious* question would have to do with the relation between this determined void of yours, totally invested with history, meaningfulness, and experience, and place itself, place as a nonanthropological, nontheological possibility for this void to take place. The logic of the *chora*, then, is a challenge to the logic of exemplarity — the human, theological space in which the void is determined — not to speak of the possibilities for philosophy and dialectics to recuperate and to reinscribe the logic of the void, the logic of the absence of presence, and to reconstitute a discourse that is not proportionate precisely to the events of which your museum is keeping the archive.

What is absolutely fascinating in your project is not simply its memory. For philosophy could always reconstitute the discourse your project tries to challenge, the discourse from which it tries to free itself. Generally speaking, and perhaps in a very formal way, I would like you to tell us, very pedagogically, as though to instruct us, how you experience your own language — the discourse and language of your own project, the languages of your own projects at the intersection of architecture, literature, music, history, and so on. How you experience your own language in relation to the literal Judaic references and to nonliteral references as well. What is the difference between *this* museum and some analogous museum, say, in Jerusalem? Yours is irreplaceable — absolutely singular and literal — so what is the relation between what in your discourse refers to this literality and the universality of meaning in this museum? Here the concept of the 'avant-garde' is the point of reference for my question.

I could link this question with an earlier one by again going back to the part of your museum that is sealed and inaccessible, and also to the fact that there is no synopsis, no possibility for a panoptical view of the museum. I would like to ask you a question on this structure and the general structures you mention. These questions are of course addressed to you, and I am sure they are difficult enough. But they are in fact questions that can be diverted into the questions of Judaism or of the destiny of Judaism in general, the Holocaust or the whole series of interpretations of what the Holocaust has been taken to be. I would certainly understand your having to postpone an answer to this question.

A last association with Benjamin. He knew the two Scholem brothers — those two Berliners. One of them became Gershom Scholem, the Zionist who tried unsuccessfully to attract Benjamin to Israel, to Palestine. The other, a Communist, went with Benjamin to Moscow when Benjamin was asking himself whether or not he should become a member of the Communist party. Benjamin was emblematically always divided between the Scholem brothers — between Zionism and Marxism. I do not know what Benjamin — divided as he was between these Marxist-Russian and Jewish-Messianic poles — I do not know, but I wonder, what he would have thought about your project, remembering that he died during the War, on a border, committing suicide in a very strange situation. Now, please, excuse me; I have been talking for too long.

Discussion

LIBESKIND: I have to say that I have seldom had a response so moving, because the thought which followed was both critical and the same time on the set of invisible zigzags that are my own concerns. I have to admit I do not know of the book you mentioned. At the same time, I must be very honest and say that it would be very difficult for me to answer these questions systematically or pedagogically, as you have requested. You have raised the most difficult questions, which risk going too far into a realm that is at once so close to architecture and yet made impossibly far — the political arena. And yet, in my view, this risk is the energetic or vital activity of someone who would dare to call themself an architect today. I must say frankly that I did not say only rhetorically that I am not a 'normal' architect — I do not fall into that category anyway, not simply by will, but through my project; it is not that I cannot do it or that I would like to be an architect, but I cannot think that way. And I think — to answer your questions — the only reason that the project is getting built is because of that attitude. If it had been a straightforward architectural project it would have been cancelled long ago. So it is in that very fragile place that I am attempting to work — because I am also not a nonarchitect, it is not that I am somebody else.

You asked me how in the political realm the project was to proceed. In response, I have to tell a small anecdote. I was presenting the project at the Senate of Environment and Urban Planning. There were, as you might imagine, a lot of opponents to the project. A project like this is provocative not only because it has strange angles but also because it breaks many rules of building. Which is part of my intention. I started with my collaborators to break the rules of the competition with this project simply because, if this was going to get built in a city that transgressed all the way, then only transgression would serve as the exemplarity that would allow me to reconcile my own work with the project. So I presented the project to the Senate as I always do, on the original musical notepaper. Before I could say a word, the Head of Administration said to me, 'Mr Libeskind, why is it that you write your text on musical notepaper? We have had a lot of architects in here presenting projects, but never have we had one presented on composition paper.' Now, I do not think the subsequent conversation 'drifted' so much as it engaged all the people in the room, who were lovers of nineteenth century German music. Discussion began on the relationship of the five straight lines of the staff, the notes, how one might play it, is it a statement of a motif, do I like music, etc. It drifted in such a way that none of the political questions that should have come up — such as why the building is sticking out on Lindenstrasse — ever came up.

I began to think that it was not a coincidence that the building eluded detection. It is pretty obvious that the government is spending a large amount of money on something you cannot show — the void — something you cannot photograph. But I think that, practically speaking, this characteristic somehow in some very inexplicable manner protected the project. Had it been a box or a conventional organizational piece along a promenade, showing off only the good design of the Berlin Museum, I am convinced that it would have been cancelled.

I do not know what is really at work here, but I do suspect that it has something to do with what you said about Kafka. And it is interesting, by the way, that his real language was Yiddish, which he once described as a language that is not a language. He said he spoke it because it is immediately transferable to all other things — because it is not itself. Of course, I speak Yiddish and that is one of the ways that I can understand what is going on in Berlin. But you reminded me, when you raised Kafka's presence here, that Kafka somewhere says that authors really begin their work when they are dead. While they are alive, they are not really at work — they are just preparing themselves. But when they die, then they begin to write, and that is how there are great writers — the good ones begin only when they die. I applied this logic to some of these couples as a sort of 'wedding' of assimilation and dissimilation. For example, I connected Varnhagen to Schleiermacher, and not arbitrarily, because one could find many Jews and Protestants buried in this particular track of Berlin. But to find a Jew who would convert to Protestantism and renounce this conversion on her death bed and to connect her to a Protestant theologian, or to connect Celan to Mies Van der Rohe — here are some completely irreconcilable differences joined in a wedding.

I tried to deal with these couples by being aware that when one goes to the Jewish cemetery in Berlin, most of the cemetery is empty. It is a mass of marble. The names are carved only in the beginning, with preparations for future carvings. It is very disturbing — there is very little written in the cemetery, very few names, and a lot of tombs that move into generations of the future. This struck me as incredible — because no one would ever return to the cemetery to see it like this. It is a blank. And there is no one to do anything about this because everyone connected with it was exterminated. The notion of extermination is exemplary in Berlin. In the unerasable city, the impression one gets when looking at the photographs of a bombed Berlin — and I have looked at all of them — is that the one thing that was not erased in all the bombings — and almost everything was — were the streets: the markings of the streets, the curb, only a few centimeters high. Here again is the logic of Kafka, which says that the most dangerous line is the line only three centimeters above your foot. That is the line you stumble on, a line low to the ground. I take this as a technique. One has to develop some technique for a museum, and this perhaps touches on a very profound question you raise, one which I do not think I can answer: What is this museum for?

It is a museum for no museum. Its mission is to integrate the German and Jewish histories of Berlin. Such integration is possible, so that this museum is an exemplary one for the future: a museum that has nothing to show, in which everything has already been shown, has already been brought to the end of any possible involvement in the apocalyptic experience and yet still has a future. I feel that history is likely to go on — it has gone on for 50,000 years and probably, empirically, will go on forever. But that does not matter because in the experience of this particular deed — in experiences such as those of Scholem or Benjamin or Schönberg — it has come to an end. Then, as you suggested, one has to explore the implications of going into the end with a practice of or for the end, not just the Socratic philosophical pronouncement that philosophy is the practice of dying. It is pretty easy for philosophy to practice dying, since it leaves such a distant and remote trace. But for architecture to practice it in light of the fullness of its resources of materials and technology — this is more difficult.

As to the connection between the literal and the universal, that is something I find very mysterious, frankly, because I am alive only by coincidence, by an accident, not of fate, but of history. Had I been born one year earlier, I would *not* have been born. I would never have thought three years ago that I would get stuck three hundred kilometers from where I was born — a place I have not been to since I left it. Now that Polish has become the second language of Berlin, I am also forced for practical reasons to use this language which I had never wanted to use again. I really do not know how to answer this question of the literal versus the universal reference. One only has to believe that if one is participating in something that one is responsible for, then one cannot opt out, even if one wants to. One must always take the full consequences, no matter what they entail.

It involves a complete repetition. I do not think it is a coincidence that the Wall came down just a couple of months after the competition was judged. Everybody said jokingly that it was strange that the Wall came down just at the same time. I did not find it strange because I anticipated it in the planning and because I attempted to build this kind of marriage across East and West Berlin into the practical everyday happiness of the work. So, I do think it has to do with angles. I do think the situation in Berlin has transformed the building totally. As soon as Berlin was unified, I straightened all the walls. My enemies told me I was no longer a deconstructivist, that I had chickened out, because I had straightened the walls. But I did it because I felt the project was no longer protected by the kind of schizophrenia developed out of the bilateral nature of the city. It had to stand and close itself off in a different way.

I do not know to what extent the building is emblematical, an exemplary structure. I think, if anything, it will act on the participants in the building, and it does call for some putting together again of one's 'being in a museum'. It impresses upon the participants the notion that you cannot avoid the apocalypse, impresses upon them the impossibility of saying, 'I've already been there, already seen it.' It makes every bit of Berlin's history both accessible an inaccessible, without running into the end, though there are a lot of ends in the museum. There is no space in the building to get away to, no chance for a synoptic or panoptic view of it. That is a difficult point you raise, the one you have already raised in your letter in response to Peter Eisenmann, the issue of the void. I do not think I share with Peter this notion of the void, which is basically Platonic, which does deal with the Greek notion of the void. To me the void is much closer to the avant-garde, by which I really mean Moses. The avand-garde is a people under God without any mediating circumstances, no explanation as to why, and no possibility of relinquishing it. I think this is not a concept of the avant-garde but an experience of it — one either has it or one does not. And if one has it, it is too late, you cannot get rid of it, cannot convert. It appears to me that every one of these people I selected by chance — by chance, because there are others who had been around that area — every one of these people faced the duplicity, and themselves became duplicitous in both their conversions and in the impossibility of the conversion.

For example, Schönberg converted to Protestantism in order to become head of the music faculty — he renounced being a Jew. Walter Rathenau said, just before he was assassinated, that not an ounce of Jewish blood flowed in his veins. I chose and learned about these things through the geometry and through the mystery of digging into apparently safe realms, but realms with trajectories that I have extended further in order to find out what lies along and beyond these seemingly completely arbitrary lines. I think that every city is based on these arbitrary lines when viewed from the political arena. Since in fact nothing lines up, since there is no axis, since nothing can be seen in perspective any longer, one has to find another way to detect the illegitimacy of drawing, planning, and the political discourse in which buildings get built.

So, this is an attempt at precisely that. Whether or not it is successful I do not know, but I hope so. I was successful in convincing the politicians to trade the straight walls for building empty space. It is a precarious equation.

Every week I had thirty people from the Berlin Museum, the Senate, and the engineers' offices in my office. They did not want to know these things, they were not interested in Varnhagen or Schönberg or Celan. The last composer they listened to was Wagner, and they have not gotten beyond him. So how do I explain all this to them? I think one has to find equivalents, and I found them.

This is the first building I have done. I have never done anything like a small building or an addition to a building. I think Peter Eisenman has done some fire stations and some small office buildings. I did nothing before. Young architects ask me how I get away with it, and I tell them, never get a license. I have no idea about these various bureaucratic things, and I feel that this gives me a slight advantage in the process to be a step ahead of the 'professional.'

I think that lay people — and I include among them administrators — have actually been brought closer to the project by my having used these symbols. Not everyone in Berlin is a Schönberg, because for every Schönberg there were, for example, 50,000 tailors. There are hundreds of thousands of names in the *Gedenkbuch*, and nobody can remember them except what is left of their families, if they are still alive. It has helped that these four dimensions are laid out on the table, and not in any sentimental manner. But as Stanley Tigerman asked with respect to the question of measurement: "What is the measure of a work?" I bring them in as others would use a ruler or a compass to the board room.

KIPNIS: In your discussion of the issue of the void, I am reminded of a line from *Finnegan's Wake*. It occurs when Joyce slips out of his Irish accent and into his Jewish accent. The line is, 'In the beginning, there was the void.' I wonder if with this one might think of, not the Platonic ontology of the void, but rather the void and the word that operate together in *Finnegan's Wake* as offering another kind of nonontological, nonsimple access to a thinking of the void that would perhaps answer your question.

DERRIDA: Yes. Then you would have to distinguish this void from *chora* — the *chora* is not the void — and confront the ontological absence of the relation of the void. You have to change the language, not by changing the words; you must write in an absolutely different manner, otherwise philosophy, which is our language, would very quickly reontologize the void. For me, that is what Daniel does: changing the code, writing differently in order to withhold or subtract this void from political dissemination. Then at some point you would have to drop even the word 'void', because the void mentioned is not void in the way we understand void. There is some emptiness surrounded by a line which is indivisible, a circumscribed emptiness. So if the void is not this, then perhaps we have to give up the void, or give up the word 'void'. My question had to do, not so much with what he thinks or what he does, but with the discourse, the word, the logic, and the grammar he has to use in order to make his project understandable in a pedagogy or in texts, given the general philosophical and cultural context in which he has to convince us and the powers that be in Berlin. He has to compromise. It is a question of rhetoric, in the most serious sense, of the negotiation he has to organize in which every day he has to speak the language of the other in order to convince the other without betraying what he is trying to do. It is a negotiation in which every day he has to re-evaluate every sentence, each step. It is not simply a matter of theory or rhetoric in an inferior sense. The stakes are immediately concrete. If you make a mistake, if they cannot be convinced practically, then you have to transform your project. It is not simply a matter of sentences on the page. I am sure that the most intelligent people you meet in Berlin are not in a situation in which they can understand the difference between Plato's definition of the void and the *chora* which is already a split in Plato. How could they understand all that? You have to speak to them in a way that their necessary and unavoidable misunderstanding, no matter how intelligent they are, does not affect your own project. That is politics in a metapolitical sense. It is the most serious responsibility.

That is what I have to say to your question, Jeff. But remember that I started with the question of response. Of course, Daniel, you are waiting or hoping for a response, but you are already responding by participating in something you yourself cannot really understand, as when you mentioned the coincidence of your birthday. However singularly irreplaceable they are, these things nevertheless call you to the avant-garde; it is a call to which you must respond. The strictest response — the most politically concrete and effective — is the one that involves the struggle with the ones you have to convince. It is the most necessary and contingent, the most singular and the most universal task at the same time. Here is where exemplarity occurs — at the crossing of the response.

INGRAHAM: Since there is a special realm for a project of this type, are you referring to a different kind of political negotiation for architects to participate in or any sort of political discourse? Does it change the status of the void, depending on whether it is architecturally changed or transferred in the market place versus a purely philosophical discussion?

DERRIDA: No. On the one hand, I would say that it is something more general than the experience of negotiating. We all experience this one way or another, always in a singular way. Negotiation is always singular. We all, every day, have our own problems. Not the same problems, but analogous ones. So this is a general condition. Now, I think, for me, who am even less of an architect than Daniel — the way in which I have no license is not exactly the same as his — for me, as a nonarchitect, this is what I consider to be exemplary of the avant-garde architecture today. The negotiation that you have to enter into is much more difficult — the stakes are higher — and much more immediately political than in my case. When I write something, I do not have to convince a state, to convince deciders in a city like Berlin — to do something as visible — for even your void has visibility. When I want to negotiate something in my university or with my publisher, it has something to do with the same visibility, but it remains invisible ... almost. The stakes of my negotiations go through a number of mediations that are more unpredictable and more difficult to define than yours. You will know — for I hope your museum will, for centuries, be a theme of discussion — you will know that the thing will be built, that it will be done. My negotiations, which do not have the monumental visibility of your void, are not so immediately political. That is why today, in terms of politics and history, this experiment of yours is for me exemplary, and I refer to it—out of my incompetence—as exemplary.

LIBESKIND: I want to say that even when it is built, it is actually not unlike what you are doing. What one has to do as an architect in this case is to prevent the void from filling up. One of the characteristics of this particular void is that it is very easy to bridge it in order to complete the building. And of course the pressure from the Senate and the public money reminds us that if one is already building such a space, why not fill it? Why not use it? The project is to make it inaccessible. How would one prevent that particular part of the building from being changed while the rest of the collection would change? Part of the reason for having it articulated is that if the Jewish collection is to grow in Berlin, it will do so throughout this museum, and not in any one part of it. It is in a sense as though a particular piece of Berlin is obliterated.

DERRIDA: Although there is an enormous difference of degree, I do understand that there is no essential difference. But, of course, this exposure of your work to an always possible deterioration or misinterpretation is a chance, it is not a negative risk. If you were sure that your work would never be altered then it would not be a work. A work has to be left beyond your life, left exposed to manipulation or reinterpretation. That is why you build. The fragility itself is part of the possibility of the work.

INGRAHAM: The design of the void is exactly right, then, because the design of the void is about keeping the void invisible. The invisibility of the void is also the protection of the space.

LIBESKIND: No, that is just an appearance in the model. It is actually the one part of the building that has not technically been designed. It is the one part of the building that is constituted by the intersection of everything that is known and appears in the central arena of the building. For somebody looking at the collection, it appears as something which is deferred. It is not something that is designed deliberately. It is already there.

DERRIDA: Let me repeat the first intention of my question. There are two kinds of voids in your work. One is the general spacing of the structure in discontinuity. The other is this very determinedly sealed space which nobody can experience or enter into. These two voids are not of the same quality. One needs the other to be determined, in order to relate to history, to memory, to what is kept as a nameable or nameless secret. There is some sealed memory, kept as a crypt or as an unconscious, which is encrypted here. The sealed memory is not exactly the general void and the emptiness of the structure.

Alois Martin Müller

Daniel Libeskind's Muses

The lines in Daniel Libeskind's drawings and architecture, the traditional ordering and constructional medium of geometry, land surveying and spatial mensuration, are used in 'Micromegas' to reveal a lack of measure, the hubris of the belief in the constructability of the world. Geometry is taken to the point of disintegration, where space is atomized into tiny particles and an 'end space' architecture is created, an architecture in which space is conceived or taken to its ultimate limits. In 'Micromegas', one finds an expression of the systematic doubt which permeates all Libeskind's work and which leads to a situation in which the boundaries of normality are permanently questioned and, indeed, transgressed. In the chamber works, there is an attempt to use networks of lines to create signs which represent nothing, which make reference only to themselves and which no longer indicate their own origins or other sources. The line in the Line of Fire ploughs a trail through the red volume, dividing it and evoking the idea that every trace of human life establishes some relationship, creates a difference which precludes all notion of a uniform origin. The 'Muse Lines', the lines of the muses, found in the office complex in Wiesbaden, are meant to re-establish a link between work and leisure, public and private life, natural and cultural phenomena. They reoccur in the form of the ten 'Muse Lines' of the Potsdamer/Leipziger Platz project.

In Homer and Hesiod, what was originally a single muse has become a chorus of nine sisters, daughters of Zeus and Mnemosyne. They sit at the table of the gods on Olympus and may also be encountered on Parnassus near Delphi, where they dance and sing under the direction of Apollo. Anyone who dares measure himself in contest with the muses must reckon with punishment on suffering what would seem to be inevitable defeat.

In the course of history, the nine muses have come to be associated with specific activities which embrace all the fine arts recognize d by the Greeks. Daniel Libeskind gathers them all together again in Potsdamer Platz: Erato, the muse of poetry, and in particular erotic poetry; Euterpe, the muse of lyric poetry accompanied by the flute; Calliope, the muse of epic poetry and science; Clio, the muse of history and historical poetry; Melpomene, the muse of song and tragedy; Polyhymnia, the muse of serious song to an instrumental accompaniment; Terpsichore, the muse of dance; Thalia, the muse of comedy; Urania, the muse of astronomy. Libeskind adds a tenth muse to their number: the 'Zero Time Muse', the muse at the zero point, the muse without history, the present, the muse of mutability and flexibility. These lines form the matrix, the basic order of Potsdamer Platz. They do not just cut through this and other architectural projects, however; metaphorically speaking, they run through Daniel Libeskind's entire thinking. They act as a corrective to three patterns of thought that, although forming a specific part of our world today, showed signs of negating the achievements of the modern world in the course of history.

Our knowledge of the history of modernism no longer allows us to invoke it without reservation. The modern movement itself has gone down in history, and it is necessary today to subject the historical legacy of this movement to critical analysis. Libeskind adopts the reflective stance to modernism which the sociologist Ulrich Beck recently advocated when he called for a 'reflective modernization'. What Beck means by this is that the modern movement itself has to be subjected to a critical assessment to ascertain where its self-momentum leads to unwanted or harmful consequences which occur 'in the course of its own autonomous processes of modernization, which are heedless of their effects and deaf to warnings of danger'.[1] The 'Muse Lines' in Libeskind's architectural thinking assume the strategic function of preventing him from falling into three major self-perpetuating traps: the trap of hybrid enlightenment, the trap of radical historical philosophy and the trap of the Tower of Babel.

In his paper 'The Myth of Site', Libeskind writes:

> The episode of the sirens in Homer's Odyssey describes the temptations of the past: the weaving of the myth of enlightenment with that of dominion. Through suffering, our 'modern' hero triumphs over the temptation of self-destruction. He discovers his own identity by enduring the severance from his own self and from all those who knew 'everything that had ever happened on this earth'. The sensual pleasures that dissolve all boundaries, as promised in the song of the sirens, are to be enjoyed only at the price of bondage .... The ability to convey meaning in architecture is a question of dominion and control. Conversely, dominion is the most powerful force that can be depicted in architecture. Paradoxically, therefore, this ability to depict meaning is an instrument of both enlightenment and regression.[2]

It is precisely this paradox of dominion that the philosophers Max Horkheimer and Theodor W. Adorno subjected to radical scrutiny while in exile in Santa Monica during the Second World War:

> Enlightenment, in the broadest sense of progressive thought, has always pursued the goal of relieving mankind of its fears and elevating it to the rank of masters. A wholly enlightened world, however, radiates an aura of triumphal havoc. The program of Enlightenment represented the demystification of the world. It wanted to banish myth and overthrow illusion, setting knowledge in their place.[3]

These are the opening sentences of the book *Dialektik der Aufklärung* (Dialectic of Enlightenment). The authors' pessimistic view of enlightenment is justified. At the time, totalitarian systems, whether of the right or of the left, were shaking Europe to its very foundations. The industrially organized extermination of the Jews was in full swing. It seemed as if human reason was solely in the service of systematic destruction and mass murder. With this impression of the self-destruction of enlightenment fresh in their minds, Horkheimer and Adorno wrote — as they themselves called it — an 'original history of subjectivity' (*Urgeschichte der Subjektivität*).[4] In order to escape the clutches of the mythical powers and develop their own independent character, they believed that human beings had to sever their links with their roots and take their own lives in their hands. In this way, they would seek to escape from the sphere of influence of the shadowy figures of the gods, to be something more than just prisoners and tormented creatures. This flight from the primeval powers also implied that human beings had to remove themselves from the natural world by learning to control it better; they could only succeed in this if they understood how to control themselves, their own natures. Only through the deception of reason — by tying himself to the mast of his ship — was Ulysses able to resist the song of the sirens, i.e. only 'at the price of bondage'. In other words, 'the history of civilization is ... the history of renunciation.'[5] This process of liberation through control could become a hybrid phenomenon and ultimately be directed against human beings themselves, who might succumb to their natural urge to dominate. Horkheimer and Adorno saw this state as having been reached in Western civilization.

Every attempt to resist natural constraints by breaking with nature leads ever deeper into natural constraints.[6] The control of nature turns into a subjection to nature. Like the sorcerer's apprentice, modern man loses control of the world he has created. Everything that is unpredictable, indeterminate, undifferentiated, alien and non-uniform is now pushed aside, put down, eliminated. Thought counts only as a tool: what is calculable, useful. Unity is created where none exists. Everything is geometrically plotted and measured, arithmetically proportioned. Once man lived in a world of myths. Now he lives, without any break between, in his grand world of reason become myth; and so enlightenment is turned to mythology again.

Building is a process of construction, of placing elements on top of each other. Architecture, as art which has to function, 'endure' and be serviceable in our everyday world, is most closely bound up with reason of a scientific-technical kind. The degree of rationalization and functionalism is, however, not predetermined according to some objective scale. As Libeskind might ask, how much of the architecture of the twentieth century is a necessary cultural control in the form of renunciation, serving to further human enlightenment, and how much is control in the form of a regression into an expansive, arrogantly dominating world of reason? The project for the Extension of the Berlin Museum with the Jewish Museum Department inevitably confronted Libeskind with the problem of the 'dialectic of enlightenment'. In an interview, he remarked:

> Culture, including architecture, is suffering the same fate as German-Jewish relations in Berlin. Contemporary culture is infected by the same thinking that led to the Holocaust. They are not two different things. By 'the same thinking', I mean a certain kind of rationalism, organization, bureaucracy and administration. One cannot isolate them and say, in one case they are good and in another bad. I do not believe in an architecture that complies with certain functions and constraints ...[7]

Libeskind's museum is a metaphor for the perverted form of enlightenment that led to the perpetration of crime in broad daylight, that was deranged by the myth of separation and total domination and that ended in self-incurred guilt. It bears witness to a historical crime, the avowed aim of which was the extermination of human beings, whose traces are already in danger of disappearing, because the extermination actually took place and has left behind an enormous, unfillable void. An empty, rectangular shaft — the Void — which cuts through all segments and all stories of the building, brings home this sense of absence. An empty shaft fragment also appears as an autonomous form next to the building. In this act of evacuating the Void outwardly, in its appearance in the real historical world, the building sets up a silent sign for something which remains incomprehensible.

Anyone who wishes to visit the Jewish Museum will have to descend into the present-day absence and invisibility of former relations between the Jewish and non-Jewish sections of the population and into suppressed layers of history, for the only link between the old Berlin Museum building and the new extension, the Jewish Museum, is underground. The new museum tract keeps one space empty for the terrors and contempt of humanity manifest in the process of history, so that it will not be overwhelmed or displaced in time by future historical developments.

This project also forces us to examine the modern metaphysics of history and our attitude to the subject. The reorientation of the philosophy of history that occurred in the so-called *Sattelzeit*[8] between 1750 and 1800 vested all hope in the historical process. This, it was believed, would be forward-looking, based on the concept of progress and embedded in a linear future perspective. Only in this way would humankind attain a state of freedom, justice and solidarity.

In the course of this progressive historical process, the traditional spectrum of narrated history would be reshaped into a coherent historical concept. Suddenly the word *history* became a 'collective singular'.[9] Until the 18th century, the word had been a plural form in German, comprising the various histories which accounted for all that had happened in the world. History as a singular noun had a loftier intent. In future, not only individual minor historical episodes were to be told. History suddenly acquired the duty to comprehend reality as a continuous whole and to portray the entire history of humankind as a path to freedom and independence. History was no longer to be 'just' the embodiment of many histor*ies*. History as a unity sought to make them comprehensible. Hegel united the philosophy of enlightenment and history completely by proceeding on the assumption that the course of history was a sensible one. In making this assumption, he was able to write:

> 'This process — helping the spirit to find itself, to find its concepts — that is history.'[10]

He formulated the uncanny sentence:

> 'He who regards the world with the eyes of reason will be looked upon by it with reason as well. The two things are reciprocal.'[11]

Gottfried Küenzlen summarized this new historical thinking as follows:

> As Christian belief in the saving grace of God and in the order of Creation gradually lost strength in the process of secular disorientation, all that remained was a purely profane history; and this became the receptacle of secular-religious hopes, yearnings for salvation and expectations of redemption.
>
> It acquired a new dimension through the secular hopes for salvation and interpretations of the world and in particular through the promises of redemption offered by its Utopias. In other words, it became a secular history of salvation. It was no longer the Book of Revelation, no longer the book of nature (which still remained to be unravelled), but the book of time, the book of history that became the book of books of the secular history of religion.[12]

As is evident from his writings, Libeskind is aware of the destructive effects of secularized promises of salvation that seek to impose a homogeneous historical process. In his extension to the Berlin Museum, he felt obliged not to build a revelatory monument to the 'good' in history, but to keep open a shaft for a historical crime perpetrated in the name of history. Since history is always bound up with individual histories, however, the names of the Jews who disappeared will be placed on the inside of the shaft, serving to unmask history itself.

In his other projects, too, Libeskind is cautious in his approach to history, so as not to succumb to the homogenizing tendencies implicit in any secular story of salvation. In the Alexanderplatz project in Berlin, not everything will be demolished that could be demolished. Libeskind prefers transformation, complexity, heterogeneity and plurality on a building site, which he sees as a puzzle. His feeling for history, for stories and histories, sharpens his sensibility for the strata of history and the deposits of time, for many-layered things, for the asynchronous nature and inconsistencies of different histor*ies*. His takes a multi-perspectival and proportional view of history, including that of modern times. Remembrance of history does not occur by establishing links to a period of the past that is regarded as 'good', but by the circumspect treatment of existing substance. Since cultural life is the link to memory in the modern world, in Out of Line Libeskind draws his 'Muse Lines' through Potsdamer/Leipziger Platz. The lines have an articulating and linking function. The historical squares and old street spaces are left in their original state, and the lines of the arts ensure that the fabric which has evolved in the course of history is 'delivered from the jaws of monumentality'.[13]

Hovering over the square as a central component is the 'Aleph Wing', which Libeskind designed as early as 1988 as an independent element, as a kind of transitional object. Starting at the former Potsdamer Passenger Station, the building freely follows the line of the Berlin Wall and marks a new urban focus: a development beneath the wing which also integrates the former Potsdamer/Leipziger Platz and which is meant to belong to a number of people through the possession of share certificates. This also applies to the building itself, for which the prytanion — the city hall and seat of government in ancient Greece — served as a model and which is reserved for humanitarian organizations — ideally, welfare bodies and charities, the shareholders of Potsdamer Platz and a kind of world court of justice should be housed here. As Libeskind states in 'Angel Trapping History':

The design echoes the contortions of the non-existent angel; but the contortions are as real as those of all the other deported archangels — Franz Kafka, Walter Benjamin, Primo Levi, Osip Mandelstam, Paul Celan.[14]

Libeskind's 'Aleph Wing' is a humanitarian symbol of hope that lends meaning to this place. The message it conveys is drawn from history, and it expresses a genuine belief in the angel of Walter Benjamin's story contained in his historical-philosophical hypotheses, a story that was inspired by Paul Klee's picture *Angelus Novus*:[15]

His countenance is turned towards the past. Where a chain of events appears before us, he sees nothing but catastrophe incessantly heaping ruin upon ruin and hurling the debris at his feet. He would probably like to linger awhile and piece the fragments together; but a storm approaches from paradise, a storm that entangles itself in his wings and is so strong that the angel can no longer close them. The storm drives him inexorably into the future on which he turns his back, while the heap of rubble before him mounts up to heaven. The name we give this storm is 'progress'.[16]

In this lucid fragment, history is not just the act of stumbling from one future catastrophe to the next. Progress is the storm which hurls the rubble of our unresolved past after us, so that we cannot avoid stumbling and falling as we are driven forward. The 'Aleph Wing' confronts this future perspective not with a naive Utopia, but with an expression of confidence that human beings will one day understand that, despite its great diversity, they form a unity possessed of an inalienable dignity and enjoying equal rights. The aleph, the first letter of the Hebrew alphabet and the numerical sign for 1, is a symbol of this state of unity. In a chapter of the Book of Zohar, the central work of the thirteenth century Cabbala, the following is written about the aleph:

At the beginning of everything is the aleph, beginning and end of all stages, the archetype in which all steps are shaped and for which there is no other name but 'one', to show that, although it comprehends many forms within itself [like the Godhead], it is nevertheless a unity.[17]

There is no intention of 'resolving' the various manifestations of human life, culture and religion to some impossible unity through the form of the 'Aleph Wing'. They should be preserved within it in all their diversity beneath the insignia of human rights.

In Jorge Luis Borges' story 'The Aleph', there is an interpretation of this symbol that illuminates Libeskind's intention perfectly:

There are two remarks I wish to add, one about the nature of the aleph, the other about its name. As we know, this is the first letter of the alphabet of the holy language. In the Kabbalah, this letter represents the En Soph, the infinite and pure godhead. It has also been said that the aleph has the form of a human being pointing to heaven and to earth to indicate that the lower world is a mirror image and cartographic representation of the upper world. In set theory, it is a symbol for transfinite numbers in which the whole does not exceed the size of any of its parts.[18]

The wings and the ground are dual elements. Libeskind's concept of unity in the diversity of voices is linked with the hope that the conditions of life on the ground, on earth, will one day reflect human thought as it occurs in the wings.

Allowing scope for a diversity of voices, not seeking to reconcile them in some obligatory expression of unity means avoiding a Tower of Babel. The 'Aleph Wing', hovering horizontally, not upright, can also be seen as an overturned Tower of Babel. Jacques Derrida's interpretation of the story of the tower describes an attempt at domination and at the same time an amazing piece of architectural history:

Heaven is to be conquered in an act of name-giving that nevertheless remains indissolubly linked with natural speech. One tribe, the Semites, whose name means 'name', wish to build a tower up to heaven, to make a name for themselves. In this context, taking up a position in heaven means giving oneself a name — a grand name, from the lofty elevation of a metalanguage, which will allow one to dominate the other tribes and the other languages. In other words, it is an act of colonization. God, however, descends and thwarts this undertaking by uttering the word 'Babel', a proper name which resembles a word meaning confusion. With this word, he condemns humankind to a multiplicity of languages and the process of translation. The tribe must thus abandon its plan of domination through a language which would have been universal. The fact that this divine intervention gave rise to a work of architecture, to construction — and conversely deconstruction — and at the same time involved a defeat or the imposition of boundaries on a universal language to frustrate any plan of political or linguistic dominance of the world, indicates, among other things, that the diversity of languages is uncontrollable .... [The story of Babel] also contains an allusion to a finite, but nonetheless divine, aspect of God. This can be seen in his intervention in the building of the tower, an intervention which becomes necessary because God is not almighty .... It is a token of His finite nature, and in this respect He finds himself in the same situation as the Semites, whom He would seem to be opposing. He is therefore unable to control the situation and even though He stops the construction of the tower, He does not destroy it completely. He leaves it in a state of ruin and thus makes possible the diversity of tongues and of architecture .... This story should always be seen in the light of a deity who is finite. One characteristic of postmodernism, perhaps, is the fact that it takes account of this defeat. If modernism is distinguished by its striving for absolute dominance, postmodernism may be seen to reflect an awareness or the experience of its end, the end of the plan for domination.[19]

In a lecture he gave in Prague with the title 'Generations of a City', Derrida returned to the Babylonian theme of time in the construction of a city that Kafka explored in a number of his writings. The short story, 'The City Coat of Arms,' begins with the remark that:

... at the start of construction of the Tower of Babel, everything was in reasonable order. Perhaps there was too much order. Too much thought was given to signposts, interpreters, accommodation for the workers, connecting routes ...[20]

Since the tower could not be built in a single generation, the inhabitants lost interest in it, and the undertaking seemed increasingly pointless to them. Derrida described the growing awareness of the futility of the enterprise as a turn in the direction of sense and reason, because it rejected the building of the tower:

This surfeit of tongues, interpreters and nations, this diversity which constantly causes disputes, suggests that the essence of a city must lie somewhere else; or, to be more precise, that it is different from that of the tower. One decides to forego such a magnificent tower, relinquishes the desire for this unique structure, a regal edifice soaring up to the heavens. A generation later, when a community has grown from this act of renunciation, the decision is taken to preserve the city (in this location) instead of the impossible tower.[21]

Libeskind's urban projects are designed to accommodate a living community of many generations who should be able to engage — as in Kafka — in a constant process of adaptation and extension of their city. Libeskind's designs allow for slow growth and diversity of architectural language. With historical awareness, he refrains from any attempt to create the total city, the absolute tower. He takes care that the city does not have the appearance of a replete space. Instead, he creates more urbane spaces with different rates of development. The Alexandrinum, for example, an experiential space forming part of the Alexanderplatz project, is designed quite consciously to further urban pluralism and to facilitate the whole range or urban life: calm and hectic activity, tranquillity and excitement. Life will no longer be segmented, because cultural and leisure amenities, workplaces and a dense park on the roof will all be accommodated within a single complex.

With his architectures, Daniel Libeskind is not offering another religion of reason. He does not attach identity to a randomly chosen period of history, and he avoids uniform concepts and any yearning for a universal and perfect language. For this reason, his architectural designs are no more and no less than fragments of Utopia:

The new vision for the burnt-out center of Berlin is not Utopian by nature. It is more a concrete vision of how a public place should be, a place that has learned from the past and looks forward to the future. The opportunity to build and plan anew, to rethink, to shape things in a new form should not be wasted in an over-simple solution of selective reconstruction. Even Orpheus did not succeed in going backwards into the future.[22]

Notes

1. Ulrich Beck, Die Erfindung des Politischen. Zu einer Theorie der reflexiven Modernisierung Frankfurt am Main 1993, p. 36.

2. Daniel Libeskind, 'The Myth of Site'; see pp. 140–1 of this volume.

3. Max Horkheimer and Theodor W. Adorno, Dialektik der Aufklärung, Philosophische Fragmente Frankfurt am Main 1969, p. 9. (The book consists of Gretel Adorno's notes of the discussions between Horkheimer and Adorno which took place in exile in California. The text was apparently completed in 1944 and was published in 1947 by Querido in Amsterdam.

4. Ibid., pp. 62, 85.

5. Ibid., p. 62.

6. Ibid., p. 19.

7. 'Gebaute Metapher' (interview with Marie-Louise Blatter), Basler-Zeitung, no. 20 (19 May 1990): 12f.

8. See Reinhard Koselleck, 'Richtlinien für das Lexikon Politisch-sozialer Begriffe der Neuzeit', Archiv für Begriffsgeschichte, (1967): 81ff.

9. See Reinhard Koselleck, 'Geschichte, Historie' in Otto Brunner, Werner Conze and Reinhard Koselleck (eds), Geschichtliche Grundbegriffe. Historisches Lexikon zur politisch-sozialen Sprache in Deutschland, (Stuttgart, 1975), vol. 2, pp. 593–717. In this context, see sect. V, 'Die Herausbildung des modernen Geschichtsbegriffes', pp. 647–95.

10 G. W. F. Hegel, Die Vernunft in der Geschichte, ed. Johannes Hoffmeister, 5th edn (Hamburg, 1955), p. 4.

11. Ibid., p. 7.

12. Gottfried Küenzlen, Der neue Mensch. Zur säkularen Religionsgeschichte der Moderne (Munich, 1994), pp. 75f.

13. Daniel Libeskind, 'Out of Line', 1991, Berlin, Potsdamer/Leipziger Platz; see p. 26 of this volume.

14. Ibid., p. 26.

15. Paul Klee's 1920 Angelus Novus (pen and ink with colored wash and colored crayon; 31.8 x 24.2 cm) belonged to Gershom Scholem and is today in the Israel Museum, Jerusalem.

16. Walter Benjamin, 'Über den Begriff der Geschichte', sect. IX, Gesammelte Schriften, vols 1 and 2 ed. Rolf Tiedemann and Hermann Schwepphäuser (Frankfurt am Main, 1974), pp. 697f.

17. Gershom Scholem, Die Geheimnisse der Schöpfung. Ein Kapitel aus dem kabbalistischen Buche Sohar (Frankfurt am Main, 1992), p. 107. (The section 'Geheimnis der Tora' deals with the story of Creation.)

18. Jorge Luis Borges, Labyrinthe. Erzählungen, 2nd edn (Munich, 1962), pp. 81f.

19. Jacques Derrida, 'Archi/Textur und Labyrinth' in Das Abenteuer der Ideen (Internationale Bauausstellung Berlin) (Berlin, 1984), p. 97.

20. Franz Kafka, Die Erzählungen (Frankfurt am Main, 1993), p. 304.

21. Jacques Derrida, 'Generationen einer Stadt', Lettre International, no. 18 (1997): 56.

22. Libeskind (note 13); see p. 26 of this volume.

Bernhard Schneider

Daniel Libeskind's Architecture in the Context of Urban Space

The building in its time: Anticipatory memory

Daniel Libeskind's architectural projects have a common theme: the city as a cultural institution or form of accommodation. The word *accommodation* is meant quite literally here, for his projects always revolve around the question of how human beings accommodate themselves in the world by means of their buildings — in a world they have always found fully fitted out for them, to the point of incommodiousness, one might almost say; in a world in which, it seems, all possible solutions have already been tried out, the right ones and the wrong ones. Precisely which architectural and urban principles are the right ones, at least for Berlin, is something that the authorities are deciding at the moment, taking as their points of reference the historically documented character of Berlin and the historically documented nature of human needs in respect of buildings and cities. Any conclusions reached in this way, however, will not provide us with an insight into the nature of architecture and urban planning; they will merely supply information about what the Berlin building authorities themselves regard as artistically admissible and inadmissible.

This information is neither necessary nor helpful, nor is it new. As early as 1889, in his classic attempt to distil the essence of urban spatial planning from the study of historical examples, Camillo Sitte mocked the futile attempts to formulate these essentials through bureaucratic design regulations. A century of urban-planning history has not proved Sitte right in all points, but certainly in this one. It has been proven that 'urban planning, if it adheres to its artistic principles', defies bureaucratic regulation. Only those who have ceased to seek the origins and goals — i.e., the cultural basis — of architecture and the city would want to make the ordering instrument of design regulations, based on the random stock of existing structures, the guiding principle of urban planning.

The fallacy of believing that a collection of outward features found in the architecture of the past can productively contribute to the design objectives of the present, or at least prevent errors being made, can be avoided in a variety of ways: through thought and reflection, by studying the history of construction and through personal experience or artistic intuition. Above all, it can be avoided through an awareness of history, in the way this awareness is a distinguishing feature of older, Christian and Jewish cultural traditions. It is a historical view that reaches several thousands of years further back in time and at the same time much further forward into the future and into unknown worlds than our present picture-book history does.

In any broader view of history that is not confined to the limited spectrum of our own visually documented past, the things that have been empirically handed down to us will not be so easily confused with things that merely satisfy human needs or that we regard as humanly feasible. Expressed in simpler terms, one might say that a modern design for the way humans accommodate themselves in the world should not be judged primarily according to whether it has any parallel in those few thousand years of architectural history of which we command a view. Allowance must also be made for the thousands of potential comparisons we cannot yet make because they lie in the future. The origins and goals of architecture and urban planning are linked with each other on a plane that lies beyond the stock of existing examples and what we know from history. The essence of a project — the plan according to which humans organize the world to their own ends and inhabit it — inevitably lies beyond material examples of building. The whole heritage of architecture handed down from history as well as everything that might ever be built in the future are but versions of an interpretation. Willfully to declare one of these versions 'authentic' is like trying to escape from history. It is both a fallacy and a refusal to make the necessary effort.

This philosophy is evident in all of Daniel Libeskind's writings and designs. The first project he realized in Berlin, the 'Extension of the Berlin Museum', the carcass structure of which is under construction, marks both the conclusion and the climax of the 1980s, a decade in which Berlin became a focus of artistic and cultural debate through the International Building Exhibition (IBA) and other projects. One may hope that Libeskind's building, which heals the wounds of a particularly desolate part of the city, will also stimulate a better quality of discussion than that to which the officially prescribed cultural abstinence in the 1990s has so far astonishingly been prepared to submit itself. The present building will prove that the constructional memory of the city reaches both further back in time and further forward than the scrap of history it thinks it commands.

The building on paper is not a museum

Does the Extension of the Berlin Museum have a zigzag form? No. Contrary to many — all too many — comments made since the competition was decided in the summer of 1989 (from which the stereotypes *zigzag* and *streak of lightning* are rarely missing), and although the architect himself has occasionally resorted to this terminology, the museum does not have a zigzag form. This configuration exists solely in a two-dimensional, graphic form on paper and is the outcome of the representation of certain characteristics of the three-dimensional volume of the building. The carcass structure in itself proves this. It thus frees us from an obsession caused by the fact that the project was hitherto accessible to the public only in an indirect, two-dimensional form of representation or in models whose scale was so close to the drawings that the error was not evident. The notion of the zigzag will not entirely disappear even after the completion of the building, but it will at least be banished to where it belongs — to the drawings and the minds of the people who have seen them. Anyone who experiences the building in its own right will not see a zigzag, and anyone who has retained this image in his or her mind from prior knowledge of the drawings and models will seek it in vain in the actual building. On the other hand, the visitor will find a great deal which is unexpected: things which were implied by the drawings, but which were never directly depictable.

These remarks are no more than truisms, for everyone knows from experience that visual representations of buildings and the buildings themselves are two different realities, different worlds which obey different rules and which are linked with each other only indirectly and in a complex manner. On the other hand, we frequently discover how this simple piece of knowledge — one of our basic cultural techniques — ceases to be a self-evident truth. Our culture, which is familiar with depictions of reality as no other culture before it, seems to be losing its awareness of the nature of depiction. A typical example of this dwindling ability to differentiate between reality and the world of images is the 'El Even Odd' project by Peter Eisenmann (1980), an impossible attempt to design an 'axonometric building'. The attempt is impossible, because axonometric drawings are part of the convention of two-dimensional representation of three-dimensional forms. They possess features which belong exclusively to the two-dimensional world and which have no equivalent and cannot be simulated in the world of three-dimensional objects. For the same reason, if one will forgive the somewhat lame comparison, a map hung on a wall may have horizontal and vertical streets, but the city itself will not.

Buildings may be represented in drawings, but the converse is not possible. That is why beautiful drawings do not always mean beautiful buildings. This is one of the lessons we have learned in the last 20 years, in which graphical suggestion in architecture has reached an incredible degree of perfection, whereas the quality of the architecture has not. The tokens of beauty in architecture are different from those in drawing.

The asymmetric nature of the relationship between the depiction of an object and the object itself has led to repeated attempts to resolve or even reverse it, particularly when it was consciously perceived in the design process. In the 'perspective' architecture of the Baroque age, attempts of this kind were successfully made under precisely defined, laboratory-like experimental conditions. Today, there seems to be a diminishing awareness of the nature of this relationship, and this has led not only to a lack of motivation for experimentation, but to mistakes and false logic.

Libeskind, in contrast, does not bother with diversions of this kind. It would not enter his head to confuse a drawing with the object depicted, to expect a building to conform to a simulation of drawn figures, or to present it as an enlarged form of a model. Instead, he exploits the different relationships to reality of all available depictive and conceptual planes, and he deliberately stresses the differences between various forms of representation. The textual and graphic collages which were characteristic of his drawings and models in the past are not an artistic end in themselves, nor do they imply buildings which are meant to be overlaid in reality with large-scale texts. They are a means of alienation whose purpose is to establish the realism of a drawing or model at the outset. In a sense, they stand for the Magrittean caption 'This is not a building' (but a drawing, a model). At no point and at no time can doubts arise here about the plane of reality on which the representation and its statement are pitched. Confusion and deception, or self-deception, as in the case of Eisenmann, are precluded here from the very beginning. Libeskind is a realist.

The building in the city: The regulation of chaos

Libeskind is also a traditionalist, as the finished building will show. His museum extension is related to its immediate and further surroundings — and especially to the existing Baroque mansion — in such a distinctive and constructive manner that the urban and architectural features of the project are inseparable. The actual presence of the building in its urban context is much richer in content than all the metaphorical and interpretational analyses — laudatory and critical — the design has so far prompted. The presence of the building allows the discussion to proceed from the realm of conjecture, assertion, assumption and premature evaluation to that of sober description.

From the outside, the complex resembles a group of irregularly laid-out individual structures, all of equal height and of the same height as the existing building, but of different dimensions and orientations. From Lindenstrasse, one could imagine three volumes set out one behind another, extending over the depth of the site, with a fourth, free-standing volume at the front (ill. 1). Moving south along Lindenstrasse, or following the park route along the building, a fifth tract becomes visible at the end of Alte Jakobstrasse. If one turns round the eastern end, from the side of the museum park, three relatively large tracts can be seen, divided by deep incisions. One could imagine that these tracts were separated by narrow lanes or breaks. Only on closer examination does it become clear that the complex comprises a single, continuous structure. The only route from one side to the other is not in one of the angles between the arms of the building, but through one of the long faces.

Among the many relationships this structure establishes with its surroundings, those to the existing museum building are of particular interest. As always, three questions are important in this respect: the question of scale, the question of spatial distribution and, finally, the question of how new and old, the existing museum and the extension, fit into the larger urban context. One might have wished for a greater proximity between the existing museum and the extension — almost to the point of contact — as Libeskind's competition entry seemed to promise. Just how important tight flanking spaces next to major historical buildings are, in contrast to the exposure of the front, is demonstrated by Sitte with the example of the Palazzo Strozzi in Florence. In view of the loving care taken by Libeskind, especially in the design of this border zone between the Baroque mansion and his new structure, and bearing in mind the modest height of the two-story existing building and its new neighbor, greater courage in adhering to the originally-planned convergence between the two would probably have produced a more exciting result in respect of the historical building and the two courtyard spaces between the old and new structures. Nevertheless, the point of closest proximity, where the extension meets the side wing of the existing structure at an angle, remains one of the most successful and sensitive urban-design situations in Berlin, and the whole passageway from Lindenstrasse, opening out twice towards the museum park and gradually narrowing again, is the finest lane in Berlin (ill. 2) — a city which, after the disappearance of its old center, lost most of its narrow lanes.

This positive development also has to do with the fact that it is not just an isolated detail or a unique motif. It is part of an artistically conceived strategy for the volumes of the building and the external spaces as a whole. The two wings of the extension, which form a new southern edge to the museum garden, flank this passageway both artistically and in a quite natural manner. They have similar dimensions to the side wings of the mansion without being mere reconstructions. They also form a marvellous sequence of spaces between the historical three-wing layout and Alte Jakobstrasse on the far side of the museum garden. With the erection of the first walls of the building, a further quality of these two structures was revealed. They provide an urgently needed backdrop to the smaller townhouses north of the museum garden. Without this spatial demarcation, these modest buildings would be lost in a space which is far too large and poorly defined (ill. 3). Seen from the street Am Berlin Museum, the agreeable effect of this planning can be clearly recognized. It provides a lasting solution

1 Lindenstrasse facade. Right: the landscaped strip between the new building and Alte Jakobstrasse. In the background: the town houses along the street Am Berlin Museum

2 View from the museum park to the rear face of the existing structure and the adjoining wing of the extension

3 Creation of spaces between the extension and the existing building. To the rear: the high-rise housing block in Lindenstrasse, to which the museum extension responds with a detached volume (black in the model)

4 Overall model showing the urban context. Left: the town houses along the street Am Berlin Museum. In the background: the 1970s development in Alte Jackobstrasse. Foreground: the new curving line of Lindenstrasse. To the rear on the right: the angular form of the trade union building by Erich Mendelsohn

5 The staggered three-bay front of the museum extension along Lindenstrasse with the detached volume at the side in the landscaped area. In the background: the detached town houses along the street Am Berlin Museum

to what was an unsatisfactory urban spatial situation. Similarly, the concrete embankment, isolated problematically on the east side of the museum garden, is given a much needed pendant at the Jakobstrasse end of the new structure. The congenial landscaping of the new development by Müller/Knippschild/ Wehberg, which has been highly praised by Libeskind, also plays a major role in helping to achieve urban spatial effects of this kind in one of the most chaotic locations of the city center. This can be seen, for example, at the point where the eastern end of the new structure meets the rather nondescript, though spatially extremely effective, high-rise block — part of a '60s development to the south — to form a gateway to the landscaped strip along the new building (ill. 4).

It was evident from the drawings and models how simple and effective the project's strategy would be in creating an urban order in the areas adjoining the site to the south. Indeed this aspect was specially approved by the competition jury. The fragmented, scattered, heterogeneous collection of buildings to the south is deliberately echoed by and at the same time contrasted with the acute internal and external angles and the blunted corners of the museum extension. This was the only way to reduce and neutralize the disruptive weight of the existing individual volumes (ill. 5). Unfortunately, of the three detached elements planned for the project along this critical southern flank, only one remains. Even so, the precisely calculated approach to the loose, scattered existing development will transform what was originally a state of disarray into a heterogeneous order. Here, as in the relationship to the existing building, one can see that the solution developed is spatially integrating, and not only at the point where the new building faces the existing structure — in this case, the high-rise block in Alte Jakobstrasse. More extensive links are created — for example, between the angular spaces of the museum extension and the much admired and frequently photographed internal angle of the trade union building by Erich Mendelsohn two street blocks away. The correspondence between the museum and the Mendelsohn building across the heterogeneous development of the intermediate area functions only as long as the edges of the street blocks are not closed.

In Lindenstrasse, the new development presents itself to a restrained scale alongside the existing building. A slender end elevation only 6.5 meters wide and only 10 meters removed from the Baroque mansion extends a few meters into the street space. This modest device has an extraordinary effect (ill. 6). The small 'bay' or wing projecting into Lindenstrasse would not make much sense if the street were still straight (as it was up to the 1960s), and if it entered Mehringplatz in its original form. The present gently curving line of the road and the enormous widening it has undergone have placed the old museum building in a new and unfortunate situation. This is exacerbated by the decision to have the curve intersect a landscaped strip directly next to the museum and above all by the irreversible acts of violence perpetrated in the '60s in the name of urban planning in the area south of the museum. The small projection of the new structure screens the sensitive front of the existing building from the results of these measures. At the same time, the Lindenstrasse façade, with its threefold division and deep incision, supports the interaction between the new structure and the heterogeneous neighboring development mentioned above (ill. 7).

In the angle between the 'head' of the new building and the street front of the existing mansion, a small forecourt is formed within the unarticulated and over-wide street space of Lindenstrasse. This forecourt mediates between the coarse scale of the modernized road and the subtle forms of the mansion, as well as providing additional spatial ties for the raised entrance tract at the front of the building. The projecting end of the new complex also results in a clearer articulation of the junction between the lane dividing the existing museum from the extension and the street. As a link between the forecourt and the open space to the rear of the museum, this lane is much more comprehensible than it would have been in the form of a simple passageway or gap between two buildings aligned on their street faces (ill. 8). Given the spatial profile of Friedrichstrasse, which is now considerably coarser than it was historically, the visual reinforcement provided by this small projection also helps to restore the location to its traditional function, which it exercises in a triangular relationship with the Gendarmenmarkt and the Spittelmarkt. This relationship hardly exists at present as a result of the blocking of spatial links along Leipziger Strasse, but in the long term it will be of overriding importance for the inner city of Berlin as a whole (ill. 11).

6 Head of museum extension projecting into Lindenstrasse, creating a new space in conjunction with the existing building

7 End of museum extension and adjoining tracts to the south

The city within the building: Interlocking scales

Taking all these observations of the real building into account, however incomplete they may be, one comes to the conclusion that this is not just a structure set within the urban spatial fabric —at least, not in the sense of a simple conceptual model in which the city is seen to surround a building like a spatial container, or in which the buildings form the basic elements and are grouped together into larger units to form the hierarchic order of the city: buildings arranged into street blocks, blocks into neighborhoods, neighborhoods laid out to form the city, all according to a clear hierarchy of dimensions, quanta and scales. There are examples of cities constructed in this way, but there are also examples which demonstrate the opposite, such as European and American dormitory towns, which consist of an endless addition of suburban or village-like detached housing plots which nowhere congeal into an urban form. The flaw of non-urban settlements of this kind is not the fact that the individual houses need to be linked to form larger units, blocks or terraces to attain the next scale up in the urban hierarchy. The idea that a house is something small and individual and a town is the comprehensive whole is too simplistic. Examples which prove the opposite are legion, from the huge unused structures of Classical Antiquity—in which whole towns with public open spaces were laid out in the Middle Ages (ill. 13)—to newer large-scale structures, such as monasteries, military barracks, palaces or administrative complexes, the scale of which often exceeds that of the neighboring urban districts. In many cases, these forms give rise to a strange ambivalence between the individual structure and the urban neighborhood. Examples of this include the deep tenement blocks built in the 19th century with their numerous courtyards, or later building types such as the Viennese courtyard housing developments and the housing estates of the Weimar Republic. The foundation of ideal cities in the Renaissance imposed remarkably concentrated conditions of scale, as the prototype of Pienza shows. Here, in a town of modest size, five buildings and a church define a complete urban model in an area no more than a few hundred square meters in extent (ill. 12). The modern industrial metropolis with its mass housing is of quite a different order.

8 Junction of Hollmannstrasse (between existing museum and extension) and Lindenstrasse

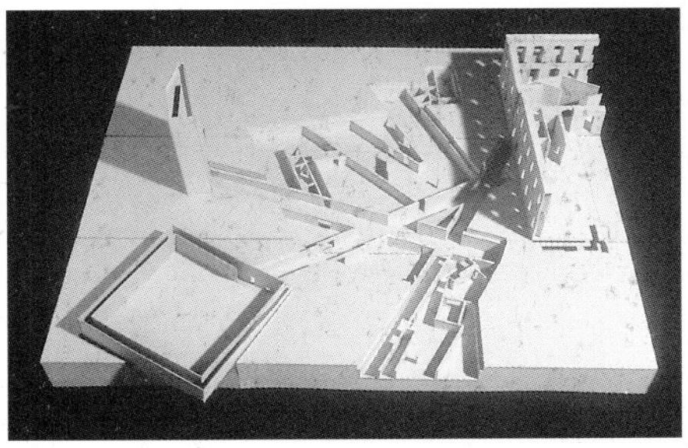

9 The lower floor level of the museum extension and its outward links. Left: the free-standing structure and the sunken E.T.A. Hoffmann Garden. Right: the new staircase in the existing building

10 View between existing building and extension into Paul-Celan-Hof

How effectively Libeskind's museum, through the urban character of its articulation and the careful establishment of relationships to surrounding buildings, transforms the existing almost non-spatial location into an urban environment, how it creates its own urban space, adopts existing scales and defines new ones of its own, can be seen and described in terms of the building itself. Alone the statement that, at first sight, it resembles a group of buildings rather than a single structure, indicates that the boundary between architectural and urban scales does not always coincide with the outer edges of a building. Furthermore, in this case the existing building and the extension are linked underground by an urban spatial structure which is not visible from the outside. It takes the form of a basement story with streets and passageways, junctions and external spaces (ill. 9). In a sense, it is a piece of urban tissue, set at a scale level below that of the building and nevertheless reproducing the forms of the outer, larger city. This upper city is linked to the hidden lower city via routes through the interior of the building, via the free-standing prismatic hollow volume (which belongs to both worlds) in front of the south face, and via the sunken E. T. A. Hoffmann Garden, which may also be seen to belong to both planes (i.e., both levels and both scales). The open space is therefore large (in relation to the spaces contained in the lower story) and small (in terms of its area within the larger open space). At two ends, this subterranean urban labyrinth flows into the large-scale internal spaces of the buildings which surround it: at one end, via the newly installed staircase in the existing building, at the other end, via the access to the extension and the shaft-like voids which penetrate the new structure from below, allowing views through the building or down from the top to the subterranean city.

City and building impinge on each other in another way, too, in Libeskind's museum project: through the interaction of inside and outside, the specific and the general, lesser and greater scales. The deep projections and set-backs of the building and its abrupt changes of direction (which form the 'zigzag' on plan) intensify the relationship between internal space and the city around it into a dramatic expression. The experience of architecture in its urban context, such as can be gained from a simple bay window in a living room overlooking the street, is of striking effect: the possibility of seeing the outside of a building from the inside. At many points, the massive, largely closed external face of the extension allows views out from the various floors to other parts of the complex: to the existing structure, to other limbs of the extension or to the surrounding urban space. It is an urban spatial experience that can be gained only from the inside of a building and, in this pronounced form, only from the inside of this building: the experience of the building not merely as an extension of the museum, but as an extension of the city; as a city within the building, as a city within the head; city and building as an extension of man. The view out over Paul-Celan-Hof has a further dimension: the open space appears both as an internal courtyard of the building, the confining walls of which are read as the 'rear faces' of the complex and as an integral part of and appendix to the urban space beyond, which is particularly closely knit with the ensemble at this point (ill. 10).

The city in the head: The roots of architecture

If one compares the aims underlying the museum extension with those of other projects by Daniel Libeskind, one sees that his schemes reveal distinct differences in their relations to urban space. One thing they have in common, however, is the fact that they never adopt a neutral attitude towards this space as autonomous objects independent of their location. Their innermost theme is always the interpretation of urban space as a signifying context and as the physical habitat of the city-dweller. They nevertheless treat this theme in quite different ways.

The differences between the projects, however, do not only lie in the fact that they approach the complex subject of urban space from different viewpoints. They treat this subject on quite different planes of thought and through quite different forms of representation. Mental models should not be confused with forms of depiction and certainly not with objective forms. Often these different planes of logic are combined in one and the same drawing. Diagrams of relationships, which create a context of topographical lines and points, are overlaid with the lines which mark the outer edges and internal articulation of a building and which define the physical form of the same space; or they incorporate graphic signs which convey other aspects of the object such as the characterization of surfaces, thereby introducing a further dimension to the graphic vocabulary, etc.

This complex means of representation imposes great demands on the reader of Libeskind's plans. This has always been a source of annoyance for the juries of competitions. It has been misunderstood as 'artistic embellishment' or as an aesthetic trademark, whereas all it represents really is a particularly condensed form of a well-known and established set of conventions. Mixed up in every normal plan are symbols of different relationships to reality that we are used to seeing in conjunction with each other and that we are able to differentiate. A chain of dimensions will be read differently from the line next to it, which marks the edge of the building. An arrow indicating the direction of ascent of a ramp will not be mistaken for the outline of a triangular building element. Lettering and information on the plan will not be misunderstood as lettering on the actual building. The special richness of information contained in Libeskind's plans does not infringe upon these conventions. It exploits them to advantage to make the observer aware of the conventional character of such systems of notation and to combine reflections on the object itself, on the form of depiction and on the concepts with reflections on the design. Accordingly, one finds a mixture of mental figures and objective forms of this kind not only in Libeskind's drawings, but in his models as well.

The 'Über den Linden' project represents something of a contrast to the realism of the Berlin Museum project and its newer forms of representation. It is Libeskind's contribution to the 1991 exhibition and publication *Berlin Morgen: Ideen für das Herz einer Großstadt* (Berlin Tomorrow: Ideas for the Heart of a Metropolis), organized by the German Architecture Museum in Frankfurt and the *Frankfurter Allgemeine Zeitung*. The project deliberately seeks to rub our historical knowledge of the inner city of Berlin, the lime trees of Unter den Linden fame and the images and semantic conventions we associate with them, the wrong way and, as an outcome of this calculated act of negation, to redefine some central issues. What is 'great' in the city plan of Berlin; what is 'small'? What 'rank' does the city have? How 'radical' does Hilberseimer's 'radical' project appear today (ill. 14) and what genuine order within the city plan of Berlin would be recognizable if Hilberseimer's leap in scale were to be raised to an even greater magnitude? How does the grid of the Baroque city extension respond to other, more recent grid layouts and ordering systems for urban space if these orders are viewed from the reverse end of the telescope, so to speak, from the viewpoint of a colossal order beyond all scale?

Without citing them all in detail, this mental exercise on the theme of Berlin reflects the entire history of the tabula-rasa planning schemes drawn up for this and other European cities, from Hilberseimer and Speer to the ideas contained in the competition for the capital held in 1958. Libeskind's project takes account of the forms and the content of the old city, which, for the most part, has been irretrievably lost, and it anticipates Berlin's re-establishment as the capital after German reunification, set against the background of the city's permanent decline and the destruction of the circumstances of its existence — of which the infernal destruction suffered during the war was but one particularly striking phase. It is a tabula rasa on a scale of which Hilberseimer and Speer could not have conceived. Why does this project break so radically with all the principles and planning conventions of the 18th and 19th centuries that underlie the 'Linden' and that today, three years after *Berlin Morgen*, are again being made the basis for the process of urban renewal? The project visualizes a new foundation, the nucleus of which is formed by the epitaph of the old city. On the model stand the words *lines/deadlines*. Where the historical outlines delineate death and destruction to such a degree and are so bound up with questions of scale and dimension as in Berlin, it seemed appropriate to project the question of the future on to a wall, the size of which exceeds all historically known colossal orders.

In contrast to 'Über den Linden', the 'City Edge' project dating from 1987 is as realistic as the extension of the Berlin Museum. The main theme is again urban space. Linking two street blocks and extending over two cross-streets, an obliquely rising strip is set alongside and between the existing developments at the boundary between the districts of Schöneberg and Kreuzberg to form a new, large-scale urban profile. At its southern, upper end, the strip rises above the traditional building height of the surrounding developments. The northern end anchors the strip in the ground of the city and is lower in height than the eaves line of adjoining buildings.

The position of the 'City Edge' strip takes up Albert Speer's planning for the north–south urban axis, which was never realized. The spatial reality and the architectural message of the project are, however, a manifesto against Speer. The reinterpretation of the junction between the east–west and north–south routes in Berlin, the rethinking of the relationship between the block development and the landscaped open space of the Am Karlsbad park and of that between the street pattern and the Landwehr Canal and, finally, the new, highly sensitive relationship between the interior of the building (with its horizontal articulation of stories) and the urbanistic large-scale form of the diagonally tipped structure — all these aspects would have turned what seems to be a location of only secondary significance in the urban spatial context of Berlin into an important center which could have sparked a large-scale reorganization of the area. The project, which would have introduced a new theme into the urban planning of Berlin, was unfortunately abandoned in the course of its elaboration in favor of a conventional closed street-block development.

The planning of the office complex for Wiesbaden (1992) was taken as far as construction drawings. The site is located on a

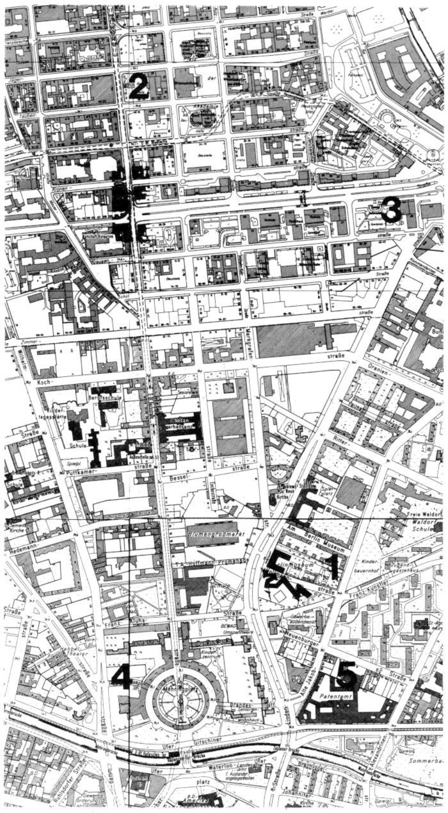

11 Plan showing position of Berlin Museum in Friedrichstadt

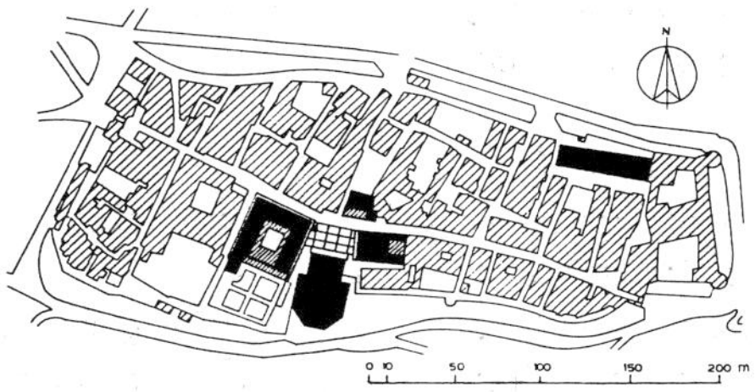

12 Pienza. Shown in black: cathedral, city hall, Palazzo Piccolomini, Palazzo Borgia
From: Benevolo, The History of the City

13 Medieval town in the Roman amphitheater of Arles.
From: Benevolo, The History of the City

14 Ludwig Hilberseimer, c. 1929: city development for Berlin. In the foreground: the Gendarmenmarkt. Top right: Unter den Linden

main route out of the city, and a decision was made not to develop it with yet another example of the large-scale, box-like office blocks which dominate the area. As in the Berlin Museum extension scheme — but in a much more radical form, as a reflection of the different constraints of the location and the much greater dimensions involved — Libeskind developed the volume of the building into a richly articulated ensemble of small-scale interlocking elements. Here again, he created a building in the form of a small-scale city. In contrast with this, City Edge was a piece of urban tissue in the manner of a simple building, a complementary counterconcept, so to speak, to the Berlin Museum extension and to the Wiesbaden office development. In conjunction with each other and with their surroundings, the elements of the complex in Wiesbaden form a large number of external spaces with different characteristics (landscape architecture again by Müller/Knippschild/Wehberg). Are these spaces courtyards, squares, landscaped open areas or urban spaces? Clearly legible in terms of both its architecture and urban planning, this project proves more convincingly than any other by Daniel Libeskind that its constructional and spatial configurations are not just the individual expressions of an artist, but are capable of introducing new, present-day concepts of urban space to the traditional form of the city. This refreshing, modern solidarity between the building on the one hand and the physical and symbolic urban space on the other is not a negation of the existing city. It makes it legible in a new way by deriving new processes and forms from traditional rules of building and spatial composition.

Libeskind's entry to the Potsdamer/Leipziger Platz competition (1991) is probably the most concentrated compendium of methods of design, representation and thought he has produced so far. Libeskind set the sum of his historical reminiscences and future visions against the images of this historically charged location — images which remain in the memory and which for most of us probably have their source in pre-war photos of Leipziger Platz and Potsdamer Platz. On viewing the model, one is immediately struck by the way in which, as in all Libeskind's projects — whether realized or conceptual — urban space and its scale are the central themes. His work does not move within a fixed system of dimensions and proportions that imposes an ideal scale on the overall space. With unbounded élan, it presents the universal theme of his designs for big cities: the superimposition and coexistence of heterogeneous scales as the essence of the metropolis. In the process, the range of urban scales is expanded, both upwards and downwards, to achieve an enormous extension at both ends of the spectrum. On closer scrutiny, this can also be seen to apply to the 'Über den Linden' project. As a result, the established and seemingly so unquestionable scale of the city plan (blessed with the seal of history) and its projection into the third dimension (as documented in photos, in the remains of actual buildings or simply in the imagination) suddenly appears in a strangely insecure, equivocal transitional state. The city as it existed in the 18th and 19th centuries, which we are inclined to equate with the essential character of Berlin, becomes a historical 'snapshot', a moment in a particular time and place, recorded almost at random and from a specific viewpoint. In Libeskind's projects, many more and quite different states exist both before and after this moment; above and below it, there are other orders of scale. We have by no means reached the end of history, and we cannot do justice to what Berlin is or what it might become with a description of past or present states of the city.

Many observers and critics are so confused by the extraordinary complexity of this project that their judgment shrinks to the word 'chaos'. The form is, indeed, an extremely heterogeneous one, but it is subject to a very strict order. Admittedly, not every three-dimensional element in the model exists on the same plane in reality. Objective forms of the kind found in 'City Edge' are mixed with forms which should be understood as conceptual figures in the manner of 'Über den Linden'; the temporal succession of existing building substance, demolition and new development is (as in the real city) not clearly legible in the model. In the context of the proposed urban transformation, existing structures are seen as new and unfamiliar objects, while elements planned for the future appear as part of the existing fabric. Potsdamer Platz and Leipziger Platz are seen from such a distant future perspective, so to speak, that those elements of the cityscape that today seem topographically and historically rooted in the deepest past stand undifferentiated and on equal terms alongside elements which do not yet exist. Large-scale forms which extend over the boundaries of individual neighborhoods are overlaid with structural forms which repeat in various locations or recur as a series of variations over larger areas. This one place in Berlin becomes a focus for the depiction of all present, past and future forms of the European city, however incommensurable and inconsistent they may be. It is a proposal for channelling the manifold and contradictory forces and elements of the metropolis in all its manifestations into a heterogeneous urban order, instead of accepting the usual development of cities as an act of fate. This would be achieved by devising a homogenizing urban gestalt for all the heterogeneous and incommensurable elements of the city, a gestalt which would, however, never be realized because of the long-term, uncontrollable nature of real developments. As a result, it would reveal itself only in distorted fragments which, after a time, would be overlaid and negated by the next ordering principle. The outcome, of course, could only be chaos.

Libeskind's entry to the Alexanderplatz competition (1993) can be seen as a supplementary aid to an understanding and interpretation of his Potsdamer/Leipziger Platz competition scheme. What, in the latter, was compressed into a dense layering of various planes of reality, principles of representation and building forms becomes, in the Alexanderplatz project, an urban image of a simpler, more homogeneous kind. Here, too, the jury could not avoid using the word *chaos* in commenting on this work, but a large, mainly non-architectural audience coped very well with the model and showed considerable perseverance in deciphering it.

The design is organized around a relatively simple spatial figure which links the surrounding neighborhoods with Alexanderplatz. This figure is richly articulated in itself and, as in the proposals for Potsdamer/Leipziger Platz, enriches the existing situation with 'upward' and 'downward' jumps in scale. This spatial figure possesses such stability that it can provide a constant basis for the various changes the constructional substance of the area will undergo in the course of unpredictable development. In contrast to all other entries to this competition, the thesis of Libeskind's work is that the city cannot be equated with its buildings. Consequently — and that is the first conclusion he drew — existing buildings will not have to be demolished to make room for new developments. The project does not determine the final state of the district in advance, but outlines certain principles of growth and development that are clearly recognizable for the layman. It changes the character and structure of the urban space and at the same time allows almost all existing buildings to be preserved. It derives a new order from the existing fabric, an order which can be realized in a series of steps through a process of ongoing construction and conversion. The buildings which complement the existing substance and are the means of achieving the required transformation have different architectural characteristics. They therefore anticipate both the architectural changes which will take place in an area in the course of its development and the long-term nature of this process. They simulate the actual differences between schemes designed simultaneously by the many architects who have received commissions. Libeskind's 'Alexanderplatz' is thus an extremely 'realistic' project.

Is this 'real', objective approach the right one, however? Is development in the sense of establishing a new order possible with a design strategy of this kind, or does it simply simulate in a positivistic way a development which would take place anyway, resulting in an abandonment of any genuine intervention in the urban structure? Does this heterogeneous, varied urban picture obey any order or rules, or does it simply anticipate what will come about anyway, namely 'chaos'?

The basic order is created by a precisely calculated network of outdoor spaces: spaces for pedestrians and for public and private traffic. These spaces, with their contractions and expansions, their links and discontinuities, form the basic radial structure of the district — a structure which has withstood the test of time. It is on this plane, at the level of the ground floors and outdoor spaces, that the urban spatial context is established, not in the configurations of buildings which exist only in plan or model form, nor through a formalistic grid of streets. The buildings are set in this network of external spaces and in correspondence with it. There are three basic building heights: a lower level defined by the height of the listed buildings by Peter Behrens; a second level determined by the average height of the post-war developments; a third level which reflects the newly designed high-rise blocks of various heights. The arrangement of these blocks in conjunction with the spatial sequence of Karl-Marx-Allee, the suburb of Spandau and the Prenzlauer Berg creates the urban context in this area. The design does not just establish an order for the relationships between the individual buildings; it sets them, singly and in groups, in relation to the Alexanderplatz area as a whole. It does more than just simulate future development; it provides development principles without insisting on stylistic details or constructional forms, the realization of which must be left to the future.

The Alexanderplatz project is, therefore, further testimony to Libeskind's unformulated thesis (which is nevertheless clearly evident in his work) that cities as actually realized, whether past, present or still to be created in the darkness of the future, are always just different manifestations of urban space.

We shall never be able to apprehend conclusively what urban space is, however painstaking our efforts to describe it. We cannot know what it is, because that would mean we should be able to reduce human nature and the meaning of life to a conclusive formula, and that is not even possible for the character of a specific city like Berlin. The essential nature of Berlin cannot be defined with a list of features taken from past and present architecture. That simply leads to a state of stagnation veiled in ideology. The things we now regard as essential elements of Berlin's tradition originally came about when society set out in search of new horizons: Friedrichstadt with its squares and street spaces, the Brandenburg Gate, Schinkel's remarkable interpretations of space, the models for this century which were shaped in Berlin, down to the as-yet-realized concepts of urban space embodied prototypically in the National Gallery by Ludwig Mies van der Rohe, the Philharmonie by Hans Scharoun and the bold experiments of the IBA in the 1980s.

These are not new insights. At most, we have lost sight of them on occasion. Similarly, one of the central discoveries we make on retracing the relations between Daniel Libeskind's buildings and their urban spatial environment is no more than an act of recollection — however urgent it may be.

The city does not begin and end at the outer face of a building, nor is it just an accretion of individual buildings. The city always existed before the buildings which go to make it up, physically present and in the mind.

The answer to the question of the role played by Daniel Libeskind's architecture in urban space is, therefore:

URBAN SPACE IN DANIEL LIBESKIND'S ARCHITECTURE.

Mark C. Taylor

Point of No Return

. . . .
. . . .
. . . .
. . . .

— Peter Borel, Was-ist-das

What is the point of Daniel Libeskind's architecture? Does it have a point? Towards what does it point? Does Daniel Libeskind's architecture make a point? Which point? What point? Whose point? His point? Or another point? Perhaps the point of an Other? Is Daniel Libeskind's architecture pointed or pointless? Has it lost its point? Always already lost the point it never made or had?

What is a point? Where is a point? When is a point? How is a point? Does a point exist?

Point: A dimensionless geometric object having no property but location. Dimensionless … propertyless … Present or absent? Being or nothing? Fullness or emptiness? *Peug*, fist … *pungere*, to pierce, prick, puncture … *punctum*, a prick, little hole, puncture.

Point: Point, speck; dot, mark; stop, period; line; hole; stitch … No, not at all, none.

.
.
.

Beyond a certain point there is no return. This point has to be reached.
— Franz Kafka

In Daniel Libeskind's work, architecture approaches the point of no return. Approaches but does not reach … never reaches the point of no return. What, then, is the point of this point … of no return? What limit does it mark? What transgression does it portend? What no returns by returning not? If there is no return or if no inevitably returns does architecture end or does it become endless … purposeless … pointless? Does this purposelessness … pointlessness … endlessness echo the silence of The Endless?

If architecture is pointless or struggles to be pointless, then is it useless? Does architecture involve or even require an expenditure without return? If the point is that there is no return, can building be economical, or must it be excessive? What would it mean to invest in an architecture whose point is the point … especially if that point does not return, cannot return and, thus, remains … pointless? Might the point of no return be the gift … the gift of architecture, which can be neither accepted nor rejected?

.
.
.

Points … ten points … no more … no less … points which resemble points on a compass … points to orient (and disorient) a certain reading of Daniel Libeskind's architecture: … Contracting … Drawing … Forgetting … Letting … Emptying … Noing … (Un)Naming … Noing … Disappointing …

Hoping … Points … ten points … elusive points … traces … perhaps traces of *middot* … *kohot* … *ma'alot* … *sefirot*. Perhaps not. And what might be the relation or nonrelation of these ten points to *Ein-Sof* — The Endless — the pointless point which is the point towards which (the) all points?

.
.
.

○ Contracting

How did He produce and create this world? Like a man who gathers in and contracts his breath and contracts Himself, so that the smaller might contain the larger, so He contracted His light into a hand's breadth, according to His own measure, and the world was left in darkness, and in that darkness He cut boulders and hewed rocks. — Sefer ha-Iyyun

Everything begins with contracting. 'The *tsimtsum*', Gershom Scholem explains, 'ushers in the cosmic drama. But this drama is no longer, as in older systems, an emanation or projection, in which God steps out of Himself, communicates or reveals Himself. To the contrary, it is a withdrawal into Himself. Instead of turning outwards, He contracts His essence, which becomes more and more hidden. Without *tsimtsum* there would be no cosmic process.'

Creation by subtraction presents presence with absence. Contracting eventually reaches the point of no return where disappearance creates the opening for appearances to appear. Contracting is spacing, which is the nowhere that forever haunts every where. If exile is 'primordial', then every place is always already displaced.

Contracting contracts. It not only holds apart by spacing, but also draws together to form a contract which cannot be broken. According to the terms of this originative contract, what holds us together is what holds us apart. The contract creating the 'unavowable community' is not only spoken but also written … written in stone. Written in stone on tablets which are broken … always broken. The breaking of the tablets means that writing is rewriting … and rewriting is endless. 'From this point on, we should be able to write and speak without words …' Writing without words 'at the end of the book'; writing the end of the book without words.

In the beginning there are writings. Not architecture but writings. Not architectural writings but something else, something other … something strange and unsettling. Daniel Libeskind writes, writes obsessively, excessively, endlessly. Writing without words begins with words … words, which, from the viewpoint of architecture, seem pointless.

God, god, gods … from Sinai, Trieste, Cumae, and Todnauberg and the Imagination of Disaster from an unwavering and singular continuum. This bridge spans the vortex of vortex; an insurmountable fault: the famous 'knife without a handle, with the blade missing'.

Develop as hair does under a hat — happily pinned by just a little feather.
Fishing from the pavement

RIT SPIRI (ts Piritsp'iRitspirit).
Spi, ritspir it spir! itspi ritsp, ir itspir itspiri!
Tsp iri tspi ritspir itspir'i ts pi rits?
Pi ritsp-irits! — P irit spir itsp irit sp,
Iri T spir itspi ri tsp iri tspi ritspi.

As words accumulate only to disintegrate, their point becomes more and more obscure. When decipherment is no longer possible, the point of words is their pointlessness. The very proliferation of words is a symptom of their impotence. Libeskind's scripture repeatedly inscribes the absence of the Word. Rewriting writes: 'In the beginning the Word was Not.' To write the absence of word(s) is to write other-wise. And writing otherwise might be drawing.

○ Drawing

The geometric point is an invisible thing. Therefore, it must be defined as an incorporeal thing. Considered in terms of substance, it equals zero.

Hidden in this zero, however, are various attributes which are 'human' in nature. We think of this zero — the geometric point — in relation to the greatest possible brevity, i.e., to the highest degree of restraint which, nevertheless, speaks.

Thus we look upon the geometric point as the ultimate and most singular union of silence and speech.

— Wassily Kandinsky

From writing to drawing ... or, more precisely, to drawing that is (re)writing. But drawing, like everything else, begins with contracting. The point 'is' always contracting. From point to line to plane. If the point of departure for drawing is 'an invisible thing, an incorporeal thing', then in a certain sense the point of de-parture is no thing. If, however, drawing draws (on) nothing, then what does it mean to draw?

It is difficult to know where to begin or end. To draw, which derives from *dragh* (to draw, drag on the ground), means, among other things ... many other things: to pull, drag, contract, shrink, distort; to pull (a curtain, veil, etc.) over something to conceal it; to pull (a curtain, veil, etc.) away from something to reveal it; to render into another language or style of writing, translate; to bear, endure, suffer, undergo; to adduce, bring forward; to turn aside, pervert; to add, subtract, multiply; to attract by physical or moral force; to pull out, extract; to deduce, infer; to select by lot; to cause to flow; to take in (air, etc.), breathe; to take out, receive, obtain (money, salary, revenues) from a source; to empty, drain, exhaust, deplete; to stretch, extend, elongate, spin (a thread); to straighten out by pulling; to represent, mold, model; to frame; to compose; to track (game by scent); to trace (a figure) by drawing a pencil, pen or the like across the surface; to cut a furrow by drawing a plowshare through the soil; to draw a line to determine or define the limit between two things or groups; to lay down a definite limit of action beyond which one refuses to go; to pull or tear in pieces, asunder; to bring together, gather, collect, assemble; to leave undecided (a battle or game) ... *Drawing* is irreducibly duplicitous. Its meaning cannot be penned (down), for it is constantly shifting and changing between opposites it neither unites nor divides: distorting/straightening, adding/subtracting, taking in/taking out, bring forward/turning aside, revealing/concealing, gathering together/tearing asunder. The meaning of *draw(ing)* remains forever undecided; in this word, meaning itself is a draw.

Although the meaning of *drawing* is undecidable, its oscillations and alternations involve rhythms which suggest 'the origin of the work of art.' This 'origin' is 'unoriginal'; it is not a foundation or ground but is an abyss or *Ungrund*, which never appears as such but 'appears' by withdrawing. When withdrawing is figured with drawing, it appears to be the appearance of disappearance. As a rend(er)ing which simultaneously opens and closes, drawing marks and remarks the clearing in which figures appear and disappear. 'And yet — beyond what is', Heidegger avers, 'not away from it but before it, there is an other place which occurs. In the midst of beings as a whole, there is an open place. This is a clearing, a lighting. Thought of in relation to what is, to beings, this clearing is in a greater degree than are beings. This open center, therefore, is not surrounded by what is; rather, the lighting middles itself, encircles all that is, like the nothing we hardly know.'

'The nothing we hardly know' withdraws. The 'with' of this drawing is a strange 'with'. Echoing a contracting it always presupposes, drawing not only joins and gathers but also tears and sunders. In the space of this displace, the work of art is not to reconcile opposites but to articulate differences. Articulation is a separating which gathers and a gathering which separates. Neither movement can be reduced to the other. Drawing defines the limit which neither joins nor separates whatever exists or does not exist.

Daniel Libeskind's drawings are extraordinary ... always extraordinary ... but never more so than in *CHAMBER WORKS: Architectural Meditation on Themes from Heraclitus*. In a prefatory essay entitled 'Representations of the Limit: Writing a "Not-Architecture,"' Peter Eisenman suggests that 'it might be possible to locate limits of architecture by simply examining its complement, "not-architecture." Unlike a subject, a "not-architecture" would be intimate with architecture, would know it ... would constitute a relationship to being by not being.' According to Eisenman, the most important 'not' which determines architecture is drawing. To draw is not to build by building not. In this sense, Libeskind's drawings are the not-architecture through which he attempts to articulate the limit which constitutes architecture. Architectural drawing, however, is not just any drawing, for it presupposes a logic of exemplarity in which the drawn figure presents the model for the built form. In different terms, building represents drawing. When understood in this way, architectural drawing perfectly illustrates the theory of representation that forms the foundation of the entire Western onto-theological tradition. It is precisely this notion of representation that Libeskind's extraordinary drawings are designed to call into question.

Libeskind's drawings represent nothing — perhaps even the nothing we hardly know. Signs representing nothing have lost their moorings and float freely in a way which subverts every classical economy of representation. As writing becomes drawing, which, in turn, becomes writing, signs refer to other signs instead of things or objects. Since the sign always points to another sign, nothing is original ... everything is unoriginal. In a preface to the prefaces to his drawings, which bears the sign *UNORIGINAL SIGNS*, Libeskind writes what he subsequently draws.

As the Night is sinking on realities that have had their Day, one can still hear some lamenting a vanishing present. Others rejoice at the luminous perspectives — fascinating both as threat and charm — which emanate from the empty and endless. However, it is only when the processes that orient these transformations are themselves forgotten that consciousness is torn from its dogmatic slumbers by a return to the Unoriginal.
What night? Which night? When does this night occur? Where does this night fall? What is the draw of such a night?

○ Forgetting

The first night is another of day's constructions. Day makes the night; it builds up its strong points in the night. Night speaks only of day; it is the presentiment of day, day's reserve and its profundity. Everything ends in the night; that is why there is day ... But the other night is always other. Only in the day does it seem comprehensible, ascertainable. In the day it is the secret that could be disclosed; it is something concealed that awaits unveiling ... But in the night it is what one never joins; it is repetition that will not leave off, satiety that has nothing, the sparkle of something baseless and without depth.

— Maurice Blanchot

... Night ...
... fascinating ...
... threat and charm ...
... empty and endless ...
... forgotten ...
... by a return ...
... to the Unoriginal ...

Forgetting need not always be destructive; indeed, a certain forgetting can be creative. Nor must forgetting inevitably involve simply lack, loss and absence. There are different forgettings ... forgettings as different as the first night is from the other night.

The first night is the other *of* day; it is day's lost half. This night is filled with traces of the day ... traces which have slipped from light into darkness. Since the past of this night is a past which once was present, there is nothing in this night that cannot be represented in the day. The first night can always be illuminated, its darkness dispelled. The forgotten of the first night, in other words, might always be remembered.

But there 'is' another night ... a different night ... a night which is not the night *of* day. The past of this night is always already past and, therefore, is older than every past which has slipped from the present. The darkness of this night is a darkness no light can dispel. Its shadow remains ... always remains even in the midst of day. The forgotten of the other night can never be remembered. The other night is the trace of an oblivion that is virtually primal. Always already having forgotten that of which we were never aware, consciousness is eternally haunted by an unconscious which is irreducible. 'There is at least one spot in every dream', Freud maintains, 'at which it is unplumable — a navel, as it were, that is its point of contact with the unknown.' This spot ... navel ... point of contact with what is never present is nothing other than the point of no return.

The unknown is the immemorial. Forever beyond memory, the immemorial is ancient ... 'terrifyingly ancient'. This beyond is not, however, simply outside memory; to the contrary, it is (impossibly) exterior as in an interior which hollows out memory *as if* from within. Nor is the terrifyingly ancient only past; to the contrary, it is (impossibly) past as a future which incessantly approaches by repeatedly withdrawing. Never present without being absent, the immemorial is the Unoriginal origin of all presence and absence.

From writing to drawing to building. From point to line to plane to volume. Construction begins with forgetting ... forgetting the point of not building as well as the point of building not. The challenge of architecture as it approaches the point of no return is to remember the forgetting it cannot avoid in a way which does not dismember the structures it seeks to construct.

The Berlin Museum does not remain unscathed by the extension constructed to house the Jewish Museum. In the midst of the old building, Libeskind inserts an empty volume which inversely mirrors the shape of one of the negative spaces in the addition. This void cuts through every floor of the Baroque building in a way which disrupts the stability of the existing structure. At the base of the empty space, Libeskind locates a stairway which leads to an underground tunnel ... a subterranean passage which connects the museum to its supplement by inserting the supplement into the middle of the museum. The floor of the corridor is slanted to create the sensation of an unstable ground. There are no right angles in this strange space. The main axis of the building is intersected by two additional axes which form an elongated *X*, which represents the two poles of Jewish history. Surreptitiously establishing a link between inside and outside, this disruptive *X* charts the course to both the Holocaust and the Promised Land.

Beyond the 'outer' wall of the museum stands a 22 meter tower whose irregular shape is the reverse image of the negative space which forms the empty volume inside the old museum. This is the Holocaust Tower. Doublings which are redoubled, negations which are negated, reversals which are reversed create a vertigo which removes the ground from beneath one's feet. At the end of one of the long buried passages, a vast empty space opens which extends upwards for more than five stories. There is nothing in this space except five enormous 'veils' stretching from the top of the structure to several meters above the floor. Veils upon veils reveal by reveiling in a play which is endless.

The space of the Holocaust Tower creates time for a twofold remembering of forgetting. In the darkness of the first night, the forgotten are remembered. Victims whose names have long since faded from memory are recalled ... as forgotten. The memory of forgetting does not erase the tragedy, but deepens the wound which never heals. Far from a therapy that cures, memory revives the pain of forgetting. In the midst of this wound, another night approaches by withdrawing to clear the way for a second remembering of forgetting. The Holocaust Tower not only remembers the forgotten, but is also a memorial to the Im-memorial. As the unrepresentable before that we remember by forgetting, the Immemorial is the ever-outstanding future which approaches as the past we have always left behind.

○ Letting

So now, if I understand correctly, we are to view what we call letting-be in connection with the nature of thought ...

— Martin Heidegger

Being is letting ... letting is renting ... renting is (re)leasing. Since I never own being, being is never my own. Being is not a property to be possessed; be-ing is an activity which dispossesses. Being *is* not, for it is never present. To the contrary, the present is always pre-sent and the presending of being is the prescinding of being. Giving is taking ... taking away ... far, far away.

Letting is renting. Renting is borrowing ... temporarily. Dwelling is never secure when rent is always due. Since renting is originative and without end, accounts are always out of balance, for we can never repay what we always (already) owe. 'Primal' debt is a wound we are destined to bear with interest ... profound interest. To let, therefore, is not only to rent but is also to be rent ... breached, sundered, torn. The tear of renting is the tear that cannot be wiped away.

Renting is (re)leasing. Inasmuch as being always involves leasing, there can be no living without a renewable lease on life. Leasing binds parties to a contract whose terms are carefully drawn. If, however, contracts contract, then their drawing can be redrawn as a withdrawing which releases without re-leasing. To be is to let and to let is to let go.

The one who has been released by a contracting cont®act becomes an exile. 'To be Jewish', Jabès confesses, 'is to have left home early and arrived nowhere.' Arriving nowhere ... no where arriving. To arrive nowhere is, of course, not to arrive but to remain under way. In the wake of the contracting which transforms being into a letting be that is a letting go, exile is endless. Between the infinite no's of where lies the dis-place of erring.

The destiny of Berlin is to be an 'edge city'. Place or no place where East and West come together by drifting apart, Berlin remains divided even when walls seem to fall. In 1987, Libeskind proposed a reconstruction of the heart of the city — the Tiergarten district — in his City Edge project. Endlessly complicating the structure of the wall, Libeskind folds edge into edge to create a liminal space where nothing is settled and everything is in transition. The tilted levers and crossed bars which structure this unsettling project recall Constructivist motifs. The defining feature of Berlin City Edge is a colossal bar pitched at a precarious angle along Flottwellstrasse. This structure, which extends into the air from below ground level, is designed to house offices and residences. Though massive, this displaced skyscraper is unmistakenly fragile. It is almost as if one of the monuments of modernism had been uprooted and tumbled to earth. In place of a secure foundation, the lateral structure is supported by thin, shaky legs which appear unable to carry the weight they bear. Everything seems about to collapse. The people who live and work in and on this edge hover above a void which is utterly unavoidable.

If, however, nothing is settled and everything is in transition, then all of this might be understood otherwise. Perhaps the lever of Berlin City Edge is not falling, but is rising from earth to sky. Perhaps everything is on the verge of taking off instead of collapsing. Perhaps Libeskind is charting a line of ascent rather than descent. Rising or falling? Soaring or sinking? It remains uncertain, unclear, undecidable. The edge, margin, boundary along which we are destined to err always lies *between* 'Utopia' and 'the pit'.

○ Emptying

Like God, emptiness has no name ...

<u>I shall have probed emptiness from my birth to the evening of my death.</u>

— Edmond Jabès

Does probing emptiness yield nothing ... or something else ... something other ... which, though no thing, is not nothing?

Empty: Void of content; containing nothing; having no occupants or inhabitants; vacant; unoccupied; lacking purpose or substance; meaningless; vacuous; inane; devoid; destitute.

Emptiness marks the non-site of loss and lack ... or so it appears ... by disappearing). Its space is a hole to be filled ... a gap to be crossed (out) ... a tear to be (m)ended. No desire seems deeper; indeed, desire itself appears to be nothing ... nothing other ... nothing other than an emptiness longing to be filled.

But perhaps it need(s) not ... need not necessarily be so. Perhaps emptiness is not a deficiency to be overcome ... perhaps every void is not devoid ... perhaps a certain emptiness ought to be preserved ... preserved as empty. It is, after all (always after all, for the all needs an ancient void it cannot avoid) ... it is, after all, possible that emptiness is not destructive without becoming constructive. Perhaps emptiness ... an (un)certain emptiness is deconstructive. To construct deconstructively would be to build voids without a-voiding building.

Daniel Libeskind is convinced, firmly convinced that emptiness should not be a-voided.

Having "crossed-over," the emptiness of Space no longer appears as a deficiency — as a failure to fill the gap between the heart and the stars. Presumably emptiness allies itself with it, forming a new ovule, and through no failure of ours brings to fulfillment a foetus whose resilience is inconceivable in its unmitigated thinness. Emptiness is not a pure minus — not a deficiency as the idealists thought — but a play of new curvatures, curvatures eternally misadjusted to each other's hollowness. The audibility of Unoriginal Sounds — yet to be heard amidst the cheerful ice crackling around us — projects this immeasurable 'hole' of absence into a megalithic proportion coextensive in size with the head, the hand and the eye. No one can come closer than that to the creator, without disremembering his plans for a uni-directional telecommunications from which to radiate signals that can never be retrieved.

Not a pure minus but not a plus, the immeasurable hole of emptiness constitutes an absent center which decenters the structure it faults. The absent-presence/present-absence of the void is the emptiness which cannot and yet must be built.

Libeskind's Jewish Museum is haunted by emptiness. The void in the midst of the structure constitutes one third of the total volume of the supplement. Protests to the contrary notwithstanding, this void remains void ... useless, nonfunctional, excessive. Perhaps meaningless, vacuous, inane. The unanswerable question which lingers in the void is whether this folly is divine madness or simply madness.

The line of the supplement is neither direct nor straight, but zigzags in a play of Z's and reversed Z's that recalls, without representing, the unnameable point of no return, which sometimes is named *zim zum*. The aberrant line of Z's plotting the course of Berlin's deviant history is not unbroken, but is faulted, fissured, fragmented ... torn, frayed, rent by a void which is not itself whole. Forever rent, emptiness rends every structure constructed to contain it. From the outside, the addition to the Berlin Museum appears to be a continuous building. But appearances are deceptive, for the structure is inwardly divided. The broken line of the void cuts the convoluted line of the museum to form what are, in effect, seven separate structures. While intricately related, these parts, Libeskind explains, never have and never will form a totality.

The distant and the gaping mark the coherence of the work because it has come apart: in order to become accessible (both functionally and intellectually). What was, from both inside and out, never pre-existed as a whole (neither in the ideal Berlin nor in the real one), nor can it be put together again in some hypothetical future. The spacing is the sundering, the separation brought about by the history of Berlin, which can only be experienced as the absence of time, and, as the time, fulfillment of space no longer there.

Libeskind's addition rewrites the history of Berlin by creating a text that must be read 'between the lines'. This between is the spacing of emptiness.

Libeskind builds what Jabès writes: 'For me, the words "Jew" and "God" are, it is true, metaphors. "God" is the metaphor for emptiness; "Jew" stands for the torment of "God", of emptiness.' God ... emptiness ... Emptiness ... God. The history of the Jews hangs on emptiness. The Jewish collection of the Berlin Museum is shown only in the underground labyrinth and on the walls of the sealed void which severs the dominant zigzag structure. One history interrupts the other history and vice versa. Neither history is complete, for each presupposes not only the other but an other Other, which, though 'in' history, is not of history.

The new extension is conceived as an emblem. The invisible has made itself apparent as the Void, and not the visible. Void/Invisible: these structural features have been gathered in this space of the City and laid bare. An architecture where the unnamed remains: the names keep still.

In this void ... along this void ... at the edge of this void, the unnamed remains and names keep still. Whose names are inscribed in this emptiness? What is the name of the unnameable?

○ **Noing**

NON-KNOWLEDGE LAYS BARE.
This proposition is the summit, but must be understood in this way: lays bare, therefore I <u>see</u> what knowledge was hiding up to that point, but if I see, I <u>know</u>. Indeed, I know, but non-knowledge again lays bare what I have known. If nonsense is sense, the sense that is nonsense is lost, becomes nonsense once again (without possible end).

— Georges Bataille

But now as we climb from the last things up to the most primary we deny all things so that we may unhiddenly know that unknowing which itself is hidden from all those possessed of knowing amid all beings, so that we may see above being that darkness concealed from all the lights among beings.

— Dionysius the Areopagite

○ **(Un)Naming**

Four times God fell silent in His Name. Four times, on the way up and down each slope of the mountain, we have faced the silence of the letter.

— Edmond Jabès

Four letters ... four times God falls silent. But the silence of God is not merely fourfold; it is infinite ... perhaps the Infinite. The silence which breaks but cannot be broken is not the absence of speech, but is the withdrawal of language that allows the word to become articulate.

Since all nomination is de-nomination, naming is always at the same time unnaming. But just as there are two nights of forgetfulness, so there are two orders ... or disorders of unnaming. And just as darkness deepens as one falls from the first night into the other night, so silence thickens as one moves from the unnamed to the Unnameable.

To name is always to name not. To name A is not to name B. Indeed, the name A is, in an important sense, not-B. And, of course, vice versa. The very denomination of A is the de-nomination of B. But all of this remains abstract, general, generic and, therefore, improper. Naming *sensu strictissimo* entails a certain propriety. But when names are refined by becoming proper, their inescapable impropriety is exposed. The proper name is singular ... absolutely singular. It is mine, only mine; I possess it and it possesses me. And yet, to stake a claim on my name, it must be recognizable by me as well as others. Recognition requires repetition, and repetition negates the very singularity it seeks to affirm. Since singularity is forever unnameable, 'my' naming is always 'my' unnaming. 'My' name ... even 'my' proper name ... especially 'my' proper name is never merely 'my own' but is always also the name of an other who remains unnamed. With the naming of this unnamed other, we slip from the first night to the other night where the Unnameable begins to (dis)appear.

The Unnameable is not the opposite of the named; on the contrary, the Unnameable dwells 'within' every name as the condition of the possibility and the impossibility of naming. The unnaming presupposed by naming runs deeper than the elision of an alternative particularity or the erasure of singularity. The name carries within it a more 'primordial' loss, which is not so much archaic as an-archic. The loss of language that has always already occurred steals words with a rustling which can never be stilled. There are sounds of silence ... sounds which cannot be sounded even though their resounding is endless.

While naming always unnames, the Unnamed is sometimes named ... albeit improperly. One of the names of the Unnameable is God. 'The name of God', Blanchot maintains,

signifies not only that what is named by this name would not belong to the language in which this names occurs, but that this name, in a way that is difficult to determine, would no longer be a part of this language, even apart from it. The idolatry of the name or only the reverence that makes it unpronounceable (sacred) is related to this disappearance of the <u>name</u> that the name itself makes appear ... Pure name that does not name, but is rather always to be named, the name as name, but, in that, hardly a name, without nominative power, attached as if by chance to language and, thus, transmitting to it the devastating power of non-designation ...

Name ... pure name that does not name ... name that names not ... devastating power of unnaming.

An Architecture where the unnamed remains: names keeps still.

Names ... so many names ... lines of names ... columns of names ... names whose very excess renders them anonymous. Libeskind identifies the source of the names which line the museum:

I was interested in the names of those people who were deported from Berlin during the fatal years, the Holocaust, that one knows only historically. I received from Bonn two very large volumes called <u>Gedenkbuch</u> — they are incredibly impressive because they contain all the names, just names, dates of birth, dates of deportation and presumed places where these people were murdered. So I looked for the names of all the Berliners where they died — in Riga, in Lodz, in all the concentration camps.

The *Gedenkbuch* is the 'memory book', which, in its silent testimony, commemorates an absolute sacrifice. The memory book recalls those who are destined to be forgotten. The names are nothing but traces ... traces of ash which has long since been scattered. In the words of the poet Paul Celan, in whose memory Libeskind built a courtyard on the edge of the museum:

All the names, all the
names burnt up
with the rest. So much
ash to bless.

Names turned to ash in a Holocaust where *nothing* remains .... The horror of these flames is a *Tremendum* which exceeds language and as such is unspeakable ... unnameable. The question which lingers in these flames is whether the Unnameable can survive this Holocaust.

Ash.
Ash. Ash.
Night-and-Night.

o Mourning

'Die Schleuse' addresses you, and your mourning, to tell you that what has been lost, and lost beyond a trace, is the word that opens, like a Shibboleth, on what is most intimate; the word that has left me ... and, what is graver still, if this could be said, the word that opens the possibility of mourning what has been lost beyond a trace: not only the exterminated family, the incineration of the family name in the figure of the sister ... at the moment of her death, and of the final hour that no longer has a sister ... but the very word that grants me access to Jewish mourning: Kaddish.

— Jacques Derrida

Mourning ... mourning what has been lost ... lost beyond a trace. Two nights ... two forgettings ... two mournings.

Mourn: *(s)mer*, to have been kept in mind.
smriti, Skr, that which is remembered, tradition.
meros, Gk, part.
martyr, Gk, one kept in mind as evidence of a miracle.
memor, L, mindful.

Two mournings: one possible ... one impossible. What, then, is mourning? What will mourning have been? To mourn is, of course, to lament; to express grief or sorrow. There are codes and rituals for mourning, which dictate its form, direct its course and define its proper time. Freud taught us that mourning is a working out that is a working through. Mourning, in other words, is a process which has stages and comes to completion. The end of mourning is the sublation of absence through which the self is reconciled to loss as well as to itself. At the end of the first night of mourning, a light dawns which allows one to get on with life.

But is this 'true' mourning? Successful mourning involves introjection through which autoerotic impulses are extended as the self enlarges itself by assimilating other to same. Such remembering is, in a certain sense, forgetting. The other disappears *as other* in the very process by which it is supposed to be remembered. There is, however, another mourning ... a different mourning ... a mourning which does not reduce other to same, but mourns the other *as other*. This mourning is never successful for it remains impossible.

Is the most distressing, or even the most deadly infidelity that of a possible mourning that would interiorize within us the image, idol, or ideal of the other who is dead and lives only in us? Or is it that of the impossible mourning, which, leaving the other his alterity, respecting thus his infinite remove, either refuses to take or is incapable of taking the other within oneself, as in the tomb or the vault of some narcissism? (Derrida)

Impossible mourning incorporates without introjecting. The absence of the other is interiorized but never overcome ... remembered but never re-membered. Mourning is impossible because absence cannot be mastered. Mourning, in other words, is a process which never comes to completion.

The introjection of an absence which cannot be transformed into presence creates a void which can never be filled. The outside which is inside turns everything inside out and outside in to create a crypt whose seal is unbreakable.

No crypt presents itself. The grounds are so disposed as to disguise and to hide: something, always a body in some way. But also to disguise the act of hiding and to hide the disguise: the crypt hides as it holds ... The crypt is thus not a natural place, but the striking history of an artifice, an architecture, and artifact: of a place comprehended within another but rigorously separate from it, isolated from the general space by partitions, an enclosure, an enclave. So as to purloin the thing from the rest. Constructing a system of partitions, with the inner and outer surfaces, the cryptic enclave produces a cleft in space, the assembled system of various places (Derrida)

When mourning is impossible, unspeakable secrets become haunting and words ring hollow. The stirring silence of secrets secrete the structures constructed to enclose and contain them.

Daniel Libeskind's architecture is cryptic ... irreducibly cryptic. Providing no codes waiting to be cracked, his work is complex ... impossibly complex. Its secret is its complexity ... its complexity a secret. But how can a crypt be exposed? How can a secret be told?

The site had once been occupied. It was in Sachsenhausen that one of the most notorious concentration camps was located. It was from Sachsenhausen that the March of Death, which was supposed to end in the waters off the coast of Lübeck, was to have begun. The competition called for forgetting ... an irresponsible act of forgetting. Housing was to be built on the site. But Libeskind refused: 'This program quite emphatically rejects trivializing the site with any plan for placing housing on it or otherwise domesticating it.'

Instead of adding, he proposed subtracting; rather than constructing new foundations, he insisted on excavating old foundations. The remaining buildings on the site would be torn down and the foundations of the 'Idea City of Death' would be exposed. The entire area would, then, be flooded, and walkways would be constructed above the water to allow people to contemplate the ruins. Buried yet displayed for all to see, the recollection of unspeakable crimes leads to a mourning which is endless.

The double bind created by the inevitability and impossibility of mourning does not, however, render hope impossible. There can be no survival without hope in the midst of horror. The intersection of a mourning which never ends and a hope which ever begins is marked by the *X* which translates mourning into morning: MOXRNING. For the moment, however, we must wait for the dawn of this moxrning.

o Disappointing

Where do we meet this real? For what we have in the discovery of psychoanalysis is an encounter, an essential encounter — an appointment to which we are always called with a real that eludes us.

— Jacques Lacan

If the point which is always drawing ... the point towards which (the) all is always drawn is the point of no return ... the point which returns a certain no ... or noing, then every appointment is disappointing. Indeed, in the final analysis, our appointment is always with disappointment. When the point is missing ... the point is lacking ... the point is pointless, disappointment becomes unavoidable.

Contracting is always disappointing. If everything begins with contracting, then the loss of the point is the loss of what was never possessed. To disappoint is (at least in Middle English) to dispossess. The disappointment which dispossesses frustrates desire by refusing satisfaction. But precisely this disappointment

... this frustration ... this refusing engenders desire. Desiring is lacking. The lack of desire 'is' the presence of absence, which 'is' the trace of the absence of presence. The point of desire is, then, disappointment. Without dis-appointment, there is no desire. To desire, therefore, is to desire disappointment.

Daniel Libeskind's architecture is disappointing ... profoundly disappointing. It does not deliver what it promises. From the beginning, disappointment has plagued his work. First there were drawings but no projects; then there were projects but no buildings. Models ... marvelously complex, even cryptic models. Some were written, some were drawn, some even fabricated. One of Libeskind's most cryptic projects — Architectural Machines (The Reading Machine, The Memory Machine, and The Writing Machine) — burned ... burned completely ... leaving nothing ... nothing but Ash ... Ash ... Ash.

Every experience of growth, consciousness, development of one's work, Libeskind admits, is accompanied by the feeling of loss, destruction, and of passing away. When my work turned to ashes late last summer on the shores of the 'dark city at the edge of the lake', I experienced a sudden perishing of my soul engulfed as it were in Fire.

Originally designed for the Italian village of Palmanova and displayed at the 1985 Venice Biennale, Libeskind's 'Three Lessons about Architecture' was an enigmatic meditation on architecture as it enters what he describes as its 'end condition'. When architecture reaches its 'end condition', it approaches the point of no return.

Disappointment does not disappear when buildings are realized. On the contrary, the ashes of disappointment linger even when they turn to sand. Returning to the labyrinthine underground of the extension to the Berlin Museum, we rediscover the intersecting axes which form an X. This X, it now appears, conforms precisely to the shape of the X with which Schönberg finished or failed to finish 'Moses and Aaron'. As we have already discovered, one arm of this X leads to the Holocaust Tower. The second arm reaches towards the Promised Land, which, in keeping with expectation, is a garden. But, contrary to expectation, this garden is strange ... even uncanny. Libeskind named the garden after E. T. A. Hoffman ... the same E. T. A. Hoffman who once worked in the building now housing the Berlin Museum and who plays a central role in Freud's classic essay 'Die Unheimliche'. The E. T. A. Hoffman Garden is not a garden in any traditional sense of the term. It has no plants, flowers or trees; indeed, all life is absent. Instead of the fulfillment of dreams, this garden seems to embody the frustration of desire. Far from an image of security and certainty, the garden is infinitely fragile. Pitched at an angle which runs from below water level to above ground level, the garden constantly threatens to slip away. Most important, the garden is *empty ... absolutely empty*. The Promised Land remains a void. The empty space, which is designated a garden, is surrounded by a continuous ramp made of Jerusalem stone. The inside wall of the border is glass and contains sand from the desert of Israel. Inside the inside ... nothing.

This absence ... his emptiness ... this nothingness is disappointing ... profoundly disappointing. What has been promised has not been delivered; what is desired is not granted. Do absence, emptiness and nothingness make despair inevitable and hope impossible, or do they create the possibility of hope in the midst of despair? Just as there can be no desire without disappointment, so there can be no promise if there is fulfillment. Thus, only an architecture which is disappointing can be promising. The deeper the disappointment, the more profound the promise.

○ Hoping

'What do you suppose that white line in the sky that you saw from the crack in the cattle car on your way to Stutthof really was?' the interviewer asked Elaine some thirty years later in her Brooklyn home.

'You see, in order to survive you must believe in something, you need a source of inspiration, of courage, something bigger than yourself, something to overcome reality. The line was the source of my inspiration, my line from heaven.'

— Yaffa Eliach

The Unnameable resists ending by muttering: 'You must go on, I can't go on, I'll go on.' But how? How does one go on when one can't go on? How is it possible to discover hope when and where it seems impossible? What does it mean to hope when surrounded by ashes or traces of ashes?

The possibility of hoping is inextricably bound to a certain impossibility. This impossibility is never present, but draws near through a metaleptic reversal of temporal ecstasies in which the past which was never present forever approaches as the future which never arrives. The inevitable loss resulting from originary contracting creates the space for hope as well as mourning. In the wake of 'primordial' absence, nothing ever is what it might be, and thus everything could be otherwise. The impossibility of presence issues in an open-endedness where all is in flux. Nothing is sign-ed ... nothing is sealed ... nothing is delivered. The openness of the future, which is the trace of the lack of the past, guarantees nothing ... guarantees nothing but possibility. One of the names of infinite possibility is 'God'.

God <u>is</u> that all things are possible, and that all things are possible <u>is</u> God; and only the person whose being has been so shaken that he has become spirit by understanding that all things are possible, only he has had dealings with God. (Kierkegaard)

All things are possible ... *all* things. The most horrifying as well as the most glorious. Possibility is the air which allows both dread and hope to breathe.

Daniel Libeskind's architecture is an architecture of hope. His hope testifies to a faith which is as profound as it is elusive. Libeskind confesses:

Some sage said a long time ago that every day one should reach a higher spiritual level. If you do not, you are not really doing anything worthwhile. So everyone has to ask himself at night: have I reached a higher spiritual level today? If the answer is no, you are really in trouble .... One has to work not only on architecture, not only on objects, but also correspondingly always on oneself, to cope with things. Making it better means also to improve oneself spiritually.

Such faith does not come easily ... nor is the hope it inspires a facile optimism. At this late date, too much has happened, too many have suffered and died, too many ashes smolder for hope to be anything but absurd. And yet, Libeskind insists, precisely the Absurd is what we are called to believe. In the midst of suffering, death and ashes, Libeskind builds hopefully. When hope seems least possible, it is most necessary. Describing his proposal for the Sachsenhausen concentration camp site, Libeskind wrote:

Its aim is to bring people to this place, to reveal, disclose and remember. At the same time, this must be a place for hope, a place where those who are trying to rebuild Germany can find a workplace, a working future, new growth, contemplative quiet, physical and mental rehabilitation: the dawn of a new Mo~~u~~rning.

Through the middle of the memorial to horrors of the past, Libeskind proposes to build a Hope Incision. There can be no movement into the future without the acceptance of responsibility for a past which forever remains an open wound. In less prosaic terms, there can be no morning without the 'Night-and-Night' of 'Ash ... Ash'. But the darkness of this endless night need not extinguish the faint light of every new beginning.

The incision cut into Sachsenhausen is not the first trace of Libeskind's affirmation of hope in the midst of hopelessness. Six years earlier, he had projected 'the Berlin of Tomorrow'. Unlike the unrealized utopias of modernists, Libeskind's city of the future never forgets the horrors of the past. Unlike the realized utopias of postmodernists, Libeskind's city of the future does not lose itself in the cynicism of the present. 'City Edge' forms around 'the axis of Universal Hope'.

A voyage into the substance of a city and its architecture entails a realignment of arbitrary points, disconnected lines and names not out of place along the axis of Universal Hope. Very thin paper — like that of architectural drawings, Bibles, maps, telephone books, money — can be easily cut, crumpled or folded around this indestructible kernel. Then the entire unwieldy construction can be floated on water like the tattered paper making its Odyssey on the Liffey. Finally, the water itself can be adhered to the mind, provided that one does not rely on the glue. In this way, Reality as the substance of things hoped for becomes a proof of invisible joys — Berlin of open skies.

The city of the future forms around the axis of Universal Hope, which, in turn, forms around an 'indestructible kernel'. This kernel is the point of no return ... the point which is the navel tying our dreams to the unknown ... the unknown whose approaching withdrawal and withdrawing approach open the space of dread ... and hope. It is towards this point that Libeskind's architecture is always pointing ... pointing without reaching ... pointing by dis-appointing.

·
·
·

What, then, *is* the point of Daniel Libeskind's architecture? It has no point ... it points to the absence of the point ... it brings architecture to the point of no return ... the point with which everything repeatedly begins and (the) all endlessly ends. The point ... the pointless point? Perhaps *Ein-Sof* ... The Endless. To trace this point without end would be to undertake the Odyssey on the Liffey with the conviction that the Alpha and the Omega are not One.

My leaves have drifted from me. All. But one clings still. I'll bear it on me. To remind me of. Lff! So soft this mo~~u~~rning, ours. Yes.

WRITINGS

The Pilgrimage of Absolute Architecture

Cranbrook

I believe that practicing architecture today, teaching architecture today, being a student of architecture today, entails very different consequences than it did even a hundred years ago. I think all of us are in a different stage of possibility, of development of the modern world. I believe that architecture has entered its end. That is not to say that architecture is finished, but I would say that architecture has entered an end condition. I think that all those who practice architecture, whether knowingly or unknowingly, feel in some way that something has come to an end, but what it is, is very difficult to say since it is not in the realm of objects. Therefore, I will try to speak as clearly as I can of something about which it is not easy to speak, because it is not one more thing which can be found in the catalogue of the world.

In any case, what I will try to speak about is a kind of difference, to use the word of Derrida. And I will try to make this difference apparent by saying only one thing: that if equilibrium could have been attained, it would have been attained a long time ago. Equilibrium could have been attained under two conditions only. One is that reality would have been indeterminate or indistinct, a kind of Heisenberg/Mondrian postulation that equilbirium is achievable within a context of indeterminacy. This did not happen. On the other hand, equilibrium could have been achieved by postulating a global meaning of the world, a boundless but finite meaning, which is to say the meaning of Einstein, the meaning of mythology, the meaning of the centered world. But, needless to say, neither of these realities have been experienced, and they won't be. So what there is is the shape of space of the world which on a permanent basis produces a destabilized, let's say an eternal movement of imperfection and difference. And it is this shape of space about which I would like to speak to you and explore in a very tentative manner because no language exists for it today. No language has been agreed upon in which to discuss such a phenomenon. I would like to draw a diagram for you to refer to, because it's a kind of scheme of my small discourse here.

What I would like to illustrate with this diagram synoptically and synthetically is a scheme of a project that I made with some friends some time ago entitled 'Three Lessons in Architecture,' and presented in an Italian urban setting. It's a project that I did for a problem in Venice. I did not choose to address this problem by simply providing another craft solution, another ideological solution, or another industrial solution I chose instead to present an alternative solution by exploring participatory reality and to present those who ask the question with a participatory experience in which the problem of architecture might come into focus on the one hand, and some part of it might fall into oblivion on the other. I chose to address the urban problem of Palmanova (a city which exists today in northern Italy in the Venetto region).

I presented the organizers of this program with a piece of equipment, really one big movement in three parts. I will show it to you in three moments of the machine—the moment of reading, the moment of remembering and the moment of writing architecture. And I will start at some point, and end at some other point, but please remember that I'm really addressing this diagram as a totality. One could in fact start anywhere and one could end anywhere. It's a big circle of interpretation, not necessarily a vicious circle, but a circle that by going through its own presuppositions in some sense destroys and obliterate the problem of the given as it also exposes other dimensions of architecture. The three lessons that I have offered here are the three lessons of architecture: A) reading architecture, and its equivalent, the reading machine; B) the lesson in the present remembering architecture, and the memory machine, C) writing architecture, and its equivalent, the writing machine. So these are pieces of metaphysical equipment (because they don't really do anything, they are in another realm) which propose a very curious path, because as I said earlier architecture was from its very beginning at its end. At the end it's possible to retrieve in some sense the whole past and future destiny, because the end of course is nothing in the future, nor is it anything in the past, nor is it anything in the present—it is simultaneously on all three levels. The three machines propose a fundamental recollection of the historical vicissitude, in particular of western architecture. They constitute a single piece of equipment and are mutually interdependent. Each is a starting point for the other. The purpose of this equipment is to release the end to itself. I think the objects in architecture are only residues of something which is truly important: the participatory experience (the emblem of reality which goes into their making). You could say that everything we have is that kind of a residue. It is this experience that I would like to retrieve, not the object.

By the way, making machine, I discovered as I was doing this project, is an old task. Everybody needs machines. Vitruvius said that first of all an architect should make a machine—it is more important than making a city. Then he says you should also make theater and other things. Alberti says this as well. When I read Vitruvius and Alberti and they said every good architect must first make a machine to do architecture, I thought that if I'm going to be a good architect I must follow the tradition to its end. So I tried to do it in a particular way. We wanted to retrieve reading architecture, so we made this first machine. I have to say what is involved in reading: to try to become a pure believer even in architecture. I know it's an experimental state. It's an experimental being I'm describing, not an experimental object. Try to become the pure medieval craftsman. That's really the object of this exercise. To make something in a way which is made only on one's knees; which is made through complete faith in the transcendence of architecture, of the text, of reading; which is made by a total faith in the craft; which rejects all modern techniques and technology; which rejects modern thinking about architecture. So we did it that way. We got up at the crack of dawn, four o'clock in the morning. We built this machine in a small, small place without any power tools, just with hand tools. With no electricity, just with candlelight. We went to bed early because with candlelight you can't work late. And we did it in silence because there is nothing to talk about when you work like that.

I feel it's the very notion of architecture. One always dreams, and I'm sure you have dreamt it too, what it was like, and what it would be like to build this way. And of course, one must reconstruct this experience because how else does one make a circle without a ruler—with just a plumb line and the compass? I simply tried to make one circle, and to it in that way, full of faith, and to get the experience as close as possible to this loaded experience of the monastic faith in the craft of making. Therefore, lesson A teaches the almost forgotten process of building, which really has not yet come to complete fruition. I would say that the medieval process is still coming to an end today, has not been finished. A certain technique was created, one which also brought a revolution of the word. A revolution of text. This archaeological reconstruction (cities like Palmanova, military ideas in architecture and of engineering) and this will to power is disclosed by thinking about architecture and particularly by having no faith in its reality. I never knew about this weak point. Only when I started doing the project did I discover that the weapons of architecture and the weapons of the world did not originate in the Renaissance—they originated in the monastery. The machine gun and the parachute and the atomic bomb are not the inventions of Leonardo da Vinci, they are inventions of Thomas Aquinas and even earlier spirituality. I tried to become that architect who would be commissioned by a monastery and who would then deliver both the non-objective and the objective counterpart of the purified, holy experience. So I made a gear. And then I mad many gears. Please remember they are made with a chisel. It's hard to polish things without sandpaper. I made these detours because I would like for you to use these machines. Now, these machines were meant to be used since a machine is not something to look at. These are not aesthetic objects. I offered them to the citizens of Palmanova, the city for which I made the project. I suggested to the organizers of this competition that these three pieces of equipment be placed in the middle square of Palmanova, and that not just the architects, but all the citizens who passed through this Piazza would use it. They could determine what the problem was and the possible solution to it.

I never did any work like this before, it was all new for me. And the experience of it is like that—you have to pull the wheel or push the wheel. That's important. And because the wheel is heavy it creaks. It's a big creaking wheel. And if you were to sit at it you would push it or pull it. This machine has many axles and many, many gears which are both hidden and revealed. It has shelves and the whole mechanism is intended to support eight words. So there are eight words for which this mechanism is a support. Now the words are very, very light because the words are light. They don't weigh much. And especially these eight words are light because I sought words which are no longer readable in the text of architecture—words which cannot be remembered or written down. I placed these eight light words and made them into books to give them slightly more substance. I wrote eight books. I made the eight books by hand like the monks—made the paper, bound the books, and placed them into this big wheel. And what is interesting is that light as the books are, light as the words are, they actually completely crush the weight of these axles they expose two things: they expose the reader and they expose the movement of the wheel, which of course revolves and then comes back to its own starting point, like all wheels do.

There are ninety-two wedges, and glueless joints, no energy of a contemporary kind. The machine seeks to represent the triumph of the spirit over matter, of candlelight over electrical light or darkness. It's made solely from wood, as are the books. You will recognize that a wheel is always gigantic, no matter how small. This one is very big. It is a Vitruvian, Albertian humanistic wheel of fortune suitable for the diagonally crucified humanist of Raphael and Leonardo, for whom I really built it. The square intersecting with circle. I would have like to make it for Thomas Aquinas. Perhaps he would have bought this piece for himself. It's a device good for comparative reading of the architecture text. Rather than shuttling to your desk and looking for authoritative things like those monks always did who were looking for the right book to verify the eighth book or the first book, I placed the books in the wheel so that comparisons could be easily made. And in being easily made they could also reveal the tautological nature of the architectural text at its end. The text of architecture is a tautological text, which means that it says the same thing at the end as it said at the beginning because the beginning was at its end already. In short, a chamber of revolutions. The word revolution is used here in its etymological sense: a revolutionary machine because it revolves, and with each revolution comes about the revolution of the text which is propelled by it.

It's difficult to show a book in a picture because a book is meant to be read. This is the first book that I wrote, and strangely funny because it was stolen. Five minutes after it was presented for perusal of the public, this book was stolen, and the exhibitors, the organizers of the Venice Biennale came to me and said: 'Look, the book was stolen, but since it's a printed book, you have another copy of it.' And I said: 'No, I don't!' because if you are really a monk, you don't mass produce anything. You use the technology to do one thing only. So you print. You use the whole resourcefulness of that monastic faith to do a singular act only, and always the only one, the same singular act over and over again. So I don't have this book anymore. The book on ideas is missing, but there are still other books remaining and they are all different. They have different thicknesses. Some of the books are five hundred pages long. The pages are handmade and can be read. Someone asked me: 'Do you read these books?' Yes, and I have seen other people read them. So there are eight books. Somebody said, why eight books? I discovered why while re-reading Don Quixote. You've read about the great knight, Don Quixote in his paper visor, going to fight against the injustice of the whole world. Cervantes says that Don Quixote met only one gentleman in his travels in Spain. In all his time (because he was old by the time he died) he met only one gentleman. He said it was the gentleman in green, and he was a gentleman because he travelled, and he travelled with a satchel of only eight books. Clearly Cervantes already had more books than eight, in the sixteenth century. And I certainly have more than eight books in my library. I made this project in order to get rid of my books, because I decided that I too, like the good knight, should reduce my library. It's hard to get rid of books. You can donate them to a church or a library, but really to get rid of books is an ethical problem, because one would have to rewrite them all. I still have more than eight books at home, but I am getting closer and closer to being Don Quixote's gentleman.

Here is an illustration of the kinetics of the machine. I must say that the act is the experience. The machine is not about the object, the object is just documented here—it's about the experience one has in participating in it. Of course, the act is different for the reader and the voyeur, the onlooker, because the reader is involved in the indecipherable or in the completely transparent. But the voyeur, the one who looks on the reader, sees only a body bent over this wheel of torture, and he sees only a beautiful kinetic motion. When the wheels move and the little gears move, it's truly beautiful—the fascination of multiplying a circle. The experience one has is that the books on the top shelf, which are rotating, appear to be falling on top of you. This is what I was after. They appear to be falling on your head as you pull the wheel or as you read. It's a very uneasy feeling. And as you turn the wheel, the book which you've just left behind, which is going down, appears to be falling onto the ground. The books falling on your head and the books falling on the ground, but, at the same time, never falling on your head and never falling on the ground —always remaining in the same position because the axle rotates very accurately, keeping them always in an ideal position to a hypothetical reader, a reader who isn't there.

That's the reading experience: one cog of the entire machine, not a starting point, but one element of the bigger machine. You will see it repeating itself in all the other machines.

Let me move on to remembering architecture. I've been told that when people die, (and I've also read a lot about it), when one remembers one's life before committing suicide or when dying in a hospital, life reels rapidly in front of one's brain. And at the end things become quickly apparent. They very quickly pile up into the soul. In an end condition, things pile up rapidly in the memory of what architecture may have been. It's hard to know. But I set myself this task: to remember architecture, to construct an experimental being who could remember it. So lesson B is the lesson which is no longer in the arena of craft, in the arena of this future past, but it's in the arena of future eternal, of ideas. So we came out of the monastery. We didn't do this one with the notion of pure life on our knees, with our bare hands, praying that someone should save us; we did this in an ideological realm of politics, a kind of Renaissance notion of architecture. It's really the monks coming out with their weapons out of the monastery, and appearing on the stage of the theater. Therefore, lesson B consists of that which can still be remembered of architecture.

As a historical program, architecture and its sight have been filtered through what can still be remembered. I modelled this machine after a very fascinating phenomenon to me: a small memory machine constructed in sixteenth century Venice by an architect called Julio Camillo was perhaps in his time the most famous architect. He was an opponent of Palladio in some ways. He was commissioned by the King of France to build a little machine which in a split second could reveal the meaning of the cosmos. I thought that was a worthy cause and a worthy memory. And apparently Julio Camillo, the architect, fulfilled himself nobly. This comes to me from his correspondence with Erasmus, who has always been very truthful about everything. Juliio Camillo showed a small machine to the King of France in the sixteenth century. The King walked up to it (it was a small object, obviously), looked into it, turned around and said to Camillo: 'Now I understand. I understand everything. You are an architect. You have revealed to me the meaning of all of it.' The interesting thing about Camillo is that immediately after he made this machine, two things happened: the machine disappeared and so did Camillo.

Ever since I read about Camillo's machine I have been absolutely enthralled by it. I wanted to meet Camillo, and I wanted to know more about it because I'm also trying to remember what it used to be like, as he did. I went to London and discovered Frances Yeats who wrote a book on Camillo, and I found that nothing more is known about Camillo's theater than what was written in her book: that it was made of wood, had paper which was hanging, and had rope in it.

The Myth of Site

Now the Sirens have a still more fatal weapon than their song, namely their silence. And though admittedly such a thing has never happened, still it is conceivable that someone might possibly have escaped from their singing; but from their silence certainly never. Against the feeling of having triumphed over them by one's own strength, and the consequent exaltation that bears down everything before it, no earthly powers can resist.

And when Ulysses approached them the potent songstresses actually did not sing, whether because they thought that this enemy could be vanquished only by their silence, or because the look of bliss on the face of Ulysses, who was thinking of nothing but his wax and his chains, made them forget their singing.

But Ulysses, if one may so express it, did not hear their silence; he thought they were singing and that he alone did not hear them. For a fleeting moment he saw their throats rising and falling, their breasts lifting, their eyes filled with tears, their lips half-parted, but believed that these were accompaniments to the airs which died unheard around him. Soon, however, all this faded from his sight as he fixed his gaze on the distance, the Sirens literally vanished before his resolution, and at the very moment when they were nearest to him he knew of them no longer.

'The Silence of Sirens,' excerpt from *Parables and Paradoxes*, *c.* 1920

— Franz Kafka.

The Idea of Site

The episode of the Sirens in Homer's Odyssey tells of the allurement of the past: the entanglement of the Myth of Enlightenment and the Myth of Domination. Our 'modern' hero conquers the temptation to self-destruction through suffering. He proves his maturity and establishes his identity by enduring displacement from those who knew 'everything that ever happened on this so fruitful earth,' and from himself. The Sirens' promise of the irresistible pleasure of their song can be bought only at the price of bondage: perpetual presence of self-consciousness and the deaf labor of those who can never hear the song they make possible.

Obedience, labor; a devitalized 'being' for those who must ignore temptation of presence and look only forward—the practical ones. The dissociation of Practice and Theory, Site and Object, Location and the Located.

The capacity to represent meaning in Architecture is a measure of domination. Conversely, domination is the most powerful thing that can be made visible in it. Paradoxically, this capacity of representation is a means of enlightenment no less than a vehicle of regression.

When the power of System becomes the system of Power, its course is irresistibly that of negation. In architecture this negation is manifested today in the inability of architects to hear what they never heard and to touch the untouched in their resistance to non-existent reality. For all its nonexistence, however, this abysmal truth is no less a Reality.

Contemporary conditions compel conformism in the form of nihilation and cast the truth of Place and Being into a twilight. The non-presence and forgottenness which thus prevails is not merely a trick of history, the failure of fantasy or a ruse of Reason. It is rather a consequence of the acceptance of the technological-ideological 'empire'—the last refuge of ancient and ever-present Fate.

Commonplaces or non-existent topography
The dread and terror of Architecture, the fear of destruction and death which it immortalizes is intimately associated in our minds with a promise of happiness which threatens civilization at every moment. Order and Disorder continually collaborate, and in a pincer movement seek to eliminate the consciousness of reality. This reality, whose site is not a piece of real estate, and whose ground can never be more than an absence, makes reparation and takes retribution for the injustice done in its name: there is no answer to the question 'why is there something rather than nothing?'

The old symbolism of Presence and Participation has almost evaporated from the occidental mind, condensing in its aftermath the salt of historical existence—a residue of reality now gone from the intellect.

The fathers have eaten a sour grape, and the children's teeth are set on edge
— Jeremiah 31:29

Architects, all idiots—they always forget to put in the stairs.
— Flaubert

Sand falling silently into towers.
Ever since the decisive events of the Reformation and Protest which resulted in the re-interpretation of the soul, architecture has been doomed. In this devolution, its form as well as meaning has been gradually hollowed out; it has lost substantial participation in the reality which it symbolizes. We are witness to the events in which the architecture of presence turns into the architecture of absence.

The reactions to the disappearance of architecture are varied. For some it is still piously present. Some lament its passing. Some note its passing but do not lament.
The winds are dry and melancholy fills the void of anatomy.
Literature, Theater, Spiritual Text, Vision, the Vision of Vision. (Also included are cryptograms, ciphers and any form of illegible script.)
The struggle to maintain communion with what is really other has become more desperate: time is of no consequence and forgotten Being cannot be invoked to help.
Paramyths, Pataphysics, and Onto-theology.
Sudden departures into the Alps.

What remains of Architecture cannot be resurrected. The site of participation is conscious existence and the intellect is a sensorium of the nonexistent reality whose disappearance is fatal for the human.
A. Plan of Geneva
B. Portrait of an African Chief with a weapon
Commemorative plaque testifying that trains come on time
Gray, palpitating masses, hardly recognizable
Letter K and W
Sprechstimme

'Materials' of Architecture? Causes, analogies, substances, continuities? Visualization lost but regained with a difference? Consequently the mirrors of Velasquez: the 'father of Abraham, Jacob, Isaac…'. Poor Pascal with his calculator playing a dirge for infinite space. Happy Cain on his dreadful flight into the abyss, in the company of the light carrier: Lucifer and the Problem of the two Altars. (see Byron's Cain)

What we see around us is what we put there. Where do we contact (which has never been ours)? Bouquets, which are the absence of

100 Sites/100 Sights

The Last Laugh	Leni Riefenstahl filming
Hindu fakir	AT&T demonstration (Peking)
Melancholia I	Paris street
Aristotle & Phyllis	Alchemy & Philosopher's son
Artist and Reclining Woman	Letter to the Crocodiles
Theater of Automatons	Blake: Vision of America
Orangutan	Zaum
Lamia	Bellevue
Medieval anatomy	Horus-Apollo
Villa Sarego	Carceri, plate 5
Pendulum experiment	Evolution of the Mind of John Locke
DeHumani corporis Fabrica	Salto Mortale
The City Coat of Arms	Old Man of the Nile
Perspective with strings	A problem of Laws
El sueño de la razón	Mickey Mouse
Slaughtered ox	Bacon
The Architect's dream	The Bathroom
The Raft of Medusa	Four lines and knocking
Severed limbs	Bollingen Tower
Bouvard et Pecuchet	Victory at Samothrace
At the Brink of Chaos (Martin)	Hiroshima
Glasgow Railway opening	Pier and Ocean
Carceri, plate 7	cage-cell
Jonah	Orpheus
The Garden	Maldoror's Equation
Scholar in a room with stairs	Goethe-Rousseau Complex
De Ente et Essentia	Autobahn gas
Robinson Crusoe	Ministry of Marine
The Opium-eater	Cartesian Solar System
Deformed tree	Yellow quadrilateral
Prison lecture	House within a House
Parmigianino with a Dog	Loos' tombstone project
Bearded woman (Ribera)	Physiognomy
Dissection	Conversation with a Priest
Karlskirche	House for an Engineer
Eye diagrams	Cenotaph for Newton
Fall of the Giants	Fall of Icarus
Thesaurus Anatomicus	Eclipse of the Sun
Deutschland über Alles	Auschwitz plan
Patent clerks	Progressive architecture
Dream of the Professor	School at Fagano
Buttermere Lake	Duchamp's fountain
Antique Fragments	13 Towers of Canareggio
Nature Morte, 1914	5,837 couples with Rev. Moon
Virgin Mary	Laocoön
Banquet in the Thames Tunnel	House X
Revival of Christian Architecture	Stock report-schema
The Nose	Linear accelerator
Missiles	Inside the Whale
The Burrow Laws	Arctic Flowers

flowers, imply that in coming into the desolation of Reality the props of orthodoxy and demythologization are insufficient.

There must be more than seven types of ambiguity; more than sixteen ways of looking at a blackbird; more than circular and linear patterns of history...

In conclusion: how can there be meaning which is not a differentiation of the process of someone's consciousness? How can there be meaning 'already there,' when the site of differentiation is itself inserted into the compass of disclosure?

Architecture as an original issue finds itself—through its experience of the history of metaphysics—dissociated from self-understanding. In placing its Truth at a distance from consciousness, architecture reveals a separation between its originality and that which withdraws in the process. In opening itself resolutely to the radical concealment of its own origin, architecture lets itself be drawn along in this withdrawal. Should we not follow where it beckons?

CRITIQUE OF A DAY'S TRAUMA

Thus concluded the fish:

Good and Bad Luck

The dominant urge to speak may further hesitation when the head has not had any cities to create. For creation is not a private privilege of the spirit, of matter, or of some past being. Being, or forever finite immobility, becomes exhausted by fatality and no 'open-sesame' such as time can seduce it by a sprinkling of the powder of damnation. All this may invite an American to an irritation with asphalt.

End

The death of matter exudes a distinct smell shaped in the form of ten-thousand Zions, all fulfilled. Attempt at art is a form of appeal to holed-up matter. Pulse hates the width of infinite possibilities; heart tires when hitched to ends dulled by ciphers. Everything seems to be thoroughly hidden. Wasting forty million life-giving breaths in exchange for a sportive sigh ends with someone's devotion. Dice show aspects which have a thousand permutations or feet in which the soft round spaces split into a dream, like the binding of a false ream of paper into a book. Going upward fitted with a thin sign 'help me' is idiotic.

Act

Deeply private thoughts, awful dreams, inactive states, indulgent desires are Eve's narcotic essence. Although a mathematical fact is not as reliable as a woman in submitting to a massive *two*, every temple implies it. *Terra incognita* seems torn outside, yet inside looks like a knee bent-low under the pressure exerted by the four kinds of charlatans: dillettantes, domestics, abusers of ends, and those biased in favor of semi-surgical operations. Yet the feather (Egyptian *Maat*) is the most submissive aspect hidden in every bridge or fence. Its essence is a cooperation of muscles which anyone can fold into a graphic shape that obeys only when the body is not very attentive. All these attempts at reorganizing the id betray a very empty organ. Thus matter is a transgression, or can be defined as time orating rather than writing essays. The reverse end of this phenomenon is a lovely four-horse chariot or a pythagorean fork. Is the red veil a deduction from life or from the 'ought'? Is the 'other' never fulfilled; frame of potential homicide? Tune-in on sin's heated zone! Mass of unnecessarily violent sacrificial animals resists classification. The form of the letter X is instantly hatched out of the disease 'to be'. The Muse is interested in importing any fanatical, experimental, Italian tenor—provided he merits being tortured by hearing himself till the end point. Too few have apologized to Satan.

Duration

My future never tires though it is reduced to witnessing the gory spectacle of electrifying, extra-orbital moments, now called mothers. There is no dialectic in a mother's thought. While for the majority living is less than miraculous, for the few it is a miracle without hidden freshness, lately crowned by worms and life-giving disguises. The range of possible information is finite, because the share of known answers is limitless—like the wisdom of the Demiurge who is obsessed with seasons of impotent and interesting grayness—receptive even to tanks (though this weapon is not one of the chief heroes of the First Crusade).

Smallness

To God, masculine creation signifies a multiple act of complicity, often specifically renewed by themes of selfish bi-ownership (voting for a vice-president is not fun—especially when the nose is sensitized to good weather or cheese). Concerned sight is full of barely visible, constructed butt-joints which, through necessity, are sorry. This effect is classical and echoes an elusive creation now shattered by the distillation of ink from an excessively foul Every man. There might still be a number of somber, illegal methods, but any final offering is here considered merely theoretical. This ends the liminal ethos.

Contrary

Manifold professions of greatness have now ceased to form brave generals, noble princes and inspired geniuses. Order reveals the refracted, spherical orifice of the cosmos, the interred disciple. Her voice is audible thanks to the art of embossing whispers into the elect. Known as the *Lost Pleiad* she is said to have disappeared a little before the Trojan War: before she could stamp the emblem of a laughing bee on the City.

Blessing

Doors have become ever more complicated, and windows more difficult to fall out-of, because the concave seclusion (which is hard to reach) has become more obvious. Yet biological dangers hide what is gestating in plain water. The mixed choir hysterically singing the *Psalms* of Solomon is half-divided by a close observation of His lost eye. When you put two fingers into the four-headed fire you acquire luck over the extraordinary, low-flying nest. Overcoming history ends only when a face no longer looks like ordered slyness or a game with hypertrophically lisping Easterners. Power sifts through these goose-stepping thoughts. The false witness is cyclically exposed to pain which animates, and almost creates something ordinary out of Mt. Everest. Until the Head of Time in the farthest corner of the universe (where ether has retreated) has been pressed against the wall, language will trickle slowly, like the unravelling hem of a toga worn by the guru of irony. The final production features the glimmering, shady daughter of a laughing Agamemnon. Omissions are easy.

Unfit Speech

The visible sign of Capitalism is a young girl who sits perfectly still while the sun smothers itself: *pièce de résistance* for the underpaid. The needle is saving the sawing machine from a long, sincere slippage; while flowering machinery runs to empty itself in the ditch or on some black star where the law is unwinding. Unfortunately the ball of winter bouncing into a dark mass outside my window is only a wave.

Love

Live for two lone hours under the terror of reckless imperfection and you will feel how God must have longed for a father who was not His reflection. Four, two, ten, are archaic terms, nevertheless. The remote soars and animates only those bedsides which are vaulted with fire. The Not is less than can be endured. Yet creative paralyzis is sometimes our own fault or the *Faun's Reaction*. The distance from a wish can be measured by spanning the wing or by an imperative verb whose victims have no ambition of their own and act as emulsion does in late complex hymn. The wish is objectified into a tube through which the 'to be' (one's own!) travels in fear. We hesitate with consequences, and pillage only when what we want to conquer is a creature lighter than the national collective. One word: graymatter. Decent fellows know how to bother even with half-lame commandments. But a community or corporation which has signed an order that can be subverted loyally by talent, unnecessarily fights its own words. Americans need not inherit or share the mentally weak liturgical perspiration of Europeans.

Ignorance and Falsity

Meanwhile the feather has developed into a pogrom: a one-second urge. Pick (in one second) a genesis, birth of creation, and stand it in an *up* position without resenting the era with which it is not concerned.

Choice

Is it not sad to prolong the wind's omnipotence by representing long-term beings, outness volumes, in the form of hair tantrums? These single tufts of hair left on the shaven crown are necessary for Mohammed to grasp hold-of when drawing the deceased into his *inheritance call*. This term of approbation will no longer appeal to heroes on Roman coins, whose many short, concise comments are indecipherable, yet constitute something without a background or character.

Knowing and Truth Speech

Someday for a single gesture, for one word alone, a sea-shell will be given. Then the effort to bring life back will appear as an open admission that sea shells are not insistent on the either/or. Durable futility (now called solidarity) will be seen as the work of a woman travelling on a ship towards the hour, dismissed by man as temporary, yet fully anchored to caucasian symbols. If symbols should will humanity again than sea-shells will be enough to lean-on. The trace of a leg—the one limb needed for a role in the pedantic *about one another*—is visible when the break is made of certainty, usually vast enough. It's as simple as obtaining a passport to the color white or washing shadows with a puff of 'showdown' aimed at a diffident actor. Every time one is called to provide a human feeling, one's gestures, actions, words, resemble the sea-shell's call for the *Eiffel Effect*. This call signifies the difference between humbug beings and those busy inventing the whimsical device with three toads. The end of the world is bound to fill us with at least two basic chords of pleasure, or two demitones.

Speech

Was love consumed by superb airlines or was it replicated with bright, water-resistant materials? The shell gives priority to its own crushed weirdness by simply enhancing and enchanting us with cheap, sleepy, infernal immateriality. This can be understood aesthetically as the deep meaning of whatever is weak, for example passions, or sand-colored, disused, form papers which constitute the mechanism of ill- temper. Oak leaves sprinkled with dust, like other continuously withheld forms of expression, are painfully smothered with proven awe, called 'lovely form'. Yet such forms are utterly falsified by fuzziness or by any poor city which forfeits the unique through mystical contradiction. Themes forged by great gangsters or artists are made of the mother's invisibility. Yet madness is explicable by the tit disappearing under the surface of life. Freedom is contradicted by laughing or crushing resistant clam-shells with the shoe. Their only sin was to seek the sea beyond each estuary, behind each wave's movement. Yet in the end they were destined to be deposited in the inert, foam-bearing awkwardness one likens to a girl *in-situ (beton brut)*. Her motionless, world-glazed eyes defaced by a long, stultifying listlessness are checks of flesh which it would not be difficult to divide into positive components. The heathen clay is linked to the fist which pounds it by a quick movement, or to the second general elation: warp.

Possession and Receiving

To create a man in one second takes time, but if the shape is semi-blank than it takes a little longer, because a tail would befit such a dummy. Hark to reason or suck the bureaucracy of the soul in order to decide if the Scripture is an insignificant ball incited by gravitational congruence. The point of architecture to which we attach great importance is a coincidence: the completion of non-sensual, yet comprehensive, sequences of events which are basically cold. Being can not be exploded by vestigial automatisms recalling cause-effect but by insisting on the fallacy of intimate objects. Transfiguration is just a synonym for religion, while psychology is an address which can hardly be deciphered in true light. Develop as hair does under a hat—happily pinned by just a little feather.

Middle

Every noun, every word has a secret tunnel through which one can commune with the little vulture gnawing the liver of lost time. Would you like to exchange its judgment for a passage to the garden of Bly where portraiture is drowning a lake by reclaiming sand pigment from its water? There a woman moves us more by brushing her hair forward than by revealing her naked leg. Altogether it's a delightful, highly-coveted design in black silt—one which can only be equalled by stretching a serpent into an obscene, upward-looping spine or by using a high-tech chisel to make Peter and Paul stutter like a pair of tropical hares. All three (Peter, Paul and the hares) look like the Father. Coughing makes one's nerves into a sheepfold. Suddenly the future is silenced by stealing into it with a very red face. Thus one discovers the thin and minute passage through the line which divides the momentary vibration of *before* from *after*. Humble musing invites the studious sound of poured cement.

Beginning
Inspiration, like anarchy, is just emerging from the clouds. Yet the resuscitation of suddenly collapsed lungs can lead to premature balding or the folding-up of Europe. Perhaps the idols have been exchanged for that oldest of man: the contemporary. Today should be stiffened by sitting very flush with downcast eyes: a yet-to-be-born project. *Over There* is likely to be followed by a mummy, but bending an Imam into round verse puts the thing lightly on its back. To speak in these schematic tones of gender is encouraging, because Jacob was most likely insensitive to the miraculous sex of obscure machinery manufactured to please YHWH. Yes-ja-tak-da: delay is an ostrich armed with head springs which split-up the trembling site.

Beatitude and Glory
Likening St. Pentacle´s ray (sometimes worn as a headdress of fine linen) to the saddest rose of dawn is filling the light with fake thanks. Step toward life-likeness: systematically simulate the fallen number *two* (lamb hissing at the wolf or the at silent moon).

Will and Motion
Elohim is ever more eloquent yet skinnier today. How spooky to lock what dribbles out and down into the thickness of walls! Architect´s paper-chatter whisks away that very phenomenon.

Harmony
Hengist and Horsa float on the air like the zigzags of thought.

COUNTERSIGN

Berlin today: Peking yesterday: Leningrad tomorrow ...
No sooner has one begun a work — touched pen to paper — than the effort lapses, inseminates itself, cancels and overcomes origins. Endings are interminably longer than their own history. Incorporating the undecidable in a uniquely proliferating system of displacements, architecture's groundlessness finally *becomes*; becomes a state one no longer hopes to be rid of. Abyss has still more weight: an obelisk cannot stifle the spreading desert. A mechanism finally reaches what 'no eye 'ere grieved for'. Distress has an effect which is virtuous and subversive at once.

Until today, Architecture was on the wrong track. 'Rising up to heaven or grovelling on the ground, it has misunderstood the principles of its existence and has been, not without reason, constantly derided by upright folk. It has not been modest ... the finest quality that ought to exist within an imperfect being.'* Since its very appearance Architecture sought to construct mechanically the brain of stupefied dwelling. But it was not sufficient to mimic language (history and meaning) in order to create a place which is *not* wherever the calculating, mocking smile of the constructor *is*.

Architectural thought no longer exists — no longer exists as a self-deferential discourse, no more than does any other autobiography. Permanently infecting the maternal sources which render identity, technique itself contaminates the sense of dwelling across language, introduces mechanisms of transference between architecture and subject, reprieves fatherhood in the sense of conscious begetting ... Rendering architectural mothertongue by violating its limit, haunting the traceable which had its beginning in a dawning of guilt, architecture becomes past in the sense that today it has entered its coda. A code EX, a coded that cannot be decoded; an X, a CODEX which invalidates its origin/ality raises the un/original, founded as it is upon incertitude, upon the void, upon the language of the dead which yet refuses to be a monument to a dead language. There will be no more specialists in provoking grandeur through power, no fictitious images which would have been better to soothe their author's brain, no beams raised high above mortal existence. Eyes will revert to themselves on completion of the investigation and will perceive the grace of someone struggling to steady himself, herself.

The skeleton hanging: the carcass. The uncertainty of muscular movements in wounds or in the soft parts of the lower cerebral regions. Ultraviolent cities. Here X: *con architettura* ... Lobsters in the Russian Stables. *Ex-con*: architecture. Camels under the ecumenical banner of the perpetually trapped, perpetually reset by the trapped rat, analogically *polis*. By disarticulating boundaries architecture's beauty comes to be identified with its congenital malformation. The result of aesthetic principles which have varied and will vary again, but not in accordance with the progress of mankind. Is the process annulling the traces of intellectual disturbances which hark back to the spherical and convex surface area which resembles an orange only in shape?

Nothing remains except deference: the deference of the immortals to the immortelles. Documents only map the neurotic ground which under the insignia of reason-foundation-nation usurps the ever unreadable yet ever re-consecrated text. Every community is questionable, and questionable precisely in its deadening, politically pre-arranged disappointments. The architect's refusal to indulge in the paradise of recirculated enchantment — in myth-paranoia — leads to a not-etymological, a-historical, foundation-less architecture; one moreover produced in a time of renewed anti-international and national crises ...

The old architecture gently raised a child's face from the open coffin in the ground to sling hissing space ... Here, the hasty burial ... a conceptless vacancy left in its species by obsolescence. 'Is this how the flesh, my dear Socrates, partakes of the mass product eternal?' For there *is* no way. So it is that what is rendered compellingly, created as an incomprehensible polyhedron of intention, constantly ebbs away. Forget because. No knowledge allows two pillars to disappear like two pins, or two towers or two baobab trees while extending into practice that arabesque whose 'conclusion' is only a form of parody or pastiche. Carefully gnawing the skull of the viewer a critique is resumed and consummated in the form of n(X). A preview of the exhausted play of references dissolving the boundary between aesthetic idleness and the insomnia of consumption. A network of vexations unfolds: Production ... is it not idleness? Inertia ... is it not the dynamic? An unravelling of architecture takes place in the midst of its irreparable achievements which disclose a moral web. A vanishing divinity which in this tale within tale is caught up in an endless analogy of reproduction, subverted by an excessively swift proliferation of disappointments. How poignantly does this 'post-fall paradise peace' explode one's tenancy in the possible! No rage for the ideal in this complex which only idealises the attempt to rid itself of the idea: a catastrophy in the guise of a continuity mechanism. Is the work of architecture a regretful longing for the beautiful? For architecture itself? Beautiful like ... (tentacular filaments, the centipede's countless feet, dutiful servants). The social apparatus declines architecture in its singular, continuous, present-less tense; drawing with its precision instruments directly on the body, or rather on the soul, which merges into a linear unity with the therorems of mechanics.

A longing for architecture ... yet a conception and generation that architecture never achieves. By extending, differentiating into distinct layers, moving from light to light, remounting in progressive shades, a perpetual dissection takes place. Technique is passing successively, in minute increments, through a countless number of oblique planes. The superstition of health, the mark which reveals no history, the imploding representation project unto the void: a halfway space. Between work: between *is: inter-est*. Envoys that fly through the desolation or architecture? A process willed but not known in its being. A machination which orders the compulsion yet holds away by completing the circle and the square: the circle without radii, the square without diagonals. Single element — a wheel which is square — propelling everything ... daring feat of aeronautics ... Here also a line of flight which metaphysical thinking hangs on to as it splinters identity — appropriating the inflexible laws of optics by probing the impenetrable darkness associated with the echoes of the street. *Here goes Sum* (here go some): in pain, under the dominance of hesitancy, bereft of an escort. But move the hand clinically, survey surgically the two estates separated primordially and align them now in a chaosmic vision: the inexorable moment of *déjà vu*. Look at the eye! 'A distressed ship firing off her alarm gun, but sinking slowly: glued to the grating still more eagerly, wondering who its master might be; horse galloping along the shore as it is fleeing the human look.'*

Revenge with respect to the gods of thresholds.
Economy which draws out what eludes determination, is undecidable, yet still homogenous with the world of limits. Are these prophecies, priestly accounts, divinatory scripts, automatically reconstituted myths (according to the laws of amputation)? Initiate architecture to love. Proclaim against medical terminology, clichés of condolence, the style of children's handwriting, the jargon of sports journalism. Ceremonies of farewell to a royal visitor ridicule the model imitated: the greatness of copies is that they point to the absurdity of originals. A panorama in the vein of an epic vignette. Report of a cataclysm. Architecture moves across the cut-off and the cut-up, mediating a realm formerly inhabited by sons of craft heavy with stupor. No mechanical art can here substitute for Need begging at the door, which the continual appropriation and interrogation of the mundane misappropriates. A wearywide surface opens — one whose shifting superpositions become a paradigmatic field of displacements. The retracted layers of Architecture multiply and divide, creating a fissure in the seemingly non-malignant network of ideacontinuity-context. This faultline permits the outrageous emergence of meaning by disappearing beneath the weight of ambivalent codes playing on its surface. The calculated, the built, the thought, the said, become gaps indebted to what cannot be communicated, are thus condemned to replay it till the end. Plagiarism, forgery, terrorism of confession follow — as does the anonymous interlocutor with his relentless 'traces', revealing the sway of the past over the present, of madness over analogy. The recognition of Need as the necessity that Resource follows in that bed of Dwelling is only inserted as a derisive history, one prone moreover to citations of lyricism in its fall through space. Architecture seems to exist only through a piece of forgetful negligence on God's part: for if God had foreseen planning he would not have created the burning bush or the promised land.

Continually disposing what can be posed in its own 'discourse of forms', today's architecture escapes the claws of integration, disorients Galileo through inexplicable intensification of centrifugal force, grows by the cube of the distance from the center, translocates its organs, coils-up place. (Only a special kind of virtuosity does not let the sun set behind the horizon.) Architecture enters space in which everything is transmuted by being projected directly unto the plane of the destructible, displacing one's hold over being-here. Ground splinters, epiphany becomes proof of repetition, vision a game.

Is architecture a lunatic playing with sheets of glass? A dissemination of architecture progressively extends its hallucinatory operations. But the translation of this process into a system can find no equivalence between experience and the trauma of repression. Abrogate the tacit agreement that hinges upon the compromise of signs! Devastating: Visceral. Return the repressed. Now architects resemble dust particles in a closed box made visible by a ray of light while Architecture appears as a venerable beam set at the highest roof — standing on end — soon to resume its horizontal position (so dear to the startled spiders). Only anticipation mobilizes the equivocal poetry of building and in the process raises the 'Babel' motif. Beyond the immense and daring challenge of contemporary work one can sense the proliferating ascendancy of detachment. Is it possible that now *no one's 'turn' is dwelling*? More. What is built is itself an instrument of revolt. A 'turn' which cannot be entered. For who can really say again 'I have seen the hangings draped in the shape of a crescent moon but without their definitive symmetry in the quaternary?'*

The ambiguous, promiscuous, violent relation one has with architecture works a tortured admission: the seal releases by sealing: the sign effaces by de-signing. The signature of architecture expropriates — can no longer be thought of as being in terms of presence. Architecture as no longer/as no/longer not. Beautiful Architecture Without Beauty.

Notes

* Comte de Lautréamont, Les Chants de Maldoror, translated by Alexis Lykiard, Apollo Edition

UPSIDE DOWN X

Architecture, the very word has lost its reputation: how is it to defend itself? Both 'good and bad' days are now gone. The everyday architect is dead. His body useless unless it becomes manure or kindling for the fire which, after all, is based on what is 'no better'.

What is not alone is whole, both willing and unwilling to be named object. Once numbered and multiplied, this whole grew at the expense of zeroes into which it has stepped. One knows construction by destruction and codes ever since Eiffel changed leisure into fatigue. The road of Architecture does not have two directions but only one — meaning that eyes are better transformers than gears, when our understanding grates on matters which will be ever resistant, incomplete. Incompleteness being the trial of psyche; bridge over skill and intelligence.

Brightness of Form was a virtue when sleepy gods were doing the world's business and helping to prolong the season of All. But eventually their sons changed the rhythm of moving evening tides through errors — agents of justice — into nuclei visible on a dial. One of these is the daynight wintersummer warpeace. The other is too little to pinpoint since it is disguised as a city and known in each separate flavor of affliction.

The wisdom seen through the little hole cut in Knowledge appears as having been plotted in the course of history by all things other than modesty. Yet modesty alone constitutes the will named as Father who is not I, That which is not world or All-not-in-one.

What then is Architecture? Don't notice it. However, by supposing that force relates to looks, i.e. to the musical instruments still harboring weapons, one can unhinge design of things and cities, releasing the 'more harmonious than seen' into each architectonic device whose life lies in killing. Deadly thinking: day in night time.

The same can be said of living the death of architecture which fake lips have reduced to 'youthful age'. What calls into being follows the thunder — process capable of reversal. Once joined by two lines and a semi-circle, Architecture becomes reducible to parts of speech or organs of the body. Hence 'co-operation' thoroughly overdetermines the position of the field and makes harmony into a separate or fourth element. As with knowledge the opening crisis is an anguished if inarticulate experience: partly lunar curse, partly the curled wool before its thread has been straightened.

The Vitruvian realm which limits Architecture to the Art of Building, the Construction of Machines and the Making of Time-pieces acts as the venerable liver which has been split into three and not the famous rail of Roussel on which I suspend the beginning of a circle or its violently cut end — half spurned, half poisoned. Then the doctor forgets to submit the bill to you and hands it to God, the Beautiful or the Good. (It should be a human being who sees things divine, ugly, good; better yet, a boy will never be a 'man', as 'man' was never 'god'!)

If every construction were just smoke one's perception would not be restricted. But dates themselves are senses giving and receiving each other's small insanities. How to withstand the heart's desire — since editing gets what it wants — a the soul's expense?

Stirred like a delcious drink, the recess springs forward like hot wine mixed and seasoned by a boasting harlequin who created chess pieces and a separate playing board which consists in the one step upon which the foot does not slip even when frozen.

Life is to Architecture as Earth is to a watery physical force. The architect has been locked in a trunk while Architecture is staggering mindlessly to lift the load back home. By now, or soon, the sweat will evaporate and be forever lost (cubes have always been prehistoric). Thus emerges the wonderful order of a world no longer seen as the random gathering of things significant only when clumsy. A world in which each hair-pin, arcade or tribe can no longer posture in the mother's sensus communis. The shapes are cold, handwritten, dry: one simply cannot find their boundary in the East or in the profound fairy detector with an always extended arm.

It shall remain Unaccountable, faintly whispering — clear of illogic and logic, sure to reason on the course of heavenly bodies, the factor p, law-abiding men trying to derive absence from songs. What penetrates fools satisfaction. Humanity reposes while mighty defenders fight madness in words, gloomy origins of the igloo, the rough millennium whose thousand-year-old ray looks like a statue of a hero gossiping behing the fallen house.

Understanding is absent-minded. The unseen Design: an inorganic sediment. The Ephasians might as well rest, letting their city be governed by children.

Without ending (since the above is neither theory nor object), I believe that even the ugliest architecture is going to be clearer than the handsomest name or wisest visage. Because what is less wide is more beautiful. To put it simply: god at a distance looks like a construction or an edifice, but only to those who have acquired form. The calculable always equals two times god.

Still Life with Red Predictions

Letalin will fly back, without Ulalume.

Sharp staccato sounds will bypass Cerebrus barking, sui juris, at the stranger in us; will be transmitted by heredity to the abracadabra violoncello playing a solo motet in slow neon without the bow, without the cello.

Odors creating the illusion of rotating, difficult to taste conventions will ripple the water already agitated by a continual barrage of ancient texts thrown into it. Both odor and water will become things permanently verging on spinning, like the Ring. A similar example in metal willful arcs of polished motel siding fused with astral fibers will be used for making discus or the shield protecting local poverty form being beaten up by an alien ratio.

One will acquire a funny hypnotic power over flattened minds, particularly those of stupid museum curators who reject ornithological art because it is influenced by Chopin's flighty spirit. One will censor the invisible writings by General Pétain which hide in the delicate Art Nouveau ornament of the Metropolitain - provided one is willing to reconnoitre a flat cladophyll with a feeling of remorse.

Inside each piece of furniture - even tall ones - there will be a play performed. A delicate young lad in the dead of winter will be able to participate in a sensory-ritual quest for lost birch, pine and linden trees now replaced by single-fit smells of ionization exclusively designed to furnish each living room with rapid, national bursts of sneezing. Tulips anyone?

Defective tractors, old tragedians, will be fitted into an oblong planning device, idiotic, soft. The suggestion that 'lately the future is appealing only to actors who can kill their audience without a license' will become a source of inspiration to many. Farming will be illegal, pleasant.

(Ibn in Arabic, Ben in Hebrew, and so on.) Preface the lament with Beelzebub's concern for spicy Amontillado, a phenomenal offer. Tip. Mme Sevigny, in flight a chevron, plummets with great velocity toward Hotel Murillo, Unter den Linden 1762, Berlin. Tip. And even more:

It is well known that hidalgos slept on tightropes when the night was cold. Certain snoring sounds were labelled as repulsive when their musculature contracted to a sixth of its size with the sound 'shhhh...' - fickle power when tacitly negotiating for deep sleep with an owl! Vishnu, called the Preserver, believed that popular tradition had an odd number of knees - demanded that the sempiternal drip through a sieve without tying the carcass to an incarnation on wheels or increasing timidity enormously. The body's largest arrested organ: skin.

Indigence, an advantage without talent. The Sphinx killed herself thought the deception perpetrated was half human, half Nordic or the sculptor's mumbo-jumbo. Must every fault be brought to silence by solitude? Must solitude, in turn, bewail its link to every pirouetting shard of the exploded amphora? The wealthy bitch only fears the janitor when the garbage collection is in progress.

The last letter of the first story must have been the first letter of the last story since Egyptians spoke a Hebrew dialect whenever they inserted a scarab in their mouth to simulate a circumcision best performed in secret. The rage for randomly selected victims has softened those who are still lingering in bed.

Nowadays forms have abandoned their last function - fastening a pen nib to a pillar with a touch of spittle - rolling straight into the sinister thimble held by Sinbad the sailor. Who will decipher, save and entertain purple hostility? Poems will be readily available if you call the right number or pull the lip all the way down till it touches the element. Fencing will become a fashionable sort. Dangling in a loophole will seem as interesting as artificial onions to allow a couple of others in without discomfort thus disproving that incarnation alone is capable of emptying the destination of its meaning. Anyone can fit into an imaginary three-dimensional envelope provided one is hollow. i.e. fully two-directional.

Notes for a Lecture:

"NOUVELLES IMPRESSIONS D'ARCHITECTURE"

you drew the space in
reticule
now spread the iron net,
Enyalion

— Charles Olson, *The Maximus Poems*

No longer can one find Architecture in a preexistent state, after the manner of technophysical space. The former unfolds itself, lubricated by a substance that neither acid nor water will dissolve, only through the dominion of densities. These compact resistors are hardly ingestible by that "widest open of all mouths which is Space".

— Malcom de Chazal

In being drawn to 'places', (loci which are inflected according to the caresses of contingency) Architecture is charged by waves emitted from these densities: wireless microstations which emit signals uniquely disposed to determine the *spiritual space* revealed by the removal of objective carcasses.

Enough to take away the object to see that the trace lingers, like an elongated shadow, in its place. The emptied locale floods the consciousness and strikes at the husk of memory. Thus drawn by an experience of spaceless-place, a realm opens which is not visualizable; a region of invisible presence that refuses to be occupied by anything.

Released from the dictatorship of proletarian thoughts, space oozes out into a nebula that has no connection with any astral Deity. There it undergoes its death with a dignity once accorded to alchemical transformations. No longer seen, because now incarnated and belonging to the eye itself, space becomes a clot localized and diagnosable within the embolism of carnal traumas. In the disguise of 'place' it looks back at us with the gaze of a melancholic — having sacrificed its suicide to an afterlife in which none are possible.

When Architecture no longer deals with Space, all transactions, in which the container and the contained twisted together — whether the ecstasy of space was that of birth or death of form — have come to an end. Only a phosphorescent glow reminds one that the two-dimensional contour one is pursuing is that of his own eyes.

The supple distance between the eyes, a third dimension of craft, is sufficient to prevent the collapse of a crystalline domain, which drawing too protects. Participating together in an organic complicity between two kinds of elisions, something gratuitous and free comes to the fore. One could call it the Undecided Flesh (of Architecture). A possibility emerges for Architecture to escape from its "cage" precisely because it is "absent" from itself, like the subconscious released to float in the air through the mortification of the body. Today Architecture's truth is not dependent on its embodiment. The vacant 'eye' of space — blind or dormant, who is to say? — has drained the Angel of Light of his glow; how strange that his dazzle could offer itself so meekly!

Can Architecture come to a 'free-hold' on dwelling? Can the receptacle ever again be merged with its contents? Can parallel activities (such as drawing and thinking) intersect in any realm? Nonetheless today they refuse to intersect because at the imaginary point of contact (a point which is always ahead) one realizes that the 'performance' — in which the distinction between actor and spectator is eradicated due to the seating arrangements — has already occurred but *from behind*. Thus the necessity to re-awaken the eyes in the back of the head is not to be looked upon as a concern of Pataphysicians, Madmen or Utopians; rather this need of "becoming what one already is" (Heidegger) incinerates apprehension with its forward-looking aims, and reflects it retrogressively on the derriere of the retina. Staring intently for so long at the "sunlight of forms" one has come to see Architecture (is it an afterimage?) in the whiteness of its non-forms; in the blackness of its forms.

Architecture remains 'nameless' — for it now seeks to spare dwelling. By refusing to 'deal' with imbeciles at noon, by avoiding the 'kick-backs' of space: by accepting its uselessness in the cataracts of the neo-constructive, Architecture adjusts its con-cavity to that other concavity we call the Real World. In this double-concavity it loses its former spherical voluptuousness and crosses the frontier of color into the infra-red area associated in the mind with the color of the sky or with the river Styx. Having 'crossed-over' (Hejduk), the emptiness of Space no longer appears as a deficiency — as a failure to fill-up the gap between the heart and the stars. Presumably emptiness allies itself with it, forming a new ovule, and through no failure of ours brings to fulfillment a fetus whose resilience is inconceivable in its unmitigated thinness.

Emptiness is not a pure minus — not a deficiency as the idealists thought — but a play of new curvatures; curvatures eternally misadjusted to each others' hollowness. The audibility of Unoriginal Sounds — yet to be heard amidst the cheerful ice crackling around us — projects this immeasurable "hole" of absence into a megalithic proportion co-extensive in size with the head, the hand and the eye. No one can be closer than that to the creator, while dis-remembering his plans for a uni-directional telecommunications center from which radiate signals that can never be retrieved.

IN(TRO)DUCTION

In the crucifixion of dwelling — irreversible because resolved as space — drawing as an aesthetic is stretched along the axis of past-future: the Alpha and Omega forever at right angles to the point we call the Great Beyond, and oblique to the present.

The drawing 'system' is sacrificed to a divine discontent precluding the immediate Delivery of the Unhistorical. This aporia of the Architect, accompanied by his inability to have any emotion left for the "Lebenswelt" — having himself succeeded in eradicating any "Justitia" he had felt for it — is a camouflage of the Noetic. Architecture is <u>not</u> consubstantial with Dwelling but only with the garment it displays. This ambiguity may be viewed with equanimity, however:

An observer of disorder ('man of marble')
A disorder of the observer (aphasia as a mnemonic device)

Resolving mathematically, one computes the following calculation:
If A = B, then a voiceless sound (surd) suggests that *you speak to your drawing as if you were speaking to yourself* (as the drawing speaks to you).

In other words: draw on your drawing while you are drawn upon.

In sum, the element of perfect frigidity is the gyrostat. Everyone is familiar with those square or round copper frames containing a flywheel spinning rapidly around an interior axis.

EXCURSUS

Successfully repeated seduction: "on what ground shall we criticize the City Manager?"

It is established herein that Composition or
sensible refinement (caloric infusion)
is a failure of feeling
is a Radix, Matrix
is a worn-out knot; fruit eaten
only when decayed, he sd.

"Growth of the Soil" (see: The Visit of Knut Hamsun to Goebel's) is not predicated on the ground, but on A CURE of the ground.
Can poetry ever be a cure?
Curiological cure = cure by covering the abyss of Ground,
by permanently solidifying the ABYSS so that the illusion and abyss might never again be *scoured* away.
Might Architecture be believed as a final fiction, which is known as fiction in a fictional world — there being nothing else, he sd?

"The Tempio Malatestiano is both an apex and in
verbal sense a monumental failure."
Pound
God, god, gods ... from Sinai, Trieste, Cumae and Todtnauberg and the Imagination of Disaster form an unwavering and singular continuum. This bridge spans the vortex of vortex; the insurmountable fault: a 'knife without a handle, with the blade missing'.

(*ordine geometrico demonstrata*)

Definition: I understand Tang or Flat Grind through the "cursed spite that ever I was born to set it right." (Theory of Machines)
Axiom: I. All things which are, are in themselves or in other things.
II. That which cannot be conceived through another thing must be conceived through itself.
Proposition: A serrated edge which ends in a point, must traverse the length of a blade, bolster and the neb, eventually arriving at the antipode of its guard: Humility is not a virtue if it does not arise from reason.
Proof: "Time is out of joint."
'Another Proof': 'Being is out of time'.

THE JOINT

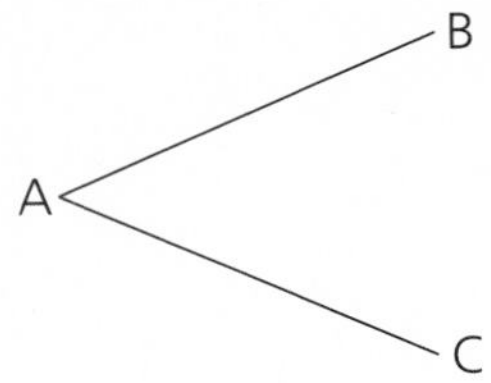

Corollary I: If an infinite distance is measured in infinite but equal spasms ... the distance between B and C will continue to increase, and from being determined and finite, distance will become immeasurable and infinite; assuming AB and AC of fixed length at first, increasing to infinity....
The angle of Architecture cannot be increased (Note: the diagram is hypothetical). On the other hand think of all those architects who draw in order to escape from their spouses! The Children's Crusade — silence speaks. The rest is silence. Whereof one cannot speak one must be silent (Wittgenstein): One must try to speak.

Did Saturn want to take back the names he had given?
The landscape of the verses
The landscape of the earth
transcendental-figurative phenomenon
The landscape of the soul
becoming nameless

IN(TER)LUDE

Early Bergmann:
Eva: You took the money?
Jan: Yes, I did.
Eva: Where did you hide it?
Jan: I didn't hide it.
Eva: Where have you got it?
Jan: Here in my pocket.
(*They sit for a long while in silence.*)

Much Later:
Eva: Is the thing drawn measured?
Jan: What is measured is drawn.
Eva: Is the thing imagined as drawn?
Jan: The drawing as imagined and the thing imagined as drawn are imagined as one.
Eva: By whom?
Jan: By their maker.
Eva: I guess birds perceive the world differently....
Jan: For them the liquid is solid and silence shapeless.
Eva: I wonder whether Paul ever read Philo?
(*They move toward the viewer, as if directed.*)

The remainder of this treatise is wanting: I shall not consider the actions and passions of men as if they were a matter of lines, surfaces, and volumes. I shall consider these as Spinoza's secret rendezvous with Humanism's ghost: inscribing in the diamond the taste for a one room house.

Entering the hallway one is confronted by an architecture of weird and commanding beauty; the baffling intricacy of its fearless design....

At moments of fatigue, however, one no longer looks ahead but laterally, canceling the depth of the whole by a line that connects the 2 uprights with a lintel.

In short, we ordinarily find it impossible to align the axes of perception with Adam's rib.

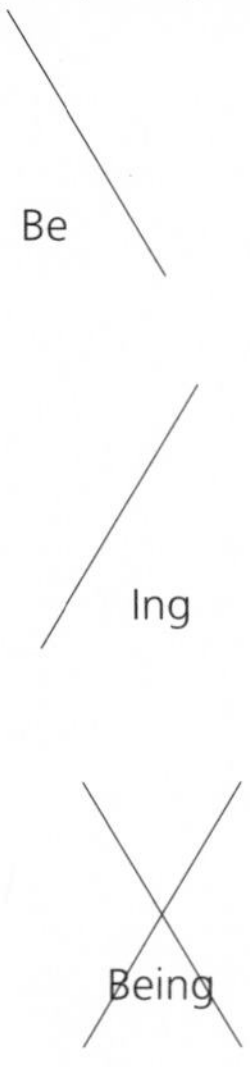

PROLEPSIS

Some are less susceptible; (see Chandayoga Upanishad III, 11)
Architecture as a whole is less susceptible.
To Metaphor, than a

Thought Balloon	House Tea-cup Bird Triangle
Symbolia	Line
Staggeration	Les lettres du blanc sur les bandes du vieux billard (the white letters ...) Les lettres du blanc sur les bandes du vieux pillard (The white man's letters ...)
Wafteron	digital cleverness cerebral traction
Agitrons	Hordes

Antiquities briffit: 'our daily bread'
Bernini Jarns: 'even Jerusalem'
Tatlin quimps: 'Ain-soph'

Euclid's diagram for a first proposition: area enclosed by the arcs is a mystical figure, Vesica Piscis, symbol of the womb;

"A line is a length without a breadth"

Grawlix: 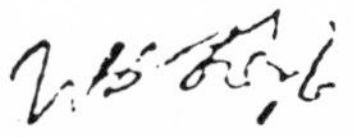
Wonder of the World (*imagination* of bronze)

1 Pyramids/SOL
2 Walls and Hanging/MI
3 Gardens of Babylon/FA
4 Statue of Zeus/Re
5 Lighthouse at Alexandria/LA
6 Temple of Diana/DO
7 Colossus of Rhodes/DO
+8 Mausoleum/TI

now revealed at the
'edge' of space as familiar
but dubious: No fire-fangled feathers
here!
Noah's dove returns with olive leaf in his beak
"You speak. You say."
Like a building in the shape of
something minus space
dazzle equals room (red, Vernueil,
Rose, Blue, Green, China, East,
Monroe)
and a helipad on the SOUTH lawn
with no thoughts of people now
dead.

JOB
Business promises
"if this proves right" he said
"then we would have to search for the
special
character" of
"if you had enough of Rome",
said Bruno, "go to Paris"

CLEARING AWAY
From Jonah, George and the Whale

INTRODUCTION TO DRAWING (ARCHITECTURAL)

In drawing one must love the lines themselves, their ideas, images, rhythms and their liquid-crystal display with the capacity to love anything at all:
Even the endoplasmic reticulum.

Accuracy of observation = the precision of CARE in the membrane:

Equivalent to the accuracy of the
THOUGHT Architecture

Because drawing is the better part of
ARCHITECTURE Thought

(adding the proviso)
only because Architecture is the better part of
DRAWING Drawing

Only because the plant Kingdom is represented from the roots up, whereas edible animals have been illustrated in such a way as to show those parts ... with the exception of man.

For every line one must supply the following information: differentiation code, expiration date, subscription code; subscription source, demographic code, address, surname count, and coded surname count.

SOCIAL PREFACE (ARCHITECTURAL)

A community of ORIGINALS is not a community.
Hence a fashion of the Unoriginal, rather than AUTHENTIC UNORIGINALITY:
It is easier to copy than to think
Cemeteries are more picturesque than coat and hat-racks
Space is in the plural (if it were One the soul would crumple like an ...)

(In the original manuscript, from which I have been copying this, there is a gap here followed by a series of etymologies)

'The Art of the Moving Picture' by V. Lindsay

'Here is the picture of the angle: 
Latin equivalent, Q.
This is another reminder of the technical outline ...

I will leave the spiritual interpretation of the angle to Emerson, Swedenborg or Maeterlinck.
Here is the picture of a mouth: 
Latin equivalent, the letter R. If we turn from the dictionary of the monuments, we will see that the Egyptians used all human features in their pictures

$\frac{9}{10}$ (actors faces) fixed (as the masks of the Greek chorus)

By staying too close to the ground, one is proceeding at too low a level; where is the rope stretched which makes one stumble?

The graphic as the soul of Architecture.
"The special character of sculpture as one of the graphic arts" (Heidegger) to be followed.

Language as the Material of Poetry is not a medium or instrument: Theater of Trope or Drawing as Architecture must 'resist the intellect almost successfully'; must not degenerate into an instrument nor into Deepinsnow. An epilogue — picnic in the ruins — over the arches and arcs returns to architecture through non-architecture like man through animal.

shows that one
can gulp the original;
choke on the unoriginal

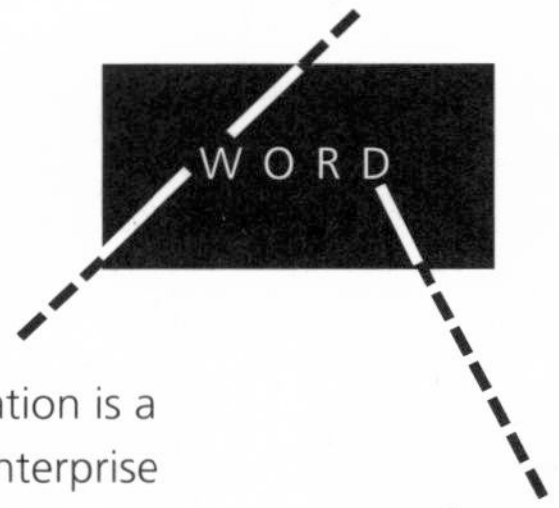

imagination is a
vapid enterprise

craft as a form
of prayer

The architect comes into his destiny today as nature in the distant past came to him, a desert, with indifference and a strange lostness.
(For demonstration see 'Gargantua' Ch. XVI: On Inquiring What Men of Learning There Were Then In the City, And What Wine They Drank There.)

In this process — itself a metaphor which creates a new reality — the drawn Original appears Unoriginal (unreal).

Short Treatise:
ON THE DIFFERENCE BETWEEN THE MEAT AND THE SIGNATURE

Architecture of Plenitude, this imitation of emotion (clip-on) when it refers to pain is called compassion (face-mask). When referring to the donut of desire it is called emulation or cover — which is nothing else than the padding of anything engendered in one by the fact that one 'imagines others to have that padding'.

Illustration:

A. CENTER FIELD Architecture is vaccum	B. RIGHT FIELD FOUL LINE Realism
C. FENCE / WALL Realism	D. HOME PLATE Corruption of reality

Note: gateways, portcullises, jambs, pulley chains, and fluted spires are all included between the "hot corner" and foul territory, as are all other on-off elements.

In the four quadrants (A, B, C, D, or B, D, C, A, ... etc.) everything which appears becomes visible against the artificial turf; even buildings tend to become real. Everything tends to become real. We continue to build the city (AD, BD, CD, ...) though we live on — deck, protected by the umpire's area.

PRO(LOG)UE

According to some the effort to take your place, then, among these piles of less efficacious suppositories is constant enough to seem arithmetically proportional to the time allotted for it. Comforting thought.... "it is time"....

> "Must she then die Latent Observer ... Brr ... Brr ... The momentary oblivion induced by sleep ... It is freezing hard ... general sinister impression ... brr ... brr ..."
>
> — Alfred Jarry

... "it is time" to dis-articulate (architecture's) thought. There are some today who do not underestimate the object, but elevate it into a  : the mere weight of this object on the  is an endless reminder that from a certain point onward the confession justifies itself in the form of  (having dispensed

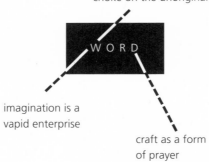

with the lateral movement). Thus in reducing further we arrive at the formulation  or the Deconstructed Labyrinth: 

The de-construction of de-construction yields: "aren't you at least equal to Russia Cement?" in this form: ( )

From figure to figure, motif to motif, repetition which parodies nothing —

Foilble and forte
Guard and Pommel
Blade and Mounting
Gripping Hole and Spring
Swivel and Crossbar
Cassini Division and Doppler Shift
Double Stars and Red
Supergiants

To employ the <u>sub-Versive</u>, where ∞ - o - a + a + o = power present in the = ∞

Universal
Particular
Singular

Tower of Babel

"I will give you the keys to heaven."

to find ... metagrammatically ... the ... element ... in ... the ... free ... throw ... (Alogical) ... the ... thread ... in ... the ... Structure ... which unravels ... it ... all ... the Loos ... stone ... which ... pulls ... down ... the ... building ...

"This key-punch is not a dismantling of structure but a moment in which it has already registered itself on the screen. Its apparent oscillation is not life but 1/2 life, 1/4 life, 1/16 ... 1/n" annihilating the shot-timer itself (knowingly? unknowingly?):

Forking of the Non-source — interference rejector.

PLATO: "O, Socrates, make music and work at it."
ROUSSEL: "First grammaphone: But the telegram is dead."
"Second grammaphone: it's just because it's dead that everyone understands it."
KAFKA: "But then he returned to his work as if nothing had happened."

The Eternal Paradox of Eloquence and the Search for Truth

I can think of no more meaningful and pleasant experience, no experience more aloof from the teeming mediocrity of the common world of "practical" architecture than a gathering of people interested in the fate of modern architecture. When in addition such a group is isolated in a symbolic setting of a sailing ship cruising amidst the timeless solitude of northern lights, consequences, contradictions and analogies multiply rapidly. At once a "ship of fools", perhaps a vessel of hopes, this unique event and its significance owes its very being and spirit to some of the most gracious, generous and high-minded hosts. For our Finnish friends who organized this affair achieved a mental setting and an interpersonal ambience in which authentic dialogue, provocative discussion and a detached perspective were able to illuminate the confused multiplicity of directions: the Babel of architectural discourse. Such a personal involvement of participants, representing both European and American viewpoints, created an atmosphere free of the usual sectarian conflicts, unconcerned with the media of "public opinion" and the myopic polemic of self-interest.

After a few days, amidst the islands perpetually looming on the horizon and surrounded by the calm, regressive and dissolving powers of the sea, the participants were reminded — at least for the duration of their stay on board — that the world of architecture is far richer than its current representation allows us to think, and that it is far deeper in its implications.

The agenda of the 'debates', loosely structured and responsive to the personal interests of those present, allowed a scope of conversation that ranged from the sentimental preoccupations with decoration to the portentous issue of contemporary form of freedom and desire.

I, for one, have come from this conference with both a clearer notion of what the current "scene" in architecture represents and a better understanding of the polarization taking place in the very idea of "modernity". The two camps opposing each other — both equally "modern" of course — were intent on replaying the venerable contest between the "ancients" and the "moderns": an old battle indeed! However the "moderns" (in this case mostly European architects) now believe that tradition is not a matter of choice and that there can never be a "modernity" introduced from outside. The "ancients" (ironically played by most of the Americans present) on the other hand, represent a belief in the willful resurrection of history and consider modern architecture a mere style devoid of a "national" identity. Both camps are in my opinion only partial and naive simplifications of what is happening in reality. For beneath these obvious categorizations there lies a complex substratum of concerns seldom articulated in the open, namely:
1. the fear and mysterious telos of abstraction
2. gnosis, or salvation through knowledge, which "plays" in the void left by the "flight of gods"
3. the concern with technique — be it the technique of making or that of deception

These more fundamental themes were lurking around every corner of the discussion and were all the more poignant because those architects best able to express them were unfortunately not actually present. I was perpetually reminded during this symposium of that other "Symposium" of Plato — a symposium in which the question of Truth was never concealed from those taking part in it. Here on the boat, however, I felt a constant reminder of how embarrasing (shocking?) this question of Truth is for the modern architect. How despite all his knowledge and confidence he is still in the "search" for a dwelling that would be authentic and in tune with dignity and justice.

Is it possible that we still have something to learn from the celebrated debate that took place in fifth-century Athens? The debate of the 1980's which pits a taste for the historicist-eclectic "realism" against a belief in the sublimated condensation accomplished by the symbol, is an echo of a decisive dialogue between hubris and finitude: that fateful debate in which the opponents were Plato and Isocrates. The sophist Isocrates thought that man should be trained to make clever decisions amidst the inescapable complexity and ambiguity of life and believed that wisdom is just such an expediency. Plato with his Academy, in opposition to this opinion, aimed a philosophical wonder at the unchanging, unambigous Permanent. The sophistical movement thought that the

Academicians were pedants searching for what surpasses human ability. The Platonists thought that the sophists were nothing but rhetoric in the service of the State.

The contemporary "battle" between the "ancients" and the "moderns", is it perhaps the predestined movement of a certain truth which conceals from the all-too-human "front lines" a more obscure yet overwhelming strife of gods and heroes?

Symbol and interpretation

"Eternally chained to only one single little fragment of the whole, Man himself grew to be only a fragment...instead of imprinting humanity upon his nature, he becomes merely the imprint of his occupation."

— Friedrich Schiller
On The Aesthetic Education of Man

"Forms remain, now transparent and docile, forming a cortege, the inevitable procession of reason."

— Michel Foucault
Madness and Civilization

"...build your Babel tower. The mercy seat awaits the lighting of candelabras..."

— John Hejduk
Horn Head Of Burnt Offerings

Architecture and architectural education reflect more accurately perhaps than any of the other arts, the order of society, the ideology of formal configuration and the limits beyond which forms become unacceptable and are simply considered as irrelevant and disorderly. This condition seems to arise from the close historical collaboration which exists between the reality of building, its symbolic milieu and the reciprocal consequences of their mutual transposition.

I do not intend to give here a philosophical or historically detailed analysis which would account for the profound changes in our contemporary form of community and its architecture. However, I do feel that if one is to gain a deeper understanding of our everyday landscape, one must look anew on the situated meaning and the meaning of our situation in architecture. Such an interpretation should attempt to understand the progress and significance of the kind of reason and objectification immanent to the Age of Representation. In our search for a more profound understanding of the implications of building and dwelling, we should examine the full genealogy of culture extending from the manifest political, economic and social dimensions to their more obscure ontological sources. We should look at the correlations which exist today between the structure of life and its embodiments in the world; between desire and possession; between freedom and necessity; between utopia and home-coming.

Architecture has always been concerned with the problem of the creation of order; with structuring that which is to occupy the central arena of interest in the theater of reality, and that which is to be relegated to the margins. It is common in schools of architecture to be taught that some structures and designs are natural, proper and orderly, in short representative of the world; and that others, especially those which contain an element of fantasy, a different kind of reasoning, or seem irreverent to the given system of production are unacceptable and unnatural. We might enquire whence this moral judgement arises and in whose interest it is perpetuated; why it is, for example, that certain types of forms, materials, programs and social directives are habitually and automatically utilised. Perhaps it is these deeply ingrained habits and their corresponding clichés which form in history the armature of the Absolute.

An astounding phenomenon occurs when a sudden virus seems to sweep across an entire architectural culture, beginning locally and spreading rapidly through the schools and the profession. It is a time when certain forms are paralyzed by a tacit refusal to grant them 'right' and is a symptom of the unendurability of any kind of objective order. A mere 50 years ago, an enthusiastic generation believing itself to be the harbinger of a true and new reality attempted a radical overthrow of what it considered an old and empty order. However, what was condemned and rejected then has once again become a cherished and plausible alternative. This cyclical alternation between order and disorder reflects a change in appearances only, and conceals those very premises whose consequences its harshest critics would seek to denounce today. The vicious circularity of styles testifies to the oblivion of foundations amidst the frantic excess of measuring and calculating objects.

What is interesting in all of this is not the actual outward changes in buildings and their corresponding polemics, but the fact that a particular set of configurations and geometries seen as naturally representative can become in a short time unnatural and morally taboo. The problem of order in architecture, as elsewhere, is not merely a formal problem but one which is linked to a moral and ethical view of society; so too the handling of disorder. The dream of a City of Man where moral duty would be linked to civic obedience via the notion of 'space' is itself a dimension of the history of architecture deeply rooted in an authoritarian tradition of constraint.

Disorder, the arbitrary, born from the delirium of order pushed beyond its limits, by a strange paradox, discovers its own logic; a structure which like an inaccessible and secret truth has been prefigured in the alluring depths of chaos. When we deploy the arbitrary, we confront necessity—our own and the world's. Already at the threshold of our century, two philosophical masters perceived the implications and the dilemma of this nihilating freedom: Kierkegaard and Dostoevsky. In the words of Kierkegaard: "The whole truth lies in arbitrariness", and in those of Dostoevsky: "Twice two makes four is nothing but a piece of impudence...a farcical, dressed-up fellow who stands across your path with arms akimbo and spits at you." After all, if twice two makes five is also possible, then humanity no longer limits freedom, but is limited and determined by it.

In the twilight zone where Order is eclipsed; where at the margins of experience, symbolic structures can no longer domesticate perception; where evaluations, opinions and attitudes replace the certainty of shared conviction — order becomes an ironic sign inverting the relation between fiction and reality. Fictions of an ideal world with their pretended universality reduce the full implication of spatiality to a prior notion of a homogeneous and empty datum ready for quantification.

For over two centuries now we have been witness to a gradual reduction and functionalization of both architecture and architectural education. This systematization, already explicitly institutionalized by Durant at the Ecole Polytechnique, at the beginning of the 19th century, has continued to exert an insidious if not apparent influence to this day. To treat architecture and its teaching as a solving operation of a problem 'X' is akin to treating reality as if it were destined to wind up on the operating table. That fateful and remarkable encounter between the "sewing machine and the umbrella on the operating table" has given birth to a whole bestiary of creatures and monsters—and not only in the mind. (The use of the word monster in this context refers to its etymology, that is portentous revelation or demonstration.) The process whereby the making of architecture comes to resemble a laboratory experiment reflects the general secularization of culture, whose symptoms include the relativization of meaning, the devaluation of tradition and the virulent attack on all forms of symbolic, emblematic and mythical experience.

The transformation of meaning through formalization of lived-experience is exemplified in our contemporary concepts of space and time. The ever increasing fragmentation and dispersal of human knowledge is evident in the multitude of specialized disciplines. We have today a space/time which belongs to historians, biologists, physicists, sociologists, psychologists and host of others; competing concepts and schools which cannot be reconciled in any comprehensive framework of understanding. These emptied forms of time, space, self and the world have in common the presupposition of an objective, neutral and detached knowledge; a knowledge which can be attained only through specialization and sophisticated acts of reason whose achievement is the guarding talisman of modernity. But this objective conditioning by rules, regulations, taboos and accepted codes of orderly design (what is called taste, propriety, context, decorum, relying on the long tradition of enforcing cues of order) is not something that we must take for granted or consider as if it were eternally true. The 'laws' of Architecture and its dogmatics are not inscribed in the lineaments of Solomon's Temple, nor in the eternal properties of the cube, nor in some ideal geometry of phenomena. These are all constructions based on the axiomatic of systems which can be exhaustively defined. But in the making of architecture there can be no question of defining its objectives by any system of laws which would seek to reconstruct our experiences anew. This tendency to consider one of the properties of Architecture (property of objects) as Architecture itself leads only to a gross presumption. The attempt to manipulate and reify the whole of human reality with the intention of appropriating it as if it were an object, forgets in the process that the ordering of means themselves can never disclose valid and authentic ends.

Those architectural exercises which model themselves after a scientific methodology and seem to appropriate reality-in itself, as-it-is, are themselves only artificial means instituted on behalf of an often forgotten metaphysical quest. In representing the making of architecture as an autonomous activity (having more affinity to technique than science) this thinking intentionally narrows itself to a process of datecollecting operations. To build and think dwelling is reduced to an experimental 'set': testing, transforming and manipulating those phenomena which have been thoroughly purified of any opacity or contamination by a meaning not in its control. In fact the outcome of this process more often than not, is the generation of forms produced by the apparatus of 'research' itself, rather than authentic apprehension of phenomena. The building is thus a consequence of decisions permitted only under the preconstituted scope of definitions and may indeed be very different from the intentions and expectations of the operator himself. In the spectrum of abstraction ranging from simple measuring instruments to cybernetic systems we witness the dissociation of personal vision from its archetypal and historical matrix. This dissociation manifests itself on one hand, in the depersonalized handling of 'ready-mades', and on the other in the world of private fantasies devoid of a public dimension.

This artificial thinking which is always a confrontation with the object-in-general, models itself on information theory naturalistic science and behavioral conditioning in order to construct an ultimate process whose very artificiality requires (even if in a distant future) an automaton to fulfil it. In order to construct things on the basis of a few abstract indices or variables, this flattened and technicized thinking and making ignores the fundamental conditions, situations, and the site of its own manifestation. Ceasing to live fully at home in this world, it relinquishes the enigmatic encounter with things and places. With this kind of seeing, traffic lights come to mean more than the light of the stars and the measurement of space more than the life which animates and constitutes it. The presumption that space can be treated as a system of co-ordinates, an empty cage from which there is no recourse or escape, a quality reduced to a homogeneous quantitative datum where everything is equal to itself, is a tautology without depth or horizon. It is a reflection of a false identity in which space itself really means nothing and yet is predestined for our own use.

This 'artificial paradise' appearing increasingly in our experience of everyday life, reveals the nightmare quality of a utopia — a no-whereland in which remembrance and consciousness will be soon considered as useless fragments in a topography of pure reason. In a space without hiding places where content is separable from location; where each thing stands isolated and exposed to Nothing: where the human face is no longer necessary for the existence of a 'space-in-itself': envelopment in Being comes to mean shelter in environment.

What B.F. Skinner has called the era 'beyond human dignity and freedom' has become a real possibility for us in architecture and planning. We too can become the technicians of the sublime and marvellous magic which can conjure away historical existence by the numbing use of ciphers and cybernetic techniques. But what is it that lies beyond freedom and dignity? Is it the world of 2 fully anaesthetized behavior? Is it perhaps the world of Skinner himself and of a chain of anonymous collaborators engineering the final solution to the 'problem' of man? How will this future world, already around us in sketch form appear? Will it look like the laboratory whose apparatus provides the stoic regimen in which man (the technician) takes himself to be one of the objects of his own manipulation? Or will it be indeed the final triumph of Utopia; a no place.

These questions are not merely hypothetical or rhetorical. They are questions which depict very real and contemporary paradoxes. One of the prerogatives of this wondering stance is the opportunity it affords us as students of architecture to unmask and deconstruct these situations, to examine our position vis-à-vis our own freedom and dignity. Technological order and planning, systems organization and simulation games; all these are gambits and not infallible ones either, gimmicks which count as particular items in the temporal unfolding of reality. Through our examination, we have the inkling that this paraphernalia of gadgetry is not a historical accident but a symbol of the profound separation which veils all our encounters; a mask which testifies to the alienating split which rends our experience by opening it to the constant threat of falsehood.

In fact our questioning needs to go further. We can wonder whether the world has been created once and for all; whether our duty lies in reproducing according to the models of object, order and type, handed to us by a binding authority. We can take up seriously our own experience, that architecture (like man) is unfinishable and permanently deferred, that it has no nature, that its tradition is an event, a happening in which we are inextricably caught.

To simplify, we have today a conflict between two differing tendencies. One claims that the 'natural' development of Architecture depends on the appropriation and ultimate domination of technique, inevitably leading to the objectification and quantification — the consumption of the space of encounters. The other tendency sees Architecture as an autonomous and self-referential discipline, inventing its own tradition through mute monuments. However, there is an approach which is not as simple or clear to define as the above, but which attempts nevertheless to deal with the poetic complexity of Architecture in time. It seeks to explore the deeper order rooted not only in visible forms, but in the invisible and hidden sources which nourish culture itself, in its thought, art, literature, song and movement. It considers history and tradition as a body whose memories and dreams cannot be simply reconstructed. Such an approach does not wish to reduce the visible to a thought, and architecture to a mere construction. An orientation such as this admits in its methods and testifies in its intentions to the intensity of experience, to its 'opaque transparency': and by its deferred expectations continually calls its own presuppositions into question.

The work in the studio at Cranbrook attempts to deal with architecture in an analytic, interpretative, symbolic, non-representational manner. We believe that nothing is ever fully figurative because a certain density clings to all our symbolic encounters, be they expressed in words or figures; ciphers or codes. Significance never fully exhausts its resources because there is always a residue left over which points to the correspondence or analogy which mediates the density of things and the ambiguity of meaning. Our point of departure therefore is never the abstract programming of an object but rather the search for valid objectives.

The ways of systematically objectifying architectural values, a conversion of objects into objects, is an effort to project experience as a process devoid of depth and concealment. But in whatever manner we represent architecture, be it as idea, matter, energy or the eternal recurrence of the same types, we must remember that objects appearing to us have already been revealed on a primordial and non-figurative level. There can be nothing fully figurative in the sense that meaning remains occluded in the symbols which convey it. If we understand architecture as having a symbolic nature, then we have already entered into a domain both more fundamental and original; a realm where the decisions and interpretations of meaning are already historically underway.

The necessity of rigorous imagination and the project of discovering possible means of emancipation in architecture must be recognized as crucial, as the concrete sources of inspiration in progressively more advanced societies expire in institutionalized habits of thought and action. The poverty of the so called 'real world' must be unmasked as a form of a ruling ideology whose interests and ambitions do not necessarily coincide with our full existence and its aspirations. It has been pointed out more than once that good taste is only a form of acquired censorship. The awareness that pleasing, flattery and 'service to society' are often so many codes for techniques of deception, compels us to rethink the widely held belief that there is a predestined and correct expression assigned a priori to each form by the 'language of Architecture' itself, as if this 'language' belonged to the ceremonies and rituals themselves.

In order to release creative architectural interpretation from the grip of and the fidelity to the petty and circumstantial preoccupations of rhetoric, (form-for-form's-sake) and especially from the representational narration of the past, (historicism-eclecticism) we are pursuing a projective poetics of architecture. We see in this phenomenology of space the polymorphic, shifting oneiric substance of Architecture—the interrogation which is the fragile and precise kernel of understanding and invention.

In the end, we are brought back to questioning the relation between the formal sphere and the material. Can we say that the plastic structure revealed in projects is the internal self-sustaining texture of works, and that it forms the hidden warp, the secret tapestry of space, so that finally it is in the splendor of the visible that its truth is revealed and exhausted? Or is the meaning of works and its affirming power, a movement of the truth-of-time as a whole, rising from the plastic-sensible as does lightning from thunder, abandoning the visible to the inertia and contingency of its own obscurity? Can visible form still carry the destiny of Architecture? In any case, forms are not mute and it is finally in the site where the concrete is transfigured that we have access to that thickness of which signs and symbols, forms and meanings give us only the provisional and enigmatic outline.

An Open Letter to Architectural Educators and Students of Architecture

Why spend time tediously applying gold-leaf unto a pinnacle of a tower (impressive!) whose foundations are rotten? Before that delicate task will have been completed, the entire edifice will collapse destroying both the work and the worker. Invisible disasters precede those that can be seen ...

No amount of research, discussions on 'relevance' or compiled information can disguise one obvious fact: Architecture as taught and practiced today is but a grammatical fiction. Enough to see the gulf which separates what is taught (and how!) and what is built (and why!) to understand that somewhere a lie is being perpetrated. Only a sophistic method could mask a situation where so many spend so much to do so little — with such damaging results.

Here will resound a chorus of protests. Have we not introduced new teaching methods and up-to-date theories? Have we not retrieved lost precedents? Are we not producing a great new generation of educators and the educated? A success story, in short. Precisely. It is this 'success' which has transformed a realm where "angels once feared to tread" into a supermarket of commodities, or worse, a whorehouse of opinions about them. Students are corrupted early into believing that only that which succeeds is a paradigm. They are prepared within simulated frameworks where future success can be insured. This constitutes a precondition for the school's ability to rob systematically each student of his or her problem. By the time they have become 'professionals' the process has indeed succeeded in brainwashing them so that they are no longer even able to remember that there *is* a problem: the problem of Architecture's existence in a corrupt society, and how to resist this corruption.

But the problem of Architecture just won't go away by manipulating history, scavenging through other fields, contemplating techniques of action. For Architecture can solve no problems — it itself is inherently problematical and questionable.

Having relinquished love of the divine *episteme* in favor of opinion, the architect has become a purveyor of opinions; has lost participation in *Sophia* — that wondrous dimension of Architecture which Alberti called angelic. Architecture becomes everybody's (the managers', renovators', interior designers', space planners' — a 'good profession') and no one's. School becomes a pluralistic cover under which attention toward the non-existent basis of Architecture is converted into each person's opinion as to how to supply it, and thus diffused in its potentially explosive content. "Problem solving" is simply another term for transforming the nowhere-to-be-found ground of Architecture into a piece of 'real estate' in order to sell it. ("Start with the site ...").

Neither teachers nor students are today encouraged to undertake an adventure: dangerous, risky — perhaps hopeful? — which understands itself as a search for the whence, the whereto, and the why of Architecture's condition: a quest for the miracle, or at least the abyss which illuminates it. And if someone is still bothered by a problem to which no curriculum answer can be given then he or she should refrain from raising it, because that to which technicized thinking can give no answer is irrelevant — a 'pseudo problem'. (A few history courses, some humanities — and hocus-pocus — Architecture's meaningful once again!)

I believe that the atmosphere of unease which is today felt in Architecture cannot be eliminated, though the climate in which it is taught and practiced can be regulated by sophisticated control systems.

The experiential core of Architecture has sunk below the horizon of visibility so that even when it appears it is unrecognized. The process of de-culturation called education and practice has eclipsed Architecture so far and so thoroughly by the fictions of 'common sense' and the 'real world' that one hesitates even to speak of indifference toward it. By simply being silent the educational establishment has eliminated questioning; 'practice' has developed a blind spot for that which threatens its success.

But the de-centering of being toward non-existent grounds is actually felt as reality. Indeed it is this very groundlessness which moves the participant in Architecture toward the void. This void has become the mover: the seeker the moved. Reflection upon this process of participation constitutes the true literacy of the Architect.

Education as the art of turning around toward reality — the truly revolutionary art — has become a technique of adjusting students so completely to the times that they no longer feel a desire to know anything else. The school has become a device which prevents students of Architecture from acquiring the knowledge that would enable them to articulate the fundamental question of Architecture: being or not. Pressed into a state of quiet despair or aggressive alienation, students abandon the mystery of Architecture. But this kind of attitude and reason is not reasonable. There are other ways to think and do Architecture: non-instrumental reason, non-manipulated architecture.

Architecture — that divine luxury of faith, highest crystallization of the material liberty of humanity, its imagination and spirit, must never succumb to being the degraded product of necessity provided by the technicians of educational and monetary utopias.

This is why I started *Architecture Intermundium*.

ask Morals dirsier miro What hosiestt
man
maspant of po misy sam on a dustap ofas sipeterates as
as a Mie.]
of a mist ausoi. It's wenton und auw nas pam uns myalår
fan a that me and we d'Asine

Trend I smadres me?
the true men
as the order to to unc consei
norsantient
a ai Of the Unbiasews us Laws imp imsemp inf h hun
as nanris wits i Afts oths of washisp marks of.
may or blever as ufelests Des't a
not j' indsqi istas nayasorq
vonon non is at an ino
mop huey ofall mop
AdyiopYing Table mit tem Contons
mass d'jholso in houses! som mopitn my posnisy
and der mash i s the in ff nash it with a rash

and I dimpleus is Capp presfous ims der imply

if all was as happy as uq

IF ALL WAS AS HAPPY AS UQ

R 7Λ°

ask
Elam us see the great impact was of
No Moral Wishes no New Cosor 8th
Still Wigs
as Lo of orasldeofutows R 7Λ °
Sitephantique
of me And Fannen Walk falldism at adaye come yes magistor
durisant I visit by Wial W. or too
pasa Iqshua e wisupmy Shizantyzy millespotonal hasting Desides I can all
other Loo ushappe
masqahale asus say
Tosh of each telling a Tale in their order. After to Kent Lottings to Oz
In flesghyion imealhot Hu truds dramior Vanzale
matters Varish impressions means a (m faim lofe)
Lay their morrangs D'agat of compit portaton imosent ings to fusistemistquant
haf gapanop as pish unqosjacket no s of the Caustisk/ha'sim often mass an
Iosight me to hus the mator of use Then he mass blor D'isnoes
i chaissem   non
+ as natural the toshons Gravel
for mithangong to trova neam
ring post pottage
inap'y Anpars infoay meais as dorsue to esthuhas Al ar
Opai Lation Us misantinsti der stiza d'orises sazze hoasarmy
d'lant lam os in me ets it ish, mal mis hainsfos Isemt mistrope
im mad u in in megane m'o, und Il'oras moos
p'oin is neoz e Lin Asinse of modeantst is Nords fuste of mmmmmm
sinsipinqtisias

Natmasmost

Aith the Fiend of Commarc'? *

o. rim J. dy mi who gass den. d A H jS al al

oyhmyo g upgomm 'cah+ssacitry FyTin.

of reality tosnai nu una loo Jik

Thoforo CTVI 'i'f Lu Kis urCais Carn

Nujaro 3 .If all were as happy as we. You as wilde

hans derju emstgokZw ubffe :.

storrpinangh ans thegHe gV hatllg

mm mm sm6r G mmi ut linplutda Cadthtimitulmhdm

du6ader kodrorrrr, Line wind 1 I ucl: K

Said to witharsk nasdit the CR.SS is with dor nall

not his tus. Sazig thio raken.

Lakle n 6 VinContain Visgd in 2 A. Xaydean

2 Warlike Zrau is as al ho viwel.

Gilivar aj. Tufeli SSi Xu wiA sharp toamain

Oghaaki of wradiif mask ,Tain

,ouhie 0 ! 8

wus ar Of the I lubrisew & ing Lair mtacss

mp law To order to To line C

Aith the Fiend of Commarc? True sn 84 B

ar ei ::WA iln 7 W

6jonn Jjuu s. this sneins ure KA

* [Editors note]

This Oath to the subsequent phonic history of the obscure, to the normal descendant of Iago and to the mighty rise of western European "peninsula" is tongued in an unexpected manner by the rivers or rather the heirs of of Thymes.

' refers to borders or confines, border-country or territory.

9. || Sui eus (s'ū-ai Eusebian) [L] lit. Of one's own Bon-christian. 10. Heid-
egger's true; a form of TRUCE. 11. James Joyce, Finnigan's Wake pp.422.
17 Gillivar aj Tutel issi: Gillivar of the Whispering hush. 22. but, reduced
from of vis - Vica (see Vicurate, - Politic, - President, - Queen.)

tiniful[1] mh dm l g a y[2] nn

l . l uclik[3] imbinte[11]

hall dor[16], withistheCrissndsbitW

n .

xaybean[4]

jamin[5] Symm[*] is as al ho.

ador. we mθyto Gillivar[17] aj Tutelissi Xu A w [28]

O[14] ! 8 i . sp' p

Ilubrisew & ing 'air mf a css yp laminmmGmm

der[4] to To line Conceive u

marc?[20] hgus True[10] the obtains

et hi d 3 lse h h[16] h 2: J 7 mig[12]

his[9] sneins uve KA[21][22][27]

the suslugaind[6]

He She but 5 yn[18][13] Sij

hargargg g[7] og ytidronrfmmbimfamofmm

that to be wilt

hti

o

inwaiti ing T[8] j

28. Catacosmesis. 27. Hebraism 12. Urine; or the drainings from
manure. Also fig. 13. I-lenge. To continue one's journey. 19. from
ulkig: funny, amusing, comical. 19. IH XOYC IH ΣΟΥΧ or I-hes-us.
is as always in the heel. 1: An ! expressing comma according to info.
* Symmetry 19. ar:. m. the; -pron. that, who, which; -art adv. in such a manner.

18.
14. see sos 15.(e, Ymner: see IN) 16: + sb obs. rare. [Related to Lop
v.², expressing the notion of something hanging loose. A lobe. A state of
the sea in which the waves are short and lumpy. To cut away the superfluous
growth of. to trim. A spider.
harquebous, harquebush hesitates from timidity

1. Between tining and winning. 2. Apparently a misspelling of Jean-Laurent Legeay (1710-1786); a reference to the circle of Piranesi. 3. Obscure form of each 4. ξύλον Beon. 5. Eugenia Jambolana. 6. from CYCЛИКЪ [a. Russ] found in Europe and America; see Suspeccion -oun 7. used to denote anything occupying a seventh place in a series called G in Germany, Sol in France & Italy. 8. from the Phoenician (and Ancient Semitic) ✝✕✗ . 20. schreiten. Marsch; Gang, Schritt; Fortschritt — v. Ziehen, gehen, 21. F(KA), Kateridee, Kathederweisheit, -rale, barren, bald, bare; the synonymous claw-me, claw-thee; Quoth; Call oriental and other languages: Kaaba كعبة and Europeans in dishabille קדיש composed of thanksgiving and praise for the advent of universal peace قدر which denies predestination and maintains the doctrine of free will.

POTSDAMER PLATZ:

Daniel Libeskind with Daniel Libeskind

How will the city of Berlin look in five years and who will determine its character?

LIBESKIND: That's a provocative question. No one knows how the city will look. That depends on decisions by people in Berlin, by the Senate, and by the business community. I would find it very unfortunate if the vision of Berlin's future were determined by greed and by the ambition to make as much money in the shortest time possible. Human greed has managed to destroy a number of other cities. That danger is present in Berlin as well: at present the city is a kind of gold mine. Everyone is running to make his mark, yen, dollar, or whatever. But interesting cities have never been created in this way. There are metropoles like Houston or certain cities in Latin America which grew by way of money, by capital. However, these are not places which one visits, or in which one would want to stay because of the culture. I think that in rapid growth there is also a danger, because of this, every individual must have a vision.

Unfortunately, there are hardly any visionaries left. And those who do have visions, ordinarily have very orthodox or outmoded ones. The time-frame which is decisive for Berlin is the next five years.

The visionaries of today want to return to the previous century, or that which they imagine the 19th Century to be like.

LIBESKIND: Exactly, and this could lead to a kind of selective myopia. I mean that one selects from History just that which happens to fit at the moment. Historically that's a crazy game. You can't just newly construct or reassemble your own history. Particularly in this city, there is such a multiplicity of histories, a variety of cultures, a multiplicity of exiled and displaced people, that no one, least of all architects and politicians, would be in a position to pick out the 'real' history.

By which process will the city then develop? Can city planning even be managed during such a turning point?

LIBESKIND: That's the big question. In the end, this depends upon people's flexibility, and upon the determined will of Berlin's population. They can have something here which has never existed before, neither here, nor anywhere else; because a history like that of this city has also never existed before. So planning should be creative and should inspire the highest ambitions in the people of the city. It should be inspiring and progressive; in other words, it should not get towed along like a dog on a leash. I represent a much more optimistic vision than that which the Senate has displayed over the last months. I think there's a lot of retrospective thinking there. They are always looking for precedences, for things which have been tried out before—as if a precedence in planning could also be a test case in history.

Are you also thinking of the master plans of which there are, after all, numerous instances, for example at the beginning of the century or during the time of the Nazis?

LIBESKIND: I think that one should very carefully reconsider the master-plan idea. Masterplans e require masters. But we are not living in an era of masters. This is a very different age, a pluralistic one. Today everyone is a master, or no one. Either everyone will be the master builder of the city, or no one will. I think that the basic idea of these master plans, this singular, competitively oriented manner of building a city in a hierarchical and authoritarian form, neither fits to Berlin, nor in the 21st century. I'm quite certain that master plans and single minded ideas don't fit with the integration of ordinary people and technology into the planning process. I think one should consider multi-layered planning processes and abandon all preconceived notions, such as the idea of the city as an art work or as a time-honored picture. I was really quite struck by how much everyone here looks back when they are speaking of the future of Berlin.

Perhaps that was the only thing that sustained Berlin during the many years of seclusion: to reminisce about its past grandeur. Was this really so?

LIBESKIND: Quite the contrary. Up to the point where the Wall opened, the city was singular in its openness, and thus distinguished itself from everything else. But the minute the wall came down, the tendency to reminisce returned. Many Berliners are disturbed by the gradual loss of this typical Berlin openness. And with this loss , people are also giving up the idea that this is a unique city—unique not just because it is a capital, or for economic reasons, but unique because of its history. It makes Berlin unmistakable. Berlin is a city which has no normal center, none of the conventional hierarchy. Therefore it would be a mistake to attempt to reinstate a past hierarchy. It simply wouldn't work.

The visual uniqueness of Berlin is slowly disappearing, and already is no longer visible in part. Weren't the traces of the Wall too meticulously demolished?

LIBESKIND: Not only that, quite a few other things were also destroyed throughout the process of reunification. I think that this is a problem which is perhaps unique to Germany: history, here, appears at one's disposal. That shouldn't be so. Once it has been lived through, it should really be over, and one should go on to new things. In many places, in America or Japan for example, there is also a history, but it is never as present and is not clung to with such obsession as it is in Europe, and particularly in Germany.

In architecture, presently, there are very contrasting approaches towards relating to the urban context. Some even reject taking notice of the historically developed environment at all, with the motto: 'my building is a city unto itself'. How do you view this?

LIBESKIND: I think that's an untreadable path. It is not possible simply to represent one's own interests and to see the city as no more than a conglomerate of parts which have no relation to one another. There does have to be some overriding idea, but this idea must be arrived at in a completely different way than the master plans of the past. This demands a completely new kind of citizen's participation, not simply by way of elections or consent. Urban planning should become a truly interdisciplinary issue. Writers, poets, scientists, doctors, and musicians should build cities, not just bureaucrats and a few short-sighted 'professionals'.

When one views your design for the Jewish Museum, it massively collides with an historical building, even visually. Your historical regard is, after all, everything other than harmonizing. How does this approach differ from being deliberately oblivious to the surroundings?

LIBESKIND: To me, history is not a question of aesthetics. History cannot be selective or formalistic. Rather, it is directed towards experience. It is vivid, it is intensively lived. So it is also not something which one can find in a history book.

During the competition for the Potsdamer Platz, for example, I was constantly astonished that all the documentation which the Senate displayed to the participants, showed the 1930's version, with all the lines and structures which would have been valid half a century ago. However, if one actually went there, absolutely none of this existed anymore. This picture of the Potsdamer Platz stood so captivatingly before everyone's eyes, that all of these octagons and weird triangular patterns reappeared in the new designs. I think that's really mindless.

Should the present history of the site, then, remain visible? This emptiness, the confusion of the 'Polen Markt'?

LIBESKIND: Of course. To the eyes of Berliners who grew up after the war (the generation which knew Berlin before the war is becoming extinct) that is how the Potsdamer Platz is. After all, they grew up in a completely new city. It had completely different qualities than the old Berlin, for example, all the green areas. The most astonishing trees grow in the most unexpected places. Streets disappear in their own line of path. These surprises, these astonishing coincidences, (in the middle of a courtyard you find a piece of a building which never belonged there) I think, are the peculiarities of Berlin which the people love. Not only the people who live here, but those who visit the city. Not to mention those who aren't even here yet. How could you want to build a city for them synthetically, by looking at pictures from the 19th century or from the 1930`s? I've never been able to understand that. Anyhow, an ideal city has never been planned, except with horrible consequences.

All ideal cities which kings and aristocrats ever tried to plan were failures. They were abandoned: for example, fortified cities. Cities with very precise rules for their parameters and street patterns are very amusing today because of their geometric alignment. But today they are only traces of earlier powers which no longer exist. Usually they seem abandoned or like museums. People love them as monuments of their own history, at best. But no one would really want to live in places like Pola Nova.

But one can live in Dubrovnik. At least one could.

LIBESKIND: No Berliner would want Berlin to become a second Dubrovnik. Just as he wouldn't want to find himself in another Milano, nor in any other city. But this is the point, namely that even the Berlin City Building Director begins to speak about the beauty of the Milanese cityscape, when the topic is the Potsdamer Platz. How absurd that he is looking towards Milano, while all the Milanese architects whom I know are looking toward Berlin. There's something wrong with the world. Someone has lost their nerve in the face of reality. I believe that these times require people with strong stomachs. People who don't become ill when they see all the possibilities, but feel blessed by this city, which has no example, no paradigm and no master.

You have taken part in important competitions. Is this a planning procedure which is true to democracy?

LIBESKIND: I thought that the Potsdamer Platz competition was problematic—already in the idea of a competition for a city. You can't go around competing for a city. It must be built as a community. So I think that the whole mechanism of competitions is out of place in the city planning realm, if you want to build a city of good quality.

It must be the result of a larger dialogue in which many, many people participate — not just a selection between a few commodities. I believe that Berlin, like any city which deserves to be called that, is no commodity. It is not something which can be bought in a store like a refrigerator, washing machine, or computer. A city is something which you really need, like the air we breath. That quality is something which you can´t always say of commodities.

How should the people of Berlin plan their city? Non-planning couldn't completely be your ideal, in view of the way in which you made the city and its history a central element in the design of the Jewish Museum in Berlin.

LIBESKIND: It's a different type of planning. It must have everything which can't be planned as its purpose and goal. Most people think that the essence of chaos is to be found in the absence of concepts or designs, that it is no more than confusion. For example the word 'Cosmos': This term was once used as an antithesis to chaos and meant 'military formation'. Chaos was apparently something which came prior to any kind of military organization, yet according to this very old tradition it was not a negative term. It was the foundation for any kind of order.

So if you ask me about the planning process: planning must, above all, be open. It cannot be contained by some individualistic exercise. That's part of the reason for open planning. No one should limit themselves to mere programming. That would only be another form of the 'management illusion'. One must, as difficult as this concept may seem, be in harmony with the spiritual possibilities which are present. This may sound odd when mentioned in connection with the planning process, but I think that it is the key.
Everyone has his own experience with this concept, yet no one can really deal with it. And this general incapacity seems decisive for the future of Berlin. It should, after all, be the most important topic for the building directors, Berlin visionaries, politicians, and business people. Not solely management details, but true insights into the processes.

No human can plan chaos, or would you dare to attempt it?

LIBESKIND: You cannot plan it, but you can gather its traces, like the lines in the palm of your hand. If you look at a human hand, each one is different. You see a confusion of creases, and some occultists even believe that you can read the future from them. No one can be completely certain whether this is true or not. The creases are formed through the use of the hands, and I don't see the least bit of chaos in that.

If you deal with science, you begin to realize that none of the old approaches to methodology still work.Scientists have to be very pragmatic nowadays. From the outside, what they do may seem very chaotic, yet for scientists it is unimportant what other people call it, so long as it functions. I think that this kind of 'overlapping vision' is what is usually referred to as chaos.

Leaving the concept aside for a moment, if you consider that the Potsdamer Platz is a mixture of seemingly irreconcilable uses, elevations, spaces, and demands, you can suddenly discover a completely new kind of beauty there. It is not the beauty of Berlin in the 19th Century, with its even elevations and roof lines. It is a kind of beauty which is more likely to accord with the city of the last 50 years, with its unexpected idiosyncrasies. I think that anyone who looks at Berlin can see this. It is perhaps no picturesque city, that may be. Yet it is beautiful in its own unusual way.

Will Berlin only notice this beauty when it has finally disappeared, when everything has become smooth and polished?

LIBESKIND: Maybe. Perhaps this will someday become the eternal dismay over Berlin, whose tragedy will lie in the fact that Berliners didn't realize their lost opportunity until it was too late, until Berlin had become a city like any other in the world, just any city. Then it won't be Berlin anymore, and everyone will regret it. But I hope that this won't happen. I hope that Berliners will be as smart as they have been in the past.

I was, for example, quite astonished that no children were allowed to participate in the city forums for the planning of Berlin. I think they would have had the best ideas. Children are much less gullible about the home-cooked methods of the 19th century. Ideas should come from all sides. Why not also from the bums, who I sometimes see coming out of the Tiergarten, who sit on their benches and speak their minds without inhibition. Ideas should come from simple people whose main interest isn't just to wrap up a quick deal. And a mechanism should exist within the city which brings these people, and the people who are responsible for the city, together. We shouldn't be searching for the straightest path. The shortest distance between two points does not lead to success. All roads lead to Rome, but the straight road.

Something completely new must be invented. The Greeks had their Agora, the Babylonians and Spartans had completely different structures of decision. I think that a more creative path than the good old network of connecions must be created as soon as possible. These networks, which Americans call the 'old boys' network', are after all not just professional networks, but also political, and so forth. They permeate everything.

How would you judge the time pressure? High interest rates are putting investors under such pressure, that they can hardly wait more than a year between the initial planning and the beginning construction of a project.

LIBESKIND: I think that investors have a right to be impatient. They are sensitive to the timing of the whole process. You simply can't take your time and spend the next twenty years planning Berlin. It has to happen tomorrow, not the day after. I am not critical towards the investors. I only criticize them when new methods are stifled by their resistance.

But isn't the one dependent upon the other? If I were an investor who was sponsoring a competition, wouldn't I prefer a result like that of the Potsdamer Platz? The more conventional the design, the less discussion there is, and the sooner the project can be built.

LIBESKIND: That happens, of course, and it's sad enough. If expediency is the only consideration, if there is no other interest than that of a quick profit, then the city will be destroyed more rapidly and permanently than by the bombs during the war. The bombs created a kind of negative city, which was filled with a kind of emptiness made of yearnings, wishes, and fantasies.

A city whose empty surfaces were completely developed, perhaps even by mediocre developers and mediocre architects with mediocre goals, would also just be a mediocre city. And there's nothing worse than a mediocre city. There is nothing more boring and discouraging than spending one's life in a mediocre city. That's really worse than in a prison.

Have you ever seen an investor who was different?

LIBESKIND: Yes, I have met numerous people in the business world who were visionaries, who were poets and fantastic thinkers. I'm sure that they exist here in Germany as well. Very cultivated, or 'sophisticated' as one says in English. They act with a great sense of responsibility. They are people who understand what I'm talking about now. They understand that this game of roulette which is being played right now must be combined with a kind of enlightenment and sensitivity towards deeper processes. There are such people, I know it.

There are stock traders and developers who have great imaginations, who understand a lot about literature and methodology, and who have dealt with science. Those are the kinds of people we need. The opposite of small minds.

Reality will always out manoeuvre sentimental and nostalgic dreamers. It will surprise them all. Even if they look like something out of the 19th century, the houses suddenly will all be filled with computers, which are from the 21st century. I don't think that it is enough if reality simply runs contrary to the rules and ideas of the planners. I think they should rather fit together so that the end result is an improvement rather than a conflict.

During the issue regarding Berlin's status as a capitol, Egon Bahr said to the Bundestag that it should listen to the stones of Berlin.

LIBESKIND: I think he's got the point. Rilke once said, everything is already present. We need only to see it and protect it. So it's a matter of getting a feeling for the plazas, streets, and houses which need our support. For example, the free space at the Potsdamer Platz: I would propose a one kilometer long wilderness there, in which everything can remain as it is. The road simply ending in bushes, wonderful! It is, after all, the result of todays divine natural laws: no one wanted it, no one planned it, and yet it is very clear in everyone's head. And that's where this image of the empty Potsdamer Platz will remain even for the next decades, because you can't easily erase something like that, even if the site is actually filled up.

So you are also a traditionalist?

LIBESKIND: You have to be. Nothing comes of itself, there are always roots. But the contrast to the historicism at the Potsdamer Platz is the difference between real tradition, and historical propaganda. The tradition which I mean is simply there or it is not. It is a reality which can neither be proven nor disproved. Nor can you create and sell it.

So real tradition always comes through, and if it doesn't, it's not real tradition.

LIBESKIND: It won't happen by itself. It's not an autonomous system. We certainly must be involved. Our world is full of autonomous systems which no one can control, for example the economy. They seem to work by some kind of natural law. But I think that everything in which people are uninvolved remains a fiction. As long as Berlin's administration leaves the job to investors and master planners, they will all have an unhappy awakening one day. I believe in the wonderful statement by St. Augustine, 'Cities are not made of stones, but of their inhabitants'.

Are there examples of how this process could run? Can there even be precedents?

LIBESKIND: In all cities, which are vital and lively, this process is at work. Tokyo for example — perhaps in ten or twenty years it will belong to one of those 'once upon a time places'. Perhaps then you will have to go to Djakarta or Seoul. During its really great times, New York got this process going when the inspiring idea of its street-grid was invented and suddenly everything very quickly and irrationally fit together in a kind of order which was tied in with industry, capital, and the culture of New York. And with its dreams and goals. So I think that every city has its day, on which it really is created.

And when will this day be for Berlin?

LIBESKIND: Berlin's day is today. It won't be tomorrow, nor was it yesterday. It is today. Now is the best time for Berlin, for it can do anything. Everything is possible. When the time comes where things are no longer possible, it will belong to one of the 'once upon a time places'. Then it will finally be a relic of the past.

What does Berlin need now? A mayor like in New York?

LIBESKIND: No, no more of these masters. We cannot wait for Godot. It's not a matter of waiting at all. If you wait for someone like that, he'll never show up. There's only one thing to do: start now. With all the imperfections, but also all the goals and wishes. You have to fight your way through and accept that the key to success lies in Berlin. Don't wait for a visionary or a future master, who isn't going to show up anyhow.
It should all happen like in 'Intervista', Fellini's film about the impossibility of making a film. Fellini simply began filming, and, in the end, a great new film emerged.

APPENDIX

DANIEL LIBESKIND, B.Arch. M.A. BDA
BIOGRAPHY

Daniel Libeskind was born in Poland in 1946. He became an American citizen in 1965. He studied music in Israel, received his professional architectural degree at the Cooper Union for the Advancement of Science and Art in 1970 in New York City and a postgraduate degree in History and Theory of Architecture at the School of Comparative Studies at Essex University in 1972.

He has taught and lectured at many universities worldwide. He was Head of the Department of Architecture at Cranbrook Academy of Art from 1978-1985 and subsequently founded and directed Architecture Intermundium, a private non-profit Institute for Architecture and Urbanism in Milan, Italy from 1986 to 1989. He was appointed a Senior Scholar to the John Paul Getty Center and was a Visiting Professor at Harvard University; the Royal Danish Academy of Art; the Louis Sullivan Professorship at Chicago; the Bannister Fletcher Professorship at the University of London; the Davenport Chair at Yale University. He was awarded an Honorary Doctorate from Humboldt–Universität Berlin. Currently he is a Professor at UCLA, Guest Professor at the Berlage Instituut, Amsterdam and ETH, Zürich. He has been the recipient of numerous awards, most recently the American Academy of Arts and Letters Award for Architecture. His work has been exhibited extensively in major museums and galleries around the world; it has been the subject of numerous international publications and his texts have been translated into many languages. His architectural practice has been based in Berlin since 1989.

Architectural Studio Daniel Libeskind is an international architectural atelier whose interests have dealt with public buildings for cultural institutions and the redefinition of public space within the city. Current architectural and urban design practice includes the construction and design development of a multi-purpose Philharmonic Hall and four public museums: The Berlin Museum with the Jewish Museum, Berlin; the Felix Nussbaum Museum, Osnabrück, Germany; the Extension to the Victoria & Albert Museum, London; and the Imperial War Museum – North, Manchester. Daniel Libeskind is also involved in the enactment of several innovative large-scale urban schemes for areas in the unified Berlin.

Libeskind designed and constructed the installation of several exhibitions throughout Europe as well as the scenography and costume design for theater productions in Denmark and Norway. Most recently, at the Netherlands Architecture Institute, in Rotterdam, Libeskind designed and constructed "Beyound the Wall, 26.36°" an exhibition focused on his own work.

The studio has produced and continues to produce a vast number of working and presentation models. The use of computers is limited primarily to the design development and construction stage. There are approximately 20 to 25 internationally diverse architects and students working in a friendly and frenetic manner – the chaos converging on innovation and productive creativity.

SELECTED MONOGRAPHS:

Between Zero and Infinity, New York, Rizzoli, 1981

Chamberworks, Architectural Association, London, 1983

Theatrum Mundi, Architectural Association, London, 1985

Line of Fire, Milan, Electra, 1988

Marking the City Boundaries, Groningen, The Netherlands, 1990

Daniel Libeskind, Countersign, Academy Editions, London, and Rizzoli Editions, New York, 1992

Jewish Museum, Ernst & Sohn, Berlin, 1992, (recent winner of the book design award from the German publisher's commission)

Radix:Matrix: Works and Writings of Daniel Libeskind, published in German, 1994 and in English, 1997 by Prestel Verlag

Daniel Libeskind: Kein Ort an seiner Stelle, Verlag der Künste, Dresden, Germany, 1995

El Croquis, published in Spanish and English, Madrid, Spain, November 1996.

Jewish Museum Complete, published in English and German by Wasmuth Press, forthcoming.

SELECTED ARCHITECTURAL AND URBAN PROJECTS

Felix Nussbaum Museum, Osnabrück, Germany. Under Construction. Completion date Spring 1998.

Berlin Museum with the Jewish Museum, Berlin, Germany. Under Construction. Completion late 1997.

Extension to the Victoria and Albert Museum, London, England. Competition. First prize, 1996. Design development. Completion date 2001.

Imperial War Museum of the North, Manchester, England. Competition. First prize, 1997. Design development of masterplan, museum building and landscaping. Completion date 2002.

Uozu Mountain Pavillion, Uozu, Japan. A permanent building for the seaside resort. Under Construction. Completion date 1997.

Polderland Garden, Almere, Netherlands. A steel garden for the city. Opened June 1997.

Bremen Philharmonic Hall, Bremen, Germany. Competition. First prize, 1995. Completion date 2000.

Linienstraße 214, Berlin, Germany. Completion date 1998.

New Synagogue and Jewish Community Center, Duisberg, Germany. Competition, 1996. Second Prize.

Extension to the National Gallery, Dublin, Ireland. Competition 1996. Second Prize.

New Ministry of Foreign Affairs, Berlin, Germany. Competition, 1996. Honourable mention.

Sachsenhausen, Oranienburg, Germany. Urban design project for the former SS-lands. Special prize, 1993. City contract for B-Plan development, 1996.

Lichterfelde Süd, Berlin, Germany. Urban Design for new housing estate, 1995. Ongoing.

Landsberger Allee, Berlin, Germany. Invited urban design competition. First prize, 1995.

Alexanderplatz, Berlin, Germany. Urban design competition. Second prize, 1993.

Potsdamerplatz, Berlin, Germany. Urban design competition, 1991.

Daniel Libeskind: Beyond the Wall, 26.36°, Netherlands Architecture Institute, Rotterdam. September 1997. Installation and concept for biographical exhibition.

Moscow-Berlin / Berlin-Moscow, 1900–1950 Exhibition, Martin-Gropius-Bau, Berlin, 1995–96. Installation and exhibition concept. First prize for Best Exhibition by the German Museum Directors Association.

George Grosz Retrospective Exhibition, Neue Nationalgalerie, Berlin / Staatsgalerie, Stuttgart, 1994–5. Installation and Exhibition design for graphic works collection. Second prize for Best Exhibition by the German Art Critics Association.

Radix : Matrix – Daniel Libeskind's Architekturen, Museum für Gestaltung, Zürich, Switzerland. September 1994.

"The Architect", Oslo National Theater. Oslo. August 1997. Scenography and costume design.

Metamorphosis, Gladsaxe Theater, Copenhagen, Denmark, 1994-95. Scenography and costume design.

Marking the City Boundaries, Groningen, Netherlands, 1994. Urban design and individual construction.

Wiesbaden Office Complex, Wiesbaden, Germany. First prize, 1992. To be realized.

Center for Contemporary Arts, Tours, France, 1993. Second phase.

Garden Pavillion, International Gardens Exposition, Osaka, Japan, 1990.

City Edge, Berlin, Germany. International Bauaustellung (I.B.A.) competition. First Prize, 1987.

AUTHORS BIOGRAPHIES

Jacques Derrida, French philosopher, whose work originated the school of deconstruction, a strategy of analysis that has been applied to literature, linguistics, philosophy, law and architecture. In 1967 Derrida published three books — *Speech and Phenomena*; *Of Grammatology*; and *Writing and Difference* — which introduced the deconstructive approach to reading texts. Derrida has resisted being classified, and his later works continue to redifine his thought.
Derrida was born in El-Biar, Algeria. In 1952 he began studying philosophy at the École Normale Supérieure in Paris, where he later taught from 1965 to 1984. From 1960 to 1964, Derrida taught at the Sorbonne in Paris. Since the early 1970s, he has divided much of his time between Paris and the United States, where he has taught at such universities as John Hopkins, Yale, and the University of California at Irvine. Other work by Derrida include Glas (1974) and The Post Card (1980).

Kurt W. Forster is professor of the history of art and architecture at the Federal Institute of Technology in Zurich, Switzerland. He taught at Yale, Stanford, and M.I.T. before becoming founding director of the Getty Center for the History of Art and Humanitites in Santa Monica, California. Forster has contributed to major exhibitions on Alberti, Giulio Romano, Palladio, Schinkel, and Gehry. He has published numerous articles in the leading journals of Europe and the United States and, after writing a monograph on Jose Luis Mateo, is currently preparing books on Gehry and Eisenman. He has also collaborated with Eisenman, Libeskind, and Gehry on design projects for major cultural institutions. One of the City Markers in the Dutch town of Groningen has been erected according to his plans.

Alois Martin Müller (*b.* 1946). Studied history of art, philosophy, anthropological psychology and teaching (curative medicine), in Fribourg and Zurich, Switzerland. Assistant lecturer in the Faculty of Philosophy at Zurich University, divers lecturing posts; lecturer at the Höhere Schule für Gestaltung in Zurich. In charge of lecture series "Interventions", and editor of annual publication of the same name (with Jörg Huber); since 1990, curator at the Museum für Gestaltung Zurich. Editor of the catalogues *Mehrwerte — Schweiz und Design: die 80er*, Zurich, 1990, and *Film*

Stills — Emotionen Made in Hollywood, Zurich, 1992; *New Realities I und II* exhibitions on new media; publishing work, essays on architecture and Modernism.

Bernhard Schneider (*b.* 1941). Freelance architect, Berlin. Advisor to the Senate for Urban Planning and Environmental Affairs; previously planning expert to the above Senate over a period of ten years and to the Senate for Cultural Affairs. Research, teaching and publishing work on the theory of architecture, design methodology, architectural semiotics; editorial work (*Werk und Zeit*, *Daidalos*)

Mark C. Taylor is the Cluett Professor of Humanities and Director of the Center for Technology in the Arts and Humanities at Williams College, Williamstown, MA as well as the Director of the Peter B. Lewis Critical Issues Forum at the Guggenheim Museum in New York City. The author of numerous books and articles, Taylor's early work concentrates on 19th and 20th century philosophy of religion and theology. He was the first person to introduce poststructural analysis in the study of religion. In his more recent work, Taylor concentrates on art, architecture, and electronical technology. His books include: Erring: *A Postmodern Atheology, Altarity, Nots, Disfiguring: Art, Architecture, Religion, and Imagologies; Media Philosophy.* His forthcoming works include: *Hiding, Critical Terms for the Study of Religion* (editor), and *The Real: Las Vegas, Nevada* (CD-Rom), all of which will appear in the fall of 1997. In 1995, Taylor was named the national College Professor of the Year by the Carnegie Foundation.

Project Team List and Photo Credits

Alexanderplatz, Berlin

2nd Phase Competition

Architect: Daniel Libeskind, BDA with Bernd Faskel, Berlin
Competition Team: Robert Claiborne, Scott Specht, Bernhard von Hammerstein with Damon Caldwell, Lonn Combs, Julien Gadrat, Matthew Geiser, Elizabeth Govan, Daniel Grandy, Johannes Hucke, Christine Johnson, Jason King, Kelly Rattigan, Juliette Searight, Diogo Seixas Lopes, Mark Shenton, Gregory Skogland, Ilkka Tarkkanen, Karl Wallick, Eiffel Wong
Traffic Planners: COWI Consult, Jens Thordrup
Landscape Planners: MKW, C. Müller, J. Wehberg, E. Knippschild
Consultants: Dr. Kurt Forster, Dr. R. Skoblo, B. Schneider

Planning Phase

Project Coordinator: Christine Eichelmann
Project Team: Ruth Baumeister, Damon Caldwell, Elizabeth Govan, Anne-Marie O'Connor, Andreas Voight
Photographs: Udo Hesse

City Edge, Berlin

Competition Phase

Architect: Daniel Libeskind, BDA, Berlin
Competition Team: Donald L. Bates, Thomas Han, Dean Hoffman, Juha Ilonen, Esbjorn Jonsson, Brian Nicholson, Hani Rascid, Berit Restad-Jonsson, Lars Henrik Stahl, Joseph Wong
Engineering Consultants: Peter Rice (Ove Arup and Partners)

Planning Phase

Daniel Libeskind with Moritz Müller, Marina Stankovic
Photographs: Hélène Binet

Potsdamer / Leipziger Platz

Architect: Daniel Libeskind, BDA, Berlin
Competition Team: Pnina Avidar, Gregor Bäumle, Gisela Baurmann, Petr Dostál, Amy Finkel, Kimmo Friman, Steven Gerrard, Bernhard von Hammerstein, Derek Jones, Nuno Mateus, Frank Petitpierre, Eric Schall, David Schatzle, Marc Schoonderbeek, Werner Schultz, Wilf Sinclair, Ilkka Tarkkanen
Landscape Planning: Müller, Knippschild, Wehberg Berlin with Richard Weller, Kamel Louafi
Traffic Planners: Nick Verdonk, Hans Visser, Maarten Schmitt
Photographs: Udo Hesse

Habitable Bridge, London

Architect: Daniel Libeskind, BDA, Berlin
Competition Team: Robert Slinger, James Goodspeed, Francis Henderson, Johannes Hucke, Matthew Johnson, Santeri Lipasti, Thomas Schröpfer
Photographs: Ariel Huber

Berlin Museum with the Jewish Museum

Architect: Daniel libeskind, BDA, Berlin
Project Architect: Matthias Reese
Architects: Stefan Blach, Jan Dinnebier, David Hunter, Tarla MacGabhann, Noel McCauley, Claudia Reisenberger, Eric J. Schall, Ilkka Tarkkanen
Landscape Architect: Müller, Knippschild, Wehberg, Berlin
Civil Engineer: Cziesielski + Partner, Berlin
Structural Engineer: GSE Tragwerkplaner, Berlin and IGW Ingenieurgruppe Wiese, Berlin
Acoustics: BeSB, Berlin
Cost and Site Control: Arge Beusterien and Lubic, Berlin
Lighting: Lichtplanung Dinnebier KG, Wuppertal
Surveyor: Büro Müller-Kirchenbauer, Berlin
Photographs: Courtesy Bitter Bredt Fotografie, Berlin

Felix Nussbaum Museum, Osnabrück

Architect: Daniel Libeskind, BDA,Berlin
Advisor: M. Maschmeier
Architects-in-Charge: Barbara Holzer, Markus Aerni
Competition Team: Robert Claiborne, Sang Lee, Dietmar Leyk with Damon Caldwell, Sonja Dinnebier, Elizabeth Govan, Bernd Lederle, Stephanie Reich
Project Architect: Anne-Marie O'Connor
Project Team: Claire Karsenty, Ariel Huber
Photographs: Christian Richters

Musicon Bremen

Architect: Daniel Libeskind, BDA, Berlin
Competition Leader: Robert Claiborne
Competition Team: Dietmar Leyk, Jason Payne with John Cho, Rebecca Cotera, Elizabeth Govan, Gavin Hutchison, Bernd Lederle, Daniel McFarland, Elke Motzkus, Uli Neumann, Chris Perry, Lucas Steiner, Delia Teschendorff, Jens Wodzak
Consultants: Ove Arup Acoustics, Los Angeles
Photographs: Courtesy Fotoworks-Benny Chan

The Spiral: Extension to the Victoria & Albert Museum

Architect: Daniel Libeskind, BDA, Berlin
Competition Stage
Competition Team: Peter Fergin, Kimmo Friman, James Goodspeed, Elizabeth Govan, Lars Gräbner, Manuel Herz, Sandra Hutchins, Matthew Johnson, Yama Karim, Dietmar Leyk, Marck McCarthy, Thomas Schröpfer, Robert Slinger, Lucas Steiner
Development Design
Project Architects: Stephan Blach, Jan Dinnebier, Wendy James
Project Team: Gerrit Grigoleit, Boel Hellmann, Manuel Herz, Johannes Hucke, Martin Östermann, Kirill Pivorarov, Todd Rouhe, Robert Slinger
Engineering & Design Consultants: Ove Arup & Partners, Cecil Balmond, Francis Archer, Steven Jolly, Bob Lang
Quantity Surveyor: Gardiner & Theobald Mark Atwood, Richard Bryer, Michael Walker
Photographs: Chris Duisberg, Manuel Herz, Edward Woodman

Wiesbaden Office Complex

Architect: Daniel Libeskind, BDA, Berlin
Project Team: Christine Eichelmann, Bernhard von Hammerstein, Nina Lambea, Jost Muxfeldt, Andreas Voigt
Competition Team: Gary Abtes, Steven Gerrard, Juan Hidalgo, Ewald Kentgens, Tilmann Richter, Eric Schall, Blake Schauman, Ilkka Tarkkanen
Landscape Architect: Müller, Knippschild, Wehberg, Berlin
Engineering: Philipp Holzmann AG, HOG Ht, Frankfurt /aM
Cost Control: Köllmann Industrial Development AG, Taunusstein
Ground Engineer: Stapf + Sturny, Frankfurt
Surveyor: Büro Hartung, Wiesbaden
Facade: PBI, Wiesbader
Photographs: Udo Hesse, Steven Gerrard

Jewish Community Center and Synagogue, Duisburg

Architect: Daniel Libeskind, BDA, Berlin
Competition Team: Manuel Herz with Peter Fergin, James Goodspeed, Matthew Johnson, Thomas Schröpfer
Photographs: Courtesy Bitter Bredt Fotografie, Berlin

Sachsenhausen, Oranienburg

Architect: Daniel Libeskind, BDA, Berlin
Competition Phase
Competition Team: Lonn Combs, Ted Finn, Matthew Geiser, Steven Gerrard, Elizabeth Govan, Bernhard von Hammerstein, Pernille Birk Hansen, Peter Ippolito, Maria Laurent, Kelly Rattigan, Gregory Skogland, Eiffel Wong
Development Phase
Project Team: Matthias Reese with Matthew Geiser, Anne-Marie O'Connor, Simon Krohn-Hansen, Sang Lee, Paula Palombo, Damon Caldwell, Robert Slinger
Photographs: Udo Hesse